The → Process → Matters

PRINCETON UNIVERSITY PRESS *Princeton & Oxford*

THE

PROCESS MATTERS

Engaging and Equipping People for Success

JOEL BROCKNER

Published by Princeton University Press
41 William Street, Princeton, New Jersey 08540

In the United Kingdom: Princeton University Press
6 Oxford Street, Woodstock, Oxfordshire OX20 1TW

press.princeton.edu

ISBN 978-0-691-16505-9

Library of Congress Control Number 2015947042

British Library Cataloging-in-Publication Data is available

This book has been composed in Sabon Next LT Pro and Univers LT Std

Printed on acid-free paper. ∞

Printed in the United States of America

10 9 8 7 6 5 4 3 2 1

Contents

Acknowledgments

It was only fitting that I started writing this book in Boston, while on sabbatical at Harvard Business School. Four decades earlier in the same city, when I was a doctoral student in psychology at Tufts, my mentor, Jeff Rubin, said I had promise but that I really needed to work on my writing. In one of my early lessons that the process matters, Jeff advised that it was necessary to pay attention not only to the "what" but also to the "how." Ever since, I have taken Jeff's words to heart while writing primarily for fellow academics. However, I wanted this book to reach a broader audience. Before gaining acclaim for his books on emotional intelligence, Daniel Goleman was a contributor to the "Science Times," a section of the Tuesday edition of the *New York Times*. I marveled at his ability to distill the essence of social science research and make it relevant and reader friendly. I decided to take a crack at writing one of those types of books.

In the truest sense, this book would not have been possible without the many forms of help I have received. I am very thankful to professional friends and colleagues who offered incisive feedback on various drafts of the manuscript: Teresa Amabile, Art Brief, Alia Crum, Adam Grant,

Eric Hertz, Joshua Margolis, Ashley Martin, Andy Molinsky, Ann Tenbrunsel, and Linda Treviño. I am indebted to my editors at Princeton University Press, Meagan Levinson and Eric Schwartz, as well as to Jenn Backer and Ali Parrington at Princeton University Press, and to Margo Fleming at Stanford University Press. I also owe a debt of gratitude to a few longtime friends who helped out by reading earlier drafts and by showing genuine interest: Steve Auerbach, Richard Gold, and Eric Stern.

I have received tremendous support from my family. Our sons, Eliot, Dustin, and Lucas, provided lots of good ideas for the book and, more generally, have inspired me in ways about which I could write yet another book. Thanks, guys! And, of course, words can't begin to describe how helpful my wife, Audrey, has been. Audrey is generally my No. 1 supporter and especially so on this project. She is incredibly wise about a lot of things, and luckily for me this includes her views on both the substance and style of my writing. Typically, after writing a few pages, I would ask for her feedback. This went on, from start to finish. Not only did she offer really useful advice, but she did so in practically record time; after all, the process matters. I dedicate this book to Aud with great admiration, affection, and love.

The → Process → Matters

1 → Introduction

See if you can figure out what these two situations have in common:

(1) John works for a high-powered investment bank. His work environment is always stressful, but this time he is really feeling the heat. His firm has had several bad quarters in a row. In a recent meeting with their boss, John and his team had been given a strict order: they needed to increase their contribution to the bottom line by 15 percent relative to the previous quarter. Seared in John's memory were his boss's parting words: "I don't care how you get there, just get there."

(2) I returned home late one night after taking part in a basketball free-throw shooting contest open to all members of the Columbia University community. I was feeling pretty good about things. Out of the fifty contestants who entered, I tied for first (making twenty-two out of twenty-five shots), which necessitated an overtime round between the other top finisher and me. The other person shot better than I did in overtime, so I finished as the runner-up. The next morning at breakfast, my three sons, then ranging in age from five to eleven, asked me

how it had gone. I decided to make this a teaching moment, as in, there's more to life than winning and losing. So I proceeded to tell them that I had tried as hard as I could, that I really enjoyed the experience, and, oh, by the way, that I had come in second out of fifty people. My sons brought me down to earth quickly: "So, Dad, you lost!" they cried out, practically in unison.

At first blush these two situations seem pretty different from one another. But they also display a noteworthy commonality: our obsession with results. Indeed, several familiar expressions reveal the great importance we assign to outcomes, such as "The bottom line is . . ." or "At the end of the day . . ." Don't get me wrong—we should care about outcomes. Obviously we would rather succeed than fail, win rather than lose, and make more money rather than less. The problem is that all too often our obsession with results blinds us to the reality that how we get there, the process, also makes a big difference.

How the process is handled really matters to those on the receiving end of decisions. Just ask Jay Leno, the longtime host of NBC's *The Tonight Show*. Jay didn't take it well when NBC replaced him with Conan O'Brien in 2009. Why? Was it because, after being No. 1 in late-night TV, he resented being told that his services were no longer needed? Was it because, at sixty, he felt hurt that someone ten to fifteen years younger would be replacing him? It is hard to know the real reasons, but his more recent reactions to being replaced by Jimmy Fallon (who is even younger than Conan O'Brien) give us some clues. As he put it himself, "The main difference between this and the other time is I'm part of the process. The last time the decision was made without me. I came into work one day and [was abruptly told], you're out. This time it feels right."

Part of Jay Leno's satisfaction the second time around was probably because NBC's CEO, Steve Burke, made a point of meeting with Jay himself before any changes were announced. As Burke said after their meeting, "Clearly our goal has been to make this a smooth transition. Jay deserves to be treated like someone who has done a wonderful thing for our company for two decades." Another important member of NBC's senior management team, Lorne Michaels (the creator of *Saturday Night Live*), agreed: "What has been key to this transition has been the absolute consideration for everyone's feelings by all involved. It has been a transparent process." Jimmy Fallon also facilitated things by saying, "I have nothing but respect for Jay. If it weren't for him, I wouldn't have a show to be taking over."[1]

The Jay Leno example illustrates three of the central points of this book. First, look at how differently Jay reacted to the exact same decision when the process was done well rather than poorly. As the old saying goes, it's not only what you do, but also how you do it. Second, doing the process well often entails simple things like involving people in decisions, showing respect, and doing things transparently. Not exactly rocket science. Furthermore, doing the process well may not require much in the way of tangible resources. For Jay Leno, it only required a few key people to show him real respect; this cost very little time or money. Third, given how much the process matters, and given the simplicity of doing it right, you would think that processes would be handled well more often than not. Sadly and alarmingly, this is not the case.

Hence this book: I will be talking about how doing things in the right way can make lots of important differences. It can have positive effects on employees' productivity and morale, on the academic performance of chronically underachieving students, on how ethically we behave, and even on how we feel about ourselves. The saga of Jay Leno is anything but an isolated case. I also will discuss what goes into doing things in the right way. The specific elements that affected Jay Leno's satisfaction with the process are part of the story, but many other factors go into a high-quality process. I also will provide answers to the puzzling question of why doing things in the right way frequently fails to happen. After all, if something so simple and straightforward can have such positive effects, shouldn't it be done more often? What is getting in the way? By identifying the obstacles, we can figure out ways to deal with them, thereby unleashing the many benefits that result from doing things in the right way.

Mapping the Terrain

Throughout the book I will consider a wide array of situations in which two or more parties are interacting with one another, or have a relationship with one another, and are trying to complete some task or attain some goal. Most of my examples come from the workplace: for instance, how employees react to a significant change in their organization such as a merger or acquisition. I also will examine more microlevel workplace encounters such as one-on-one interactions employees have with their bosses. The book's contents are also relevant to people in authority positions, such as parents, educators, and politicians. Moreover, the importance of how things are done also applies to our encounters and relationships with others who are important to us (family, friends) as we go about our various life activities.

In all of these situations, Party A is taking some action toward Party B that, from Party B's perspective, consists of both a "what" (outcome) and a "how" (process). For example, an organization may decide to introduce a new strategic initiative, leading to downsizing parts of its operations. Or a boss may give feedback to one of her subordinates about the latter's recent performance. Or, on a more personal level, a spouse may make plans for the next family vacation. In all of these examples, based upon what Party A is doing, Party B can make a pretty good guess as to what the outcomes will be. Naturally, the more Party B perceives the outcomes to be favorable, the better she responds. For instance, Party B will embrace the organizational change, will support the boss, and will go along with her spouse's suggested vacation spot.

In all of these situations Party A also is carrying out a process, which refers to *how* things are done. For example, in conducting the performance review, the boss may be very top-down, taking into account only her own views. Alternatively, the boss may be more open in her approach. For instance, if this particular organization uses "360-degree" feedback processes, the boss may consider the views of the employee's peers or direct reports, or even the views of the employee himself. Furthermore, the boss may conduct the performance review in ways that indicate how interested she is in her subordinate's development, such as by conducting the review on its scheduled day rather than postponing and rescheduling it multiple times. And a wife's reaction to her husband's vacation recommendation also depends on whether she believes she made the suggestion in a timely fashion or listened to her reactions to his suggestion.

How things are done is especially important to employees during times of organizational change. Regardless of the nature of the change (e.g., whether the organization is downsizing or growing), the *process* must include a remarkably similar set of attributes for employees to embrace the change. I will have a lot more to say about the process of managing change in a later chapter. For now, suffice it to say that the pathway leading to the result is very important to people over and above the result itself.

Process + Outcome, and Process × Outcome

You have probably heard the expression "adding insult to injury." It is a reminder of how we care about the process in addition to the outcome. Sometimes we don't like what was decided (a bad outcome: the injury), and at the same time we don't like how the bad outcome was decided or communicated (a poor process: the insult). We usually feel quite resentful when both of these things happen at the same time. For example, if a friend breaks a date with me that I was looking forward to (bad outcome), and, moreover, didn't call me beforehand to say that he would be unable to meet me and I found this out when I called him to finalize the plans (bad process), I experience a double whammy. This is usually even worse than suggested by the expression "*adding* insult to injury." Many studies show that a more accurate expression of what people experience when they get a bad outcome accompanied by a bad process is *"multiplying* insult times injury." Usually the product of two numbers (e.g., 3 × 3) is greater than the sum of those same two numbers (3 + 3). So if the bad outcome produces three units of pain and the bad process also produces three units of pain, the net experience is not six units of pain but nine units. An analogy from the field of pharmacology may be helpful here. When a patient is given a new prescription (Drug A), he may be advised to evaluate how it may *interact* with another one that he is already taking (Drug B). There may be few problems with taking Drug A and Drug B separately. However, if those same drugs are taken simultaneously they may have harmful effects. In like fashion, we often experience the combination of a bad outcome and a bad process as an especially toxic mix.[2]

Regardless of whether the combination of a bad outcome and bad process is best described as "adding insult to injury" or "multiplying insult times injury," the experience of the process affects many things that employees and employers care about. For example, in the workplace the process affects employees' motivation, which is comprised of several elements. Much like a vector, motivation has both direction and magnitude. To be motivated means that employees will do some things *and not others* (direction) and that they will put forth effort in performing those behaviors (magnitude).

One illustration of how the process can affect the direction and magnitude facets of motivation comes from the well-established finding that employees tend to be more motivated and hence productive when they work on a task with a specific and difficult goal in mind than if they have (1) no goal, (2) a difficult but nonspecific goal, or (3) a specific but not difficult goal.[3] For example, suppose you fell behind in your reading and decided to play catch-up one evening. Before starting to read, you set the challenging goal of reading sixty pages. What is likely to happen? Although you may not read as many as sixty pages, you are likely to read more pages than if you did not set a goal, or if you set a difficult but nonspecific goal ("as much as I can"), or if you set a specific but less difficult goal, say, thirty pages. Why do specific, difficult goals have this effect? For one thing, goals provide direction. If your goal is to read sixty pages, then you pretty much know what you need to do: read. Anything other than reading will not get the job done. In the words of Steven Covey (the author of *The Seven Habits of Highly Effective People*), if you "begin with the end in mind," it is easier to know when you are (or are not) doing the things that will get you to where you want to go.

One situation in which people may be susceptible to losing focus is working at the computer. All too often, I go to my computer fully intending to accomplish the goal of making headway on some challenging activity, say, writing this book. (Note the nonspecific nature of this difficult goal: "making headway.") Unfortunately, working at the computer lends itself to doing so many other things that are a mere few clicks away. For example, I sometimes tell myself that I will get to my writing "just after I check my e-mail." Upon emerging from my e-mail, sometimes hours later, I often find that I no longer have the energy to do what I initially set out to do. On the other hand, if I make the challenging goal more specific ("write five pages"), I am much more likely to remain on task. Why? If I wander over to "just check my e-mail," I know that this activity will be at cross-purposes with the specific goal I set for myself. In short, specific, difficult goals provide direction; they make it harder to veer off course.

The presence of a specific, difficult goal also affects the magnitude or intensity of our efforts. This often happens when we see ourselves making progress toward the goal. The perception of getting closer to our goal increases the effort we put forth to achieve it, a tendency known as the "goal gradient effect." Have you ever waited in a common area in a bank for the next available teller? My guess is that when you reached the point at which you were the next in line, each minute that you had to keep waiting felt interminable. Why? You were experiencing the goal gradient effect: the closer you were to your goal, the more motivated you were to get there, and therefore the more painful it was to *not* be there.

Of course, sometimes we may not be making progress toward the goal. We may have set a goal to read sixty pages, only to find two hours later that we have only read five pages, perhaps because we got involved in distracting alternatives ("just checking e-mails"). In this instance, the *negative* feedback may motivate us to redouble our efforts to get going. The point is that goals set the stage for us to receive feedback about how we are doing, and it is the receipt of the feedback that leads us to increase the intensity of our efforts.

In much the same way that specific, difficult goals affect what we do (direction) and the intensity with which we do it (magnitude), so does a high-quality process. Throughout the book, we will consider how the quality of the process influences both the direction and magnitude facets of motivation. For example, how things are handled influences whether people choose to behave ethically or unethically (direction). The quality of the process also influences how much effort employees exert to further their organization's interests (magnitude).

What Goes into a High-Quality Process?

Assuming you are onboard with the idea that the quality of the process can make a big difference, let's try to delineate the essence of a high-quality process. When people say "the process was handled really well," what do they mean exactly? There are a few ways to depict a high-quality process, as illustrated in a classic field experiment Ellen Langer and Judith Rodin conducted in a nursing home. At the beginning of the study, the nursing home administrator told all of the residents in a warm and friendly way that the staff wanted them to have a good experience living there.

From that point on, the participants were randomly assigned to one of two groups, a high responsibility group and a low responsibility group. Those in the high responsibility group were told that they had a lot of responsibility in how they wanted to live their lives whereas those in the low responsibility group were told that the staff would be taking care of and making decisions for them. For example, each individual in both groups was given a plant. Furthermore, the two groups were told that they would have the opportunity to see a movie on one of two nights during the following week. Those in the high responsibility group were asked whether they wanted the plant (all of them did) and were told that it was up to them to take care of the plant however they saw fit. They also were asked to select which of the two nights they wanted to see the movie. Those in the low responsibility group were given the plant (they were not asked if they wanted one) and were told that the staff would take care of it for them. Moreover, they were told which night of the week they would be viewing the movie.

It could be argued that the objective difference in how residents in the two groups were treated was relatively small. After all, both groups were told by the administrator that the staff wanted them to be happy. Whereas the high responsibility group made certain decisions for themselves, in the low responsibility group the same decisions were made for the residents by the no doubt well-meaning staff. However, the differential effects of how the two groups were treated were anything but small. In the short term (three weeks later), those in the high responsibility group were significantly happier, more active, and more alert relative to their counterparts in the low responsibility group. In the long term (eighteen months later), those in the high responsibility condition continued to be more active and alert, and moreover they were in better health and were even less likely to die, relative to those in the low responsibility group.[4]

There are two ways to talk about the quality of the process being higher when people were given responsibility than when they were not, and I will talk about both in this book. One way is to focus on *attributes of the process*. For example, the general thrust of the message given to the residents in the high responsibility group was that they can and should take more responsibility for their lives; this was not the case in the low responsibility group. A second way is to focus on the *experience* of those on the receiving end of the process. In this instance, those in the high responsibility group likely felt more of a sense of *control* over their environments than did those in the low responsibility group. Either way, as we saw with the example of Jay Leno's departure from *The Tonight Show*, "simple" differences in process can have demonstrably large effects.

Attributes of the Process

A widely discussed area in the management literature is organizational justice, which refers to employees' beliefs about whether they are being treated fairly by their employers, as well as the causes and consequences of those perceptions. Initial research suggested that people evaluated fairness based on the distribution of outcomes.[5] For example, in many situations it is only fair if rewards or benefits are doled out to people in proportion to their contributions. More recent evidence indicates that people also care a lot about the fairness of the process accompanying the outcome.[6] But this begs the question: What do people have to perceive about the process for it to seem fair? I will have much more to say about the perceived attributes of a fair process in the next chapter, but for now consider the following examples of a process low in fairness. During a round of layoffs at a global asset management firm, employees were let go with virtually no warning and even less explanation. To make matters worse, they were not even allowed to return to the workplace to say their goodbyes. Instead, they were called after-hours and told not to return the next day and that their belongings would be sent to them. One employee received her call while she was at her doctor's office and not even from her boss but from her boss's administrative assistant.

In a similar vein, consider this situation:

To some employees in Chicago, it seemed like a Halloween prank. But when they showed up on Saturday for work, they learned that it was a very real trick: their employer had fired them through a Robo call according to *The Times of Northwest Indiana*. [Robo calls use a computerized autodialer to deliver a pre-recorded message, which makes the message sound as though it is coming from a robot.] The workers received a message on Friday that they were no longer needed and were now out of a job. *The Times* reported that dozens of workers either missed the call or thought it was a prank, and so showed up to work anyway only to learn that their ID badges no longer functioned and to hear from security that they were out of a job.

A few days later the organization "explained" its actions as follows: "As part of our business process, we have temporarily adjusted our workforce numbers at the Chicago Assembly Plant by approximately 90 team members. Our goal, as always, is to return the workers back to their positions as soon as possible based on the needs of our business. We do not typically use Robo call to notify employees of layoffs. The plant elected to use Robo call in this situation because it is temporary in nature and we intend to recall all employees as soon as possible."[7]

In yet another case, a European-based insurance company mistakenly sent a layoff notice to 1,300 employees when in fact the notice was intended for a single individual. Essentially 1,300 people received a terse e-mail telling them that their services were no longer needed. A much more humane way to communicate major news like this would have been to have it delivered by a person, preferably someone respected by those on the receiving end. The dismissing (and dismissive) e-mail also rather sternly reminded people of their "obligations" to the company, which included retaining confidential information about its operations, systems, and clients. The final straw was the one in which the senior executive sending the layoff notice said, "I would like to take this opportunity to thank you and wish you all the best for the future."

To its credit, the company quickly sent a second e-mail to the other 1,299 people explaining that the layoff notice they had just received was sent by mistake, along with an apology. But how would you feel if you were one of those 1,299 people upon learning the way in which the organization chose to deliver its layoff notice to one of your colleagues? Losing a job is painful enough, but does the process of losing the job have to be so unfair? Talk about multiplying insult times injury.[8]

The Effects on Those on the Receiving End

Another way to talk about the quality of the process, reflected in the subtitle of this book, is in reference to its effects on people. The behaviors we engage in, and how well we do so, depend on two things: how hard we try (effort, a facet of motivation) and how skilled or capable we are (ability). We usually need both, that is, to be willing and able, to make our way through life successfully. When someone is described as having great "potential," it may be code for saying that s/he is not living up to that potential, probably due to a lack of effort. Or, alternatively, when people "get an A for effort," it means that they didn't perform well, probably due to a lack of capability. So here's another way to define a high-quality process: it *engages* people (for example, induces them to put forth a high level of effort) and/or it *equips* people (provides them with the resources they need to be successful). In later chapters I will elaborate on these points; among other things, getting people to put forth high effort requires knowing what they *want*.

Many of our encounters, both in and outside the workplace, occur in the context of ongoing relationships. Therefore, for a process to truly be high quality it needs to engage and equip people in both the short term and the long term. For example, when organizations downsize, in the short term they need to think through exactly how they will inform people that they are losing their job. A lot is at stake here. One study has shown that a powerful predictor of whether laid-off people will sue their employers for wrongful termination is how they felt they were treated when they were told that they were losing their job. If they were treated in a way that preserved their dignity and respect, they were very unlikely to sue; only one out of a hundred did. On the other hand, if they felt they had been treated disrespectfully in the course of hearing that they were losing their job, they were much more likely to sue; one out of every six people who had this type of experience sued. From the organization's perspective, that's a nearly seventeenfold difference in the likelihood of having to defend itself in a court of law, simply on the basis of how it treated people at the crucial moment of telling them that they were being laid off.[9]

Similar findings have emerged in studies of patients who have sued their doctors for medical malpractice. Doctors are not likely to be sued if the only factor under consideration is the patient's perception of how well or how poorly a certain medical procedure went. However, doctors are much more likely to be sued when a patient perceives that the procedure went badly *and* the doctors demonstrated poor "bedside manner."[10] Remember the combustible mix of a bad outcome combined with a bad process? Here we see it again, in both organizational and medical settings; Jay Leno's situation was not an isolated case.

The medical profession is beginning to recognize the importance of how doctors interact with their patients. The Association of American Medical Colleges (AAMC) recently announced plans to change the standardized test given to prospective medical students (the Medical College Admissions Test, also known as the MCAT) to include questions measuring people's interpersonal competencies. According to Darrell Kirch, the president of the AAMC, "The public had great confidence in doctors' [medical] knowledge but much less in their bedside manner. The goal is to improve the medical admissions process to find the people who[m] you and I would want as our doctors. Being a good doctor isn't just about understanding science, it's about understanding people."[11]

The notion that the quality of a process is defined by both its immediate as well as its longer-term effects also may be found in the literature on group behavior. The prominent group psychologist Richard Hackman has identified three criteria for team effectiveness: (1) *productivity*, such that the group's output should meet or exceed the standards of those responsible for evaluating the output; (2) *satisfaction*, in that the members of the group should feel that their personal needs are being met; and (3) *staying power*, in which, as Hackman puts it, "the social processes used in carrying out the work should maintain or enhance the capability of members to work together on subsequent team tasks."[12] In like fashion, a high-quality process engages and equips people in the short term without sacrificing (and, in a best-case scenario, actually strengthening) their engagement and capabilities to perform in the longer term.

A Roadmap of What's to Come

The nursing home study illustrates two complementary ways to talk about a high-quality process: by focusing on attributes of the process, which reside external to people on the receiving end of decisions, and by attending to the internal experience that the process elicits in people on the receiving end. Chapters 2 and 3 take the external approach whereas chapter 4 takes the internal approach. Chapter 2 focuses on an attribute that has received an enormous amount of attention in the past forty years: the perceived *fairness* of the process. We will consider the many aspects that go into what people perceive to be a fair process and how perceptions of process fairness combine with the outcomes people receive to influence their productivity, morale, and how they feel about themselves.

As important as the fairness of the process is, however, in reality it is part of a bigger set of things managers need to do when they are trying to engage and equip their employees to change, be it a large-scale change such as an organizational merger or a small-scale change such as when a manager is trying to persuade the people in her immediate work unit to adopt a new technology. As Mike Beer at Harvard Business School suggests, successful change requires managers to do the following: (1) get employees to be dissatisfied with the current state; (2) show employees a feasible and better alternative to the current state, typically in the form of a compelling vision of the future state; (3) have a plan in place that moves employees from the dissatisfying current state to the better future state; and (4) deal with employees' resistance to the change.[13] Chapter 3 presents a way for managers to think broadly about how to be more effective as agents of change, while simultaneously offering specific examples of best practices used in forward-thinking organizations.

In chapter 4 we consider the quality of the process based on what people experience. While not the complete story of human motivation, a significant chunk of what we strive for is to feel good about ourselves (esteem), to see ourselves as integrated and real persons (identity), and to feel that what we do matters (control).[14] Certain organizational and managerial processes enable employees to experience a sense of esteem, identity, and control. Furthermore, the extent to which this happens begins when employees join the organization and recurs throughout their tenure in the organization. Recent research has shown that employees who experience esteem, identity, and control based on how they are treated respond with greater productivity, have higher morale, and, not trivially, have a greater sense of psychological well-being.[15]

Regardless of whether the quality of the process refers to its attributes (chapters 2 and 3) or to the psychological state it elicits in those on the receiving end (chapter 4), we would be remiss if we failed to consider the ethical dimension. If how managers treat their employees boosts productivity, morale, and well-being but also leads to lapses in morality, can we really call that a "high-quality process"? Hardly. Chapter 5 is reassuring in this regard. It discusses how the elements of a high-quality process discussed in chapters 2–4 as well as other elements nudge those on the receiving end to behave with integrity. By the end of chapter 5, then, we will have identified a set of very actionable ways for managers to proceed that bring out the best in their employees.

The sixth and final chapter takes as its point of departure the observation that nearly everything discussed in the earlier chapters is "easier said than done." Most managers readily agree with the recommendation that they try to ensure that their process is fair, to be the kind of change agent that Mike Beer advocates, to ensure they treat their employees in ways that allow them to experience esteem, identity, and control, and to not neglect the ethical dimension in how they treat their employees. Why, then, aren't managers implementing these policies more often? To foreshadow the discussion in chapter 6, I will suggest that some of the barriers reside in managers' motivation to enact a high-quality process whereas others relate to their ability to do so. As any good doctor will tell you, diagnosis should precede and inform treatment. Having identified some of the things that get in the way of managing with a high-quality process, we are in a much better position to offer solutions. After all, if this really is going to be the how-to book that it aspires to be, it needs to do more than provide a checklist of things for managers to do. It requires asking why they are not doing these things in the first place, that is, identify the obstacles and then offer guidance on how the obstacles may be overcome. In short, I want to help managers translate their *mental model* of a high-quality process into how they *actually behave* when making decisions and interacting with their employees. Moreover, by completing the surveys in the appendixes, readers also will have opportunities to assess where they stand along numerous dimensions related to the quality of their own processes in dealing with others, both in and out of the workplace.

Let's get started.

2 → It's Only Fair

The following three scenarios represent a smattering of the different kinds of situations people face in their jobs:

Vignette A: Paul is about one year into his expatriate assignment, which is expected to last for three. Overall, the experience has thus far been a mixed bag. Things are going well enough at work, but his family is having a difficult time adjusting. His wife is a high-powered professional in her own right who has put her career on hold so that she could accompany Paul. Unfortunately the laws of the host country prevent her from seeking employment, so she finds herself bored and irritable much of the time. Their two children are in high school. They resented having to leave home in the first place, and they have had a lot of difficulty mastering a new language, learning a new culture, and the like. Paul feels torn. On the one hand, his boss has told him how much better it would be for the organization, and, by extension, for his career, if he could stick it out for the entire three-year assignment rather than return home prematurely. On the other hand, his family situation is such that he thinks it might be best if they all return home within a few months.

Vignette B: Annabel smokes cigarettes. She tried for many years to quit but has been unsuccessful. Up until now, her place of employment has allowed employees to take several smoking breaks during the workday. However, her company has just introduced a policy that strictly prohibits smoking on the grounds. Needless to say, this new policy poses quite a challenge for Annabel, so much so that she is seriously considering leaving the company to find another job, one in which she would not have to deal with the hardship of forgoing smoking breaks.

Vignette C: Tom is working in a manufacturing organization that is going through tough times. The president of the company recently announced that all employees will have to endure a sizable pay cut for at least three months. Prior to this announcement, Tom had no intention of leaving his employer. He enjoys the work and living in the nearby community. The pay cut has forced him to reconsider his priorities, however. He is now contemplating looking for a job elsewhere.

What do you think people will do in these situations? Will Paul end his overseas assignment early? Will Annabel leave the organization? Will Tom start looking for a new job elsewhere? Moreover, if your answer is "it depends," on what does it depend? We know at least one answer to this question: the fairness of the process. As we will see later in the chapter, studies have shown that employees exhibit greater commitment to their employers when the latter practice process fairness.

Organizational Justice: A Brief Tutorial

Concerns about fairness go back at least to the ancient Greeks (Plato and Aristotle, among others), and, much more recently, it has received a lot of attention from social and organizational psychologists. Initial theory and research posited that employees' fairness beliefs were based on the substance of their exchanges with their employers. J. Stacy Adams's equity theory suggested that people experienced fairness when the relationship between what they offered to their employers (inputs) and what they received from them (outcomes) was equal to that of some relevant standard of comparison, for example, the input/outcome relationship of coworkers.[1] If the employees who perform better are paid more, we tend to view this as fair. A concept closely related to outcome fairness is outcome favorability, which refers to people receiving the outcomes they *want* from their employers. Outcome fairness and outcome favorability have significant effects on productivity and morale in the workplace.

By the mid-1970s it became clear, however, that outcomes didn't tell the whole story. Thanks to the pioneering efforts of John Thibaut and Laurens Walker, we learned that people's perceptions of and reactions to fairness also depended upon the process accompanying the outcomes. Many of us intuitively recognize the difference between the outcome and the process. For example, it is entirely possible for us to be unhappy with an outcome, seeing it as unfair or unfavorable, but also to believe that the process accompanying it was fair. Thibaut and Walker, and then a decade later scholars such as Robert Folger, Jerald Greenberg, Allan Lind, and Tom Tyler, showed that even when outcomes were held constant, people reacted more positively (e.g., they were more satisfied with a decision) when they perceived the process as fair.[2]

Two developments followed. Justice scholars identified the many specific elements of a fair process, and they began to examine how outcome fairness (or outcome favorability) and process fairness *interact* with each other to affect what employees think, feel, and do. I elaborate on each of these developments in the next sections.

Elements of a Fair Process

Thibaut and Walker initially conceived of process fairness on the basis of whether people were given the opportunity to voice their opinion during a discussion or decision-making process, in terms of either being allowed to give their input prior to the making of the decision (process control) or being given a say in the actual making of the decision (decision control). Gerald Leventhal and his colleagues subsequently identified six additional attributes of a decision-making process that influence perceptions of fairness. Examples include consistency (in which the method for making decisions is the same across persons and time; this also is called a "level playing field"), accuracy (in which the information decision makers rely on is appropriate and valid), and bias suppression (in which decision makers put their self-interests aside). The transparency of the decision-making process also affects its perceived fairness. It is one thing for accurate information to be used to make a decision. It is another thing for everyone to be able to *see* that presumably accurate information was used to make a decision.[3] A few years later, Bob Bies observed that our perceptions of process fairness also depend upon the interpersonal behavior of the parties responsible for making and carrying out decisions. For example, whether implementers provide explanations for their actions affects perceived fairness, as does whether they implement decisions in dignifying and respectful ways.[4]

Yet another important element is the timeliness with which decisions are made. For example, when a U.S. employer is planning to close its operations or lay off a significant number of employees, it is legally obligated to give at least sixty days' advance notice. Howard Metzenbaum, the late senator from Ohio and the original sponsor of the Worker Adjustment and Retraining Notification (WARN) Act, argued that if people were about to lose their jobs, it was only fair that they be given time to prepare. In short, various features of the decision-making machinery as well as the behavior of people operating the machinery influence our perceptions of process fairness.

The Joint Effects of Outcome and Process

Having shown that the fairness of the process affects employees over and above the influence of outcomes, scholars also began to examine the joint and *interactive* effects of outcome and process on how people react to organizational events and decisions. Some of this work was done in the legal arena, in which people's reactions to the police and the court system were examined, but most of it was undertaken in workplace settings. Some studies examined people's reactions to organization-wide events affecting many people, such as downsizing, pay cuts, and various sources of work-life conflict, while others investigated more individually targeted events and decisions, such as how people reacted to their overseas assignments or to their negotiations with their bosses. A wide variety of reactions were examined in these studies, but they all reflected the same themes of employee productivity and morale: How well did employees do their jobs? To what extent did they do more than what they were required to do? To what extent did they feel aligned with what the organization was trying to do? To what extent did they plan to stay at their current job rather than look for employment elsewhere?[5]

The remarkably consistent pattern of results emerging across many dozens of studies may be described in a variety of ways. As can be seen in table 2.1, when people received an unwelcome outcome (either unfair or unfavorable) that was accompanied by an unfair process, they were particularly aggrieved; injury was multiplied by insult. Another way to state the findings shown in table 2.1 is "the ends justify the means." In other words, as long as people ended up in a good (i.e., fair or favorable) place in terms of outcome, whether they thought the process was more versus less fair made relatively little difference. Table 2.1 shows that process fairness had much more of an effect, however, when people were unhappy with their outcomes. A third way to describe the findings in table 2.1 is that "the means justify (or make justifiable) the ends." Looking at the numbers horizontally, you can see that when the process was fair, the outcome had *less* of an effect on employees' productivity and morale, relative to when they thought the process was unfair.

I have had the opportunity to show this pattern of results to thousands of people over the past decade, often during executive development training programs at Columbia Business School. Whenever I present the findings to this kind of audience, I acknowledge that I might be taking a bit of a risk. After all, they are attending the training program to learn about practical strategies and tactics

Table 2.1. Employees' Reactions to Organizational Events and Decisions

		Outcome Favorability		
		Low	Moderate	High
Process Fairness	Low	1	4	7
	High	5	7	8

Note: Scale Range: 1–10. Higher numbers reflect better employee reactions (e.g., productivity, morale).

they can take back to the workplace. By showing them the results of studies, I may come across as too theoretical or "academic."

However, I am willing to take this risk because I believe that the results convey practical messages that business professionals can use to be more effective leaders, managers, and agents of change. Indeed, I even ask *them* to tell me how they might apply these findings in the workplace. They quickly understand my intent, often saying things such as "Well, when I can give my people the outcomes they want, I probably don't have to worry quite as much about how I go about it." I tell them that I agree with this conclusion, as long as they truly mean "I don't have to worry *quite as much* about the outcome" and not "I don't have to worry *at all* about the outcome." The results show that employees will generally react better when the process is fair; furthermore, the enhancing effect of a fair process is stronger when employees are unhappy rather than happy with their outcomes.

Additionally, my professional audiences often recognize that as long as they handle the process fairly (e.g., involve people in decision making whenever possible, explain why certain decisions are being made, and communicate decisions respectfully), those on the receiving end are likely to be less affected by the fairness or favorability of their outcomes. This is not to say that when the process is fair those on the receiving end will be unaffected by their outcomes. They appear to care significantly less about their outcomes when they perceive the process to be fair.

Audiences sometimes interpret the findings in table 2.1 as indicating that as long as managers either give their employees the outcomes they want or treat them with high process fairness, they don't have to worry as much about the other element: fair or favorable outcomes reduce the need for high process fairness, and high process fairness reduces the need for fair or favorable outcomes. Although the results seen in table 2.1 seem to suggest this, this is hardly a case in which giving people good outcomes or treating them with high process fairness is an example of "six of one, half dozen of the other." Giving people the outcomes they want and treating them with high process fairness may be similar in terms of their effects, but they are quite different in terms of their costs.

I will explain with an example. For many years my colleagues and I have examined how layoffs affect the productivity and morale of the employees who remain, also known as the "survivors." We wanted to find out whether survivors *always* responded negatively to layoffs or whether there were conditions under which they responded more versus less negatively. We wondered, for example, whether survivors' perceptions of the favorability of the layoff outcomes and the fairness of the layoff process would make a difference in how they reacted to the layoffs.

The outcome factor we investigated actually pertained more to the people who had lost their jobs than to the survivors. In particular, we wanted to find out the extent to which the survivors believed that the organization provided a safety net for those who had lost their jobs in the form of severance pay, help in finding employment elsewhere (e.g., through outplacement counseling), and continuation of health insurance or other benefits. In human resources (HR) parlance, this safety net is known as "the package." Even though the package pertained only to those who had lost their jobs, it was meaningful to the survivors. As word spreads, survivors are influenced by what they hear. In fact, downsizing organizations often make the mistake of referring to the people who are losing their jobs as the "affected" employees, implying that the remaining employees (the survivors) are *not* affected. However, most people who have worked in an organization going through layoffs will be quick to tell you that *everyone* is affected, both those who leave and those who stay. For instance, survivors often infer that the generosity of the package offered to the people who are losing their jobs may say something about what they can expect from the organization going forward. Among other things, it may tell them what kind of package they might receive if they were to lose their job in a subsequent round of downsizing.

The process fairness factor in these studies consisted of the softer skills of management, such as whether the reasons for the layoffs were explained well, or whether a reasonable amount of advance notice was given, or whether the news was delivered to the people who lost their jobs in an empathic and sensitive way. Survivors' reactions were quite similar to those shown in table 2.1. The perception that outcomes were favorable reduced the effect of process fairness on their productivity and morale. Moreover, the perception that the process was fair reduced the influence of perceptions of the package on survivors' productivity and morale.[6] At first blush, then, it may seem that the effects on survivors of a generous package and a fair process were largely interchangeable. For example, table 2.1 shows that survivors responded about the same when they believed the package was moderately generous and the process was handled fairly as they did when they believed the package was highly generous and the process handled not so fairly. Note, however, that the financial costs to the organization of offering a very generous package with low process fairness are likely to be far greater than those incurred if the organization were to offer a moderately generous package with high process fairness. If you were concerned about your organization's bottom line, would you now say that the relative influence on survivors of favorable outcomes and fair processes is a case of "six of one, half dozen of the other"? Probably not.

The more general principle here is that, en masse, it is typically much easier for managers to achieve high process fairness than it is for them to deliver favorable outcomes. Have you ever heard the expression (first uttered by President Abraham Lincoln) "you can't please all of the people all of the time"? I believe that this saying is much more applicable when we are talking about giving people the outcomes they want than when we are talking about delivering those outcomes with high process fairness. Most of the time managers *can't* give everyone the outcomes they want; it just isn't financially possible. However, it often is financially feasible to plan and implement decisions with high process fairness. This allows managers to come closer to "pleasing all of the people all of the time." Even when managers have to make "tough" decisions (meaning that at least some people on the receiving end are going to be unhappy with the outcomes), such decisions still can be made with high process fairness. Indeed, not only *can* the tough decisions be made with high process fairness, but the research suggests that they *should*: the fairness of the process has much more of an influence on employees' productivity and morale when outcomes are bad than when they are good.

This brings us to a related irony: If managers can and should make the tough decisions with high process fairness, why is it that all too often they do not?[7] The short answer is that although high process fairness often is not financially costly, it is not cost-free. In chapter 6 we will consider the nonfinancial costs that managers are likely to experience if they plan and implement tough decisions with high process fairness. We will also discuss some ways that individuals and organizations can address these nonfinancial costs, thereby making it more likely that managers will do their jobs with high process fairness.

Clarifying Some Misconceptions

I am hopeful that by now you see how the research findings summarized in table 2.1 have practical implications for a wide range of organizational events and decisions. Sometimes, however, the findings have been misconstrued.

Misconception #1: Fake It Until You Make It

Some people say that it is not important for managers to truly practice high process fairness; instead, what matters is that they be perceived to be practicing it ("perception is reality").[8] For the results in table 2.1 to emerge, I certainly agree that it is necessary for those on the receiving end to believe that their managers are practicing high process fairness. In that sense, perception *is* reality. However, what sometimes gets glossed over is the fact that managers are much more likely to be perceived to be practicing process fairness if they genuinely are motivated to practice process fairness than if they merely want to appear to be doing so.

Most of us pick up on inauthenticity very quickly. A midlevel executive in an arts organization once told me a story of how the senior team in his company had attended a workshop on the virtues of adopting a more participatory management style, which is one of the hallmarks of high process fairness. They had attended the workshop to see if there was anything that could be done about the sagging morale in the organization. After the workshop the bosses came back to work resolving to appear more participatory. They asked employees for their input on various topics and in numerous ways (e.g., by establishing a task force in which lower-level employees were asked to make recommendations to senior management, by instituting an employee suggestion box, and by having more frequent town-hall meetings in which employees were encouraged to express their opinions). The problem was, however, that the bosses were not genuinely motivated to be more participatory—they just wanted to appear that way. It didn't take long for the employees to figure out that their input was being ignored, which made them even more demoralized than they had been in the first place.

"Inauthentic high process fairness" is an oxymoron. Part of what high process fairness entails is treating people with dignity and respect. Imagine the likely reaction of the employees in the situation we just discussed. Upon realizing that their bosses were asking for a lot of input but not actually considering any of it, they felt deceived. You can imagine the conversations they probably had with one another: "Do our bosses think we are such idiots that we would not notice that they are ignoring our suggestions?" Hardly the stuff of which dignified and respectful treatment is made.

Misconception #2: Don't Worry about the
Outcome as Long as the Process Is Fair

Since practicing high process fairness is a cost-effective way to lead and manage (in that giving people the outcomes they want usually costs a lot more money than does practicing high process fairness), managers may be tempted to infer that they need not concern themselves with their employees' outcomes provided that they practice high process fairness. Such an inference is misguided in two ways. First, what the studies are suggesting is that people seem to care *less* about their outcomes when process fairness is high rather than low. This is not to say, however, that they don't care about their outcomes *at all*. When process fairness is high, employees' productivity and morale are still higher when they receive better outcomes; it's just that people are even more affected by their outcomes when process fairness is low than when process fairness is high.

Second, if it is possible to deliver very favorable outcomes en masse and to accompany those outcomes with high process fairness, this is what managers should do. However, quite often it simply is not possible to deliver very favorable outcomes en masse. When this is so, the best thing for them to do is to deliver *moderately* favorable outcomes (which is likely to be much more affordable en masse) and to do so with high process fairness. Table 2.1 shows that employees' productivity and morale may not even be that much higher when they receive very favorable outcomes accompanied by high process fairness relative to when they receive moderately favorable outcomes accompanied by high process fairness. If employees treated with high process fairness react only slightly more positively when their outcomes are very favorable rather than moderately favorable, managers need to ask themselves whether the sometimes nontrivial difference in expense associated with very favorable versus moderately favorable outcomes is worth it.

Misconception #3: High Process Fairness Can Even Get People to React Quite Positively to Bad Outcomes

Even though the virtues of high process fairness can be great, it also is important to be realistic about its limits. High process fairness causes employees to react better (e.g., they will exhibit greater productivity and morale) than when process fairness is low, and this is especially so when outcomes are unfavorable or unfair. This is not to say, however, that a fair process will override or eliminate the effects of bad outcomes. When managers have to make tough decisions and do so with high process fairness, they should not expect the affected parties to react *very* positively. For example, in a downsizing situation in which people lose their jobs (or watch other people lose their jobs), even if the process is impeccably fair, we should not expect those who go and those who stay to be jumping for joy. At best, their reactions are likely to be lukewarm. But if the same bad outcomes were accompanied by an unfair process, the results would be a lot worse. For example, in a downsizing situation in which the process is unfair, the people who leave are much more likely to sue their former employers and the people who stay are likely to become demoralized.[9] More generally, when managers make tough decisions with high process fairness but still encounter some grousing among the troops, they should not conclude that the high process fairness didn't make a difference. In all likelihood, there would have been *a lot more* grousing if they had made the same tough decisions but did not plan or implement them with high process fairness.

Why Do Outcome and Process Work Together This Way?

Although the results shown in table 2.1 have been found to hold true in many different types of workplace situations, we have yet to discuss why this is so. In fact, there are two related "why" questions worth considering. First, why is it that the fairness of the process has more of an effect on employees' productivity and morale when they are on the receiving end of bad outcomes rather than good outcomes? Second, why is it that high process fairness reduces the impact of outcome favorability on employees' productivity and morale relative to when process fairness is low? It is important to answer these questions for both theoretical and practical reasons. Advancing theory and advancing practice need not be at cross-purposes with one another. Taking this point one step further, the founder of the field of social psychology, Kurt Lewin, famously claimed that there is nothing so practical as a good theory. If we truly understand why people think and act in the ways that they do, we can make better decisions that affect both ourselves and others.

One answer to the first question rests on the assumption that bad outcomes capture our attention more readily than do good outcomes. Perhaps it's a survival instinct, hardwired into us over thousands of years. Naomi Eisenberger coined the term "human alarm system" in describing the part of our brain that is particularly sensitive to events, experiences, or stimuli that threaten our well-being, such as being on the receiving end of bad outcomes.[10] The human alarm system does a few other things besides detect threatening stimuli. It leads us to be more alert to our environment, particularly to information that may help us figure out a way to reduce or at least manage the threat. Enter process fairness information. When the potential threat posed by the bad outcome is accompanied by high process fairness, the situation feels a lot less scary; as a result we are likely to be at least reasonably engaged. For example, employees may give their managers the benefit of the doubt when they receive bad outcomes accompanied by high process fairness and, as a result, pull in the same direction as their managers. On the other hand, when the potential threat of a bad outcome is accompanied by low process fairness we experience the situation as particularly aversive; the insult is multiplied by the injury. In this instance, employees will be far less forgiving of their managers and much less engaged with them.

This entire sense-making process simply does not happen as much when people receive favorable outcomes. Favorable outcomes don't activate our survival instincts the way that unfavorable outcomes do. Hence we don't pay nearly as much attention to process fairness, which may explain why it has so much less of an impact on employees' productivity and morale in the face of good outcomes rather than bad ones.

Research by Kees van den Bos and his colleagues has shown that we don't even have to receive bad outcomes in order for our human alarm system to be activated. Stimuli that merely symbolize threat or danger also may trigger our alarm system and thereby make us more attentive to fairness information. In one study participants were asked to stare at an exclamation point for a short while. Exclamation points symbolize warning signals, especially in Europe, which is where the study was conducted. After looking at the exclamation point, participants read a brief vignette in which they were asked to imagine that they had applied for a job. Half were given information suggesting that the selection process was fair (the decision was based on accurate information) while the other half was led to believe that the process was unfair (the decision was not based on accurate information). Another group of participants (those in the control condition) did not look at the exclamation point before reading the vignette. All participants were then asked to rate the fairness of the selection process. The results were rather alarming. The participants who saw the exclamation point perceived the accurate procedure as more fair and the inaccurate procedure as less fair, relative to those who did not see the exclamation point. In other words, information about the accuracy of the selection process had much more of an effect on perceived fairness among those who saw the symbol of alarm, the exclamation point.

A second study by Van den Bos and his colleagues examined a very different symbol of alarm: a flashing orange light. The study took place in a shopping area in a

medium-sized city in the Netherlands, in which participants were approached by the researcher and asked to read
a vignette. The vignette asked them to imagine that they
were working for an organization and that they had just
completed an important assignment. An orange light was
situated on a pedestal directly behind the researcher; it
flashed on and off for some participants (alarm condition);
for others, it remained in the off position (control condition). Half of the participants read a vignette in which
they were led to believe that the amount they were paid
was fair, whereas the other half read a vignette in which
they were led to believe that the amount was unfair. As
in the preceding study, participants rated how fairly they
had been treated. Not surprisingly, they said that they had
been treated more fairly when the amount they were paid
was fair rather than unfair. However, this tendency was
significantly stronger in the alarm condition than in the
control condition. For participants who were told that
they were paid a fair amount, *perceived* fairness was higher
in the alarm condition than in the control condition. And
for participants who were informed that they were paid an
unfair amount, perceived fairness was lower in the alarm
condition than in the control condition. In short, when
we receive bad outcomes, it is likely to trigger our alarm
systems, thereby heightening our sensitivity to the environment in general and to cues that may help us manage
the threat we are experiencing in particular. Information
about the fairness of the process is one such cue. The Van
den Bos studies are particularly intriguing because they
suggest that we don't actually have to be on the receiving
end of bad outcomes for our alarm systems to be activated.
Symbols of alarm can do the trick as well, which explains

why participants who saw exclamation points and flashing lights were more attuned to and influenced by the fairness information that they had read about.[11]

Here's another way to think about why outcome and process information combine to affect us in the way that they do. Bad outcomes *may* make us feel vulnerable (and cause us to disengage as a result), but bad outcomes by themselves often are not sufficient to produce vulnerability and disengagement. Upon receiving bad outcomes we have to decide whether we are willing to be vulnerable, and we use process fairness information to decide one way or the other. Organizational scholars such as Roger Mayer, Denise Rousseau, and their colleagues have defined trust as a willingness to be vulnerable to the actions of others, based on the expectation that the others will do the right thing without having to monitor them.[12] When others dole out unfavorable outcomes but do so with high process fairness, those on the receiving end are likely to believe that, going forward, the others will do the right thing without having to be monitored.

In short, managers' process fairness is one of the main determinants of how much we trust them. Our trust in managers, in turn, will influence how much we are affected by the outcome they deliver to us. For example, if they mete out an unfavorable outcome but do so with high process fairness, we trust them and therefore won't get overly bent out of shape by the unfavorable outcome. If the process is fair, we figure, we are likely to get our share of desired outcomes over time, even if we don't get a very good outcome in the current situation. If, however, the process is unfair, we feel far less reassured about the favorability of our future outcomes. And when we don't have faith that our future outcomes will be at least reasonably favorable, we are likely to assign much more importance to, and hence be much more affected by, the favorability of our current outcome.[13] The results shown in table 2.1 support this; the favorability of the outcome had much less of an effect on employees' productivity and morale when the outcome was accompanied by high rather than low process fairness.

If managers understand that high process fairness reduces the influence of outcome favorability *because* high process fairness is an indicator that they can be trusted, other factors suggesting that managers can be trusted should have the same effect. When managers have to dole out unfavorable outcomes, the thing they really need to discern (if they want to predict how engaged their employees will be) is how much their employees trust them. The amount of process fairness accompanying the unfavorable outcome is one determinant of trust, but it is not the only one. Some people are more inclined to see the world through rose-colored glasses, hence they should be more trusting of their managers; it's an "eye of the beholder" type of thing. Emily Bianchi and I recently completed a study in which we asked participants to read about certain managers and then evaluate their process fairness. Some participants read about managers who acted with high process fairness whereas others read about managers who acted with low process fairness. Naturally, perceptions of the managers' process fairness followed suit: those who read about managers exhibiting high process fairness rated them as higher in process fairness relative to their counterparts who read about managers exhibiting low process fairness. More interestingly, regardless of whether the managers they read about practiced high or low process fairness, participants with a stronger dispositional tendency to trust also *per-*

ceived the managers as having practiced higher process fairness.[14]

Furthermore, employees' trust in their managers sometimes is less a function of managers' process fairness in a given instance and more dependent on the managers' prior behavior or on what employees' coworkers say about whether and how much they trust their managers.[15] Consequently, there are several things managers can do to increase the likelihood that they will be seen as trustworthy when they have to make tough decisions. First, they can remind their employees that they have a history of generally being trustworthy. Second, they can solicit the help of other influential people in the organization to spread the message that they are trustworthy. Whether they make the case themselves or with the help of others, the presentation needs to be credible. Credibility may be achieved, for example, by careful fact-checking prior to making the case on their own behalf, or by ensuring that the people selected to lobby for them are known to be "opinion leaders," people whose points of view are taken seriously precisely because of their credibility. In summary, since it is the high level of trust elicited by high process fairness that makes outcomes less consequential, managers who have to make tough decisions should be on the lookout for various ways to ensure that they are seen as trustworthy. Again, as Kurt Lewin suggested, there is nothing so practical as a good theory.

More on the Joint Effects of Outcomes and Process

Thus far, the research results summarized in table 2.1 suggest that managers have a way to reduce the harmful effects of tough decisions on employees: by planning and implementing decisions with high process fairness. Other research findings suggest, however, that when we are on the receiving end of the so-called tough decisions (e.g., in which outcomes are unfavorable), high process fairness may have some adverse effects. We may feel especially bad about *ourselves* if we believe that our bad outcome was arrived at or delivered with a fair process. Several years ago a friend of mine, a professor at a prestigious business school, received the bad news that her case for being promoted to a tenured faculty position was turned down. One of her well-intentioned colleagues tried to console her by saying, "Well, you shouldn't feel too bad; after all, the process was fair." My friend smiled politely at her colleague but thought to herself, "Thanks a lot. With friends like this, who needs enemies?"

When we get an unfavorable outcome, in some ways the *last* thing we want to hear is that the process was fair. As outraging as the combination of an unfavorable outcome and an unfair process is (it "multiplies insult times injury"), this combination also brings with it a consolation prize: the possibility of attributing the bad outcome to something other than ourselves. We may reassure ourselves by believing that our bad outcome had little to do with us and everything to do with the unfair process. If the process is fair, however, we cannot nearly as easily externalize the outcome; we got what we got "fair and square." When the process is fair we believe that our outcome is deserved, which is another way of saying that there must have been something about ourselves (what we did or who we are) that caused the outcome.[16]

When we are on the receiving end of a bad outcome we may have different types of negative feelings depending upon whether we see the accompanying process as fair or unfair. On the one hand, if we see the accompanying process as fair, we feel *bad about ourselves*. On the other hand, if we see the accompanying process as unfair, we feel *angry and resentful toward the decision maker*.[17] I recently saw these two very different reactions (self-loathing versus resentment) demonstrated by the same individual before my very eyes. One of my students came to speak to me about his grade on the midterm exam, on which he had performed poorly. At first we talked about the reasons why he had not done well and what he could do to improve on future exams. During our conversation it became obvious to me that he was being very hard on himself for not doing well. He blamed himself a lot and, as a result, was feeling very bad about himself. I suggested that perhaps he didn't need to be so self-critical, and in a good-faith effort to console him, I casually mentioned that no test is a perfect measure of one's ability. After all, I said, exams usually cannot measure all of the material that was covered, so perhaps he had the misfortune, as sometimes happens, to be well prepared for material that was not on the exam and to be less well prepared for material that was on the exam. He thanked me for my time and consideration of his needs, both intellectual and emotional, and left my office. He reemerged, however, a few minutes later by which time he had transformed from being down on himself to being resentful toward me. Though it was not my intention, he took what I had said about the exam as evidence that it was not an accurate measure of knowledge—in other words, that the test process was unfair. So much for my trying to attend to his self-esteem needs.

When managers have to make tough decisions, they can't satisfy all of their employees all of the time. Some of them are likely to see their outcomes as unfavorable or unfair. Managers face a difficult challenge when dealing with this particular group. If managers demonstrate low process fairness, employees will feel angry and resentful and their productivity and morale will suffer accordingly. If managers exhibit high process fairness, employees may feel bad about themselves. Assuming that managers care about their employees' productivity and morale on the one hand and how they feel about themselves on the other, it sounds like managers who have to make tough decisions are stuck between a rock and a hard place. Does this have to be the case?

Not necessarily. My advice is to practice high process fairness while also being alert to the possibility that those on the receiving end of dissatisfying outcomes may blame themselves. The self-blame resulting from high process fairness may produce the unwanted side effect of people feeling bad about themselves. But even here there are things that managers can do to reduce the severity of this side effect. Let's look more closely at the different ways in which people blame themselves for their unfavorable outcomes. Psychologists such as Ronnie Janoff-Bulman have made an important distinction between *characterological* self-blame and *behavioral* self-blame.[18] Characterological self-blame refers to attributing bad outcomes to something about who we are, such as our personality or level of chronic ability. Behavioral self-blame refers to seeing our bad outcomes as resulting from things that we did or did not do. For example, imagine that you didn't perform as well as you wanted to on some important task. With characterological self-blame, you may conclude that this happened because you just do not have what it takes to succeed; your lack of ability is the perceived cause. With behavioral self-blame, you may decide that it was because you didn't try as hard as you could have; a lack of effort is the culprit. Ability and effort both pertain to the person experiencing the outcome, but they differ in important ways. Relative to effort, ability is seen as less changeable and less controllable. Indeed, when people attribute bad outcomes to a lack of ability they are pessimistic about their future chances for success and they don't try as hard, whereas when they attribute those same outcomes to a lack of effort they are more optimistic and motivated going forward.[19] Many studies also have shown that a person's level of depression is related to characterological and behavioral self-blame in very different ways: characterological self-blame for negative events is positively related to depression whereas behavioral self-blame for those same events is negatively related to depression. In other words, it is only characterological self-blame for bad events that causes people to feel bad about themselves; behavioral self-blame for those same events leads people to feel *less* depressed.

The implications of these findings for managers making tough decisions are clear: they should plan and implement them with high process fairness, be aware of the fact that those on the receiving end of the unfavorable outcomes may blame themselves, and then help them to make self-blame attributions that are more behavioral and/or less characterological. Indeed, the idea that people should be encouraged to make self-blame attributions that are more behavioral and less characterological dovetails nicely with one of the cardinal principles for providing people with constructive negative feedback: the feedback always should be in reference to people's behavior and not to their character. For example, rather than telling their employees that they are "unreliable," managers should give behaviorally based feedback about the various ways in which their unreliability is evident (e.g., by producing work of inconsistent quality or by showing up late for meetings). Behaviorally based feedback is more effective precisely because it conveys the same message to people as does behavioral self-blaming: that change is possible and that things are under a person's control.

And there may be another benefit in addition to resiliency of encouraging behavioral rather than characterological self-blame: it may encourage employees to behave more ethically. Consider the case in which unfavorable outcomes refer not to what employees receive but rather to the harm they cause other people in the organization. For instance, employees sometimes do what is in their own best interest or that of their unit, even if it is not what is best for the organization. Or the harm could take the form of what employees do *not* do, such as not being willing to go the extra nine yards to give their group a better chance to succeed. When contemplating the harm they have caused, it is common for people to feel shame or guilt. While related, these two emotions differ: shame reflects a tendency to blame the person ("I felt so ashamed of myself") whereas guilt reflects a tendency to blame behavior ("I felt guilty about what I did"). As Adam Grant recently observed, people are much more likely to do the morally correct thing when they feel guilty rather than ashamed. Shame causes people to lash out or withdraw, whereas guilt makes people more likely to empathize with the person they harmed and to make amends.[20]

When bad outcomes are accompanied by high process fairness there are other things that managers can do (besides encouraging behavioral self-blame) to help employees deal with the possible side effect of feeling bad about themselves. Essentially what people need in moments like this are boosts to their sense of self. Moreover, the boosts do not even need to be big. In their recent book *The Progress Principle*, Teresa Amabile and Steven Kramer showed that when people consistently took small steps toward completing work that they found meaningful they felt better about themselves and their work, which fueled motivation, performance, and creativity.[21] Hence a manager's job is to create conditions that allow employees to have these "small wins" types of experiences, such as by setting clear goals, allowing autonomy, and providing resources. By articulating the ultimate goal along with the necessary subgoals along the way, managers enable their employees to experience small wins by celebrating the moments when the subgoals are met.

Furthermore, the boosts to the sense of self can occur in arenas other than the one in which people feel self-threatened. Many workplace situations that cause people to feel self-threatened (such as getting a bad outcome accompanied by a fair process) are bothersome precisely because of their implications for people's global or overall sense of self. The good news here is that when employees feel self-threatened they may benefit from doing something self-affirming even in areas other than the one that is self-threatening. For instance, if employees who receive a bad outcome accompanied by a fair process do something that causes them to feel good about themselves as members of their community (say, by doing some meaningful volunteer work), the volunteer experience may actually cycle back positively to affect how they are feeling about themselves as members of their organizations.[22] We will have much more to say about the kinds of experiences that employees find self-affirming or self-restoring in chapter 4.

Let us now return to the three individuals mentioned at the beginning of the chapter, all of whom were facing a decision about being engaged with their employers even though they were on the receiving end of a bad outcome. Paul, our expat, had to decide whether to continue with his overseas assignment, which is what his employer wanted him to do, even though his family was having a difficult time adjusting. Annabel, our smoker, had to decide whether to stay with her employer even though its newly instituted smoking ban was making it a lot harder for her to continue working there. And Tom was deciding whether he should cut ties with his longtime employer and seek a job elsewhere in light of the pay cut that his employer was about to impose. Many studies have shown that one factor that makes a big difference in situations like these is employers' process fairness. Ron Garonzik, Phyllis Siegel, and I found that expats who found themselves in situations like Paul's were much less likely to consider returning home prematurely if their employers allowed them to have input into decisions and if they felt that their employers generally treated them with dignity and respect.[23] Jerry Greenberg found that people like Annabel were much more accepting of a smoking ban when the president of the company offered a lot of information about why the smoking ban was being introduced and when he expressed genuine concern and caring for the smokers, for whom the ban was going to be a hardship.[24] In a different study, Jerry Greenberg found that people like Tom were a lot less likely to look for a job elsewhere in the face of pay cuts when the president of the company went to some length to explain the reasons for the pay cuts and when he authentically expressed his regrets about having to implement them.[25] In these and in many other instances, employees' commitment to their employers is much greater when their managers practice higher process fairness, and this is especially so when employees have to endure some type of bad outcome.

Chapter Summary

I first discussed the many factors that affect people's judgments of process fairness. Some refer to a property of the decisions (e.g., whether people were allowed to provide input) while others refer to the interpersonal behavior of the people planning and implementing decisions (e.g., whether they treat the affected parties with dignity and respect). Next we considered how the outcome of a decision (its fairness or favorability) interacts with the fairness of the process to influence employees' productivity and morale. Whereas chapter 1 portrayed the "process-outcome interaction" as a toxic mix resulting from a bad outcome accompanied by an unfair process ("multiplying insult times injury"), here it was described in two other ways: (1) a good outcome can compensate significantly (but not entirely) for an unfair process, and (2) a fair process can compensate significantly (but not entirely) for a bad outcome. Lest you conclude that a good outcome and a fair process are functionally equivalent (in that the presence of one makes it less important to have the other), the two have different financial cost structures. More often than not, it will cost organizations a lot more money to give most employees the outcomes they want than it will cost them to treat most employees with high process fairness. If organizations wish to maximize employees' productivity and morale and do so in cost-effective ways, the "sweet spot" is to deliver moderately favorable outcomes with high process fairness.

In this chapter I also discussed why the favorability of the outcome and the fairness of the process interact with each other to influence employees' productivity and morale. The two explanations overlap to some degree, but they have different starting points. The starting point in one is the outcome, that is, whether it is perceived to be bad or good. Bad outcomes are threatening; they ring the bell of the human alarm system, heightening our sensitivity to information that helps us reduce or manage the experience of threat. Process fairness is one such source of information. With our attention drawn to process fairness information, it stands to reason that we are going to be affected by it. This whole dynamic doesn't happen as much when outcomes are good, which helps explain why process fairness has more of an effect on employees' productivity and morale when they are on the receiving end of bad outcomes rather than good ones.

The starting point in the other explanation is the fairness of the process. One thing employees really want to know about their managers is how much they can be trusted. The results of many studies have shown that there is a direct relationship between managers' process fairness and how much their employees trust them. Managers who practice higher process fairness are trusted more, and when managers are trusted more their employees are less concerned with and therefore are less affected by whether their current outcomes are good or bad. This may be because (1) higher process fairness makes people more optimistic about their longer-term outcomes, and (2) people are willing to trade off their short-term outcomes if they believe they are likely to get a reasonable share of good outcomes in the long run. Knowing why the outcome and the process interact with each other is important not only theoretically but also practically: it can help managers reach more informed judgments of how much their people trust them, and it suggests that managers should consider other ways (besides practicing high process fairness) to heighten their employees' trust in them.

Finally, an additional wrinkle is that outcome favorability and process fairness interact with each other in a different way to influence how people feel about themselves. Whereas an unfair process accompanying a bad outcome provokes employee anger, resentment, and perhaps even outrage directed toward managers, a fair process accompanying the same bad outcome may cause people to feel bad about themselves. Does the latter finding suggest that when managers have to make tough decisions they should use low process fairness to soften the blow that bad outcomes have on people's self-esteem? No. Instead, they should plan and implement tough decisions with high process fairness. They should be aware, however, of the possibility that their employees may experience a threat to their sense of self; therefore, when appropriate, managers should be prepared to take action to help them deal with the threat.

For instance, since high process fairness causes people to make self-attributions for their bad outcomes, managers should encourage the self-attributions to be behavioral rather than characterological. In fact, clinical psychology research has suggested that the nature of people's self-attributions for their unfavorable outcomes is a watershed moment with respect to how negatively they will feel about themselves. The more that they attribute the bad outcome to who they are (characterological self-attribution), the more unfavorably they will view themselves. However, the more that they attribute the same bad outcome to what they did or didn't do (behavioral self-attribution), the *less* negatively they will view themselves.

3 → Making Change Happen: It's All (or at Least Largely) in the Process

Process fairness has a huge impact on how well employees react to a wide array of organizational events and decisions. Whether you are trying to gain support from many people or even a single person for a particular decision, you better make sure that they believe the process is fair. But gaining support for organizational decisions through a high-quality process entails much more than considerations of fairness. In this chapter we take as our point of departure an organization trying to persuade its employees to embrace some change and ask the question: What would the process have to look like? You may have noticed my use of the words "an organization" and "some change" in the previous sentence. I chose these words intentionally, in suggesting that the features of a high-quality process cut across many different types of organizations and many different types of changes. Regardless of whether you are working at a Fortune 500 company, at a government agency, or at a nonprofit organization, and regardless of the substance of the change (e.g., whether your organization is trying to grow or to downsize), the principles for getting the process right are much more similar than they are different.

Change initiatives are introduced in organizations on a regular basis and for a simple reason: dynamism in the external environment. The world is often in flux. Sometimes the external environment becomes more threatening, constraining, and demanding. For example, sometimes we have to deal with new competitors that we may even find surprising. For many years I planted a vegetable garden in our backyard in the spring, tended to it carefully for weeks and months, and saw the fruits (vegetables) of my labor as the crops grew by the end of the summer: good process (I found it relaxing to work in the garden) and good outcome (it was a lot of fun to have some delicious vegetables to eat and to share with others at the end of the summer). One year, however, my good outcome came to a grinding halt: animals had eaten the plants. I remember thinking, how could this happen? I did everything the exact same way that I had for many previous years, only this particular year I had nothing to show for it. Then it hit me: I faced a new source of competition. If I wanted to continue to have the enjoyable experience of a fully grown garden, I would have to go about things in a different way. The next year, for the first time, I put wire mesh fences around the garden, which allowed me to "beat the competition." What I learned, as should managers trying to make change happen, is that we have no entitlements to our external environments. There are things we can do to try to influence what is happening out there, but oftentimes our degree of influence over the environment is limited at best. We need to monitor our environments on an ongoing basis and be proactive in anticipation of where we think the world is going or, at the very least, be appropriately reactive when the world has already shifted.

Sometimes a new environmental constraint comes in the form of regulations. Those working in the financial services industry both before and after 2008 know what I am talking about. The Dodd-Frank Wall Street Reform and Consumer Protection Act, which was signed into law in July 2010 after the global financial crisis in 2008, expanded the regulatory role of the federal government in the financial markets. For example, the government created a bureau to protect consumers from fraud and cut the fees that banks can charge consumers for using their debit cards, among other things. The new world order in the regulatory environment has forced financial service companies to change their basic ways of doing business. Michael Cavanaugh, a longtime senior executive at JP Morgan Chase, widely considered the heir apparent to current CEO Jamie Dimon, announced his departure to take a position with the Carlyle Group, a private equity firm. A major reason for Cavanaugh's surprise departure is that big banks such as JP Morgan Chase face a much more exacting regulatory environment than do their counterparts in private equity.

Changes in the external environment may not only pose threats to but also provide opportunities for organizations. Changes in consumers' taste or changes in technology may enable organizations to provide new products or services, or to offer existing products and services in new ways. New markets may emerge as well. For example, the BRIC report released by Goldman Sachs in 2001 suggested that by the middle of the twenty-first century the four countries represented in the acronym (Brazil, Russia, India, and China) will be among the most dominant global economies.[1] As opportunities present themselves in these new markets, multinational organizations are positioning themselves to take advantage.

Thus the world is in flux and in response to or (even better) in anticipation of where the world is going, organizations change. They introduce new strategic and cultural initiatives, often accompanied by downsizing, growth (either organically or through mergers and acquisitions), relocation, restructuring, outsourcing, new technology, and the introduction of new policies, systems, and procedures. It also seems that organizational change has become, if anything, even more pervasive. When I ask participants in executive education programs to describe the salient changes in their organizations, they frequently say that two or more of the aforementioned changes are taking place at the same time—or, if not exactly at the same time, they are occurring in rapid-fire succession. In short, as the ancient Greek philosopher Heraclitus said circa 500 B.C., "the only constant is change." Isn't it a compelling commentary on the appropriateness of Heraclitus's quote that it was first uttered more than 2,500 years ago?

Do the Right Thing, and Do Things Right

It's often said that great leadership and management are about doing the right thing *and* doing things right. This expression certainly applies to successful organizational change. For a change to better position an organization, senior executives need to do the right thing. In light of what is going on in the external environment, in light of the resources or assets that the organization has to work with, and in light of where it is in its life cycle, an organization needs to craft an appropriate vision and strategy. More often than not, the research suggests, organizations do pretty well in this area. The substance of both the vision and the strategy usually is on target. Quite often, however, the problem is that organizations don't do things right. The process for planning and implementing the change is flawed; in particular, it underattends to the human element.

Whenever change is introduced it may elicit two very different reactions. On the one hand, it sometimes leads people to feel rejuvenated and excited. For example, they may believe that the change is long overdue, and, as a result, they may embrace the change. On the other hand, it sometimes causes people to be confused, angry, or apathetic; as a result they resist the change. What makes employees' reactions go one way or the other? One of the main determinants is the quality of the process that managers use to plan and implement the change. Fairness certainly is in the mix of factors that affect the quality of the process. But there are many more determinants of a high-quality process than its perceived fairness.

These additional aspects of a high-quality process will be discussed at two levels in this chapter. First, at a broader conceptual level, we will consider the set of factors that need to be in place for change to be embraced rather than resisted. This is a "big picture" way of thinking about a high-quality change management process. Second, at a more specific level, I will discuss some concrete examples of best practices that companies have introduced in the process of trying to make change happen.

Paying Homage

Much of this chapter has its roots in the writings of three of the world's foremost authorities on organizational development and change: Mike Beer and John Kotter at Harvard Business School and Todd Jick at Columbia Business

School. Beer introduced the broad framework, derived from none other than Kurt Lewin himself, which posits that in any situation involving change people are subjected to diametrically opposite forces, some of which motivate them to change and others of which serve as impediments. We are caught in an internal struggle between change and stability, much like the "pushmi-pullyu animal," the fictional character in children's books about the life and times of Doctor John Dolittle. Astute change agents recognize that people are subjected simultaneously to the forces for change and the forces for stability. A well-managed change process therefore consists of creating conditions that turn up the volume on the *driving* forces that motivate change while also turning down the volume on the *restraining* forces that block change. Jick and Kotter provided more in the way of specific advice to managers who are trying to make change happen.[2] First, we will talk generally about what change agents need to know about the process of change. Second, because the devil is in the detail, we will consider some of the specifics of a high-quality change management process.

Doing Things Right, Generally

The driving forces that motivate people to change behavior are threefold: (1) they need to feel dissatisfied with the way things currently are ("things are not good"); (2) they need to believe that there is an attractive alternative to the current state ("things could be so much better"); and (3) there need to be mechanisms in place that will move people from the dissatisfying current state to the better future state ("I can and I want to go from here to there").

More on the Driving Forces

People have to want to change; they feel this way when their current situation is simply not acceptable. Most of us have heard the expression "If it ain't broke, don't fix it." To make people want to change they have to believe that things are indeed broken. A well-managed change process illuminates dissatisfaction with the current state. Of course, if change agents focus *only* on what's broken or wrong, they will be seen as too negative or as a wet blanket, hardly the stuff of change-motivating leadership. Therefore, the process also needs to show people that there is a better alternative to the current situation. That better alternative is captured by the word *vision*. The vision provides people with a mental image of the desired future state that gives them a reason to make the journey. Visions need to be clear, achievable, and motivational. Bringing dissatisfaction to the surface and providing a better alternative in the form of a vision are not enough, however. Unlike the Nike commercial that tells us to "Just do it," people need a roadmap of how to go from here to there. In addition to providing a roadmap, change agents need to do a host of things in the process that make people willing and able to make the journey.

Restraining Forces

People often resist change because they view it as costly. They may believe that the change will mean a loss of power, prestige, control, or job security. Interestingly enough, this can happen even when the change being implemented gives the organization an opportunity to change for the better. In the fascinating case study "Gunfire at Sea," Elving Morison describes how senior executives in the United States Navy reacted to a technological breakthrough at the turn of the twentieth century that enabled naval officers to improve their shooting accuracy by no less than 3000 percent. It would seem to be a no-brainer that this breakthrough would be readily accepted by the naval power structure in Washington, D.C. However, a midlevel officer by the name of William Sims was repeatedly ignored or rebuffed when he made numerous attempts to persuade the senior-level decision makers in the navy to take this breakthrough seriously. It was only when Sims wrote directly to the president of the United States (Theodore Roosevelt) that the innovation gained traction. Why did Sims's earlier requests go nowhere? Among other reasons, Morison suggests that it was because Sims was criticizing the prior work of the very people to whom he was sending his complaints. This example is a sobering reminder of how people may have a vested interest in maintaining the status quo (read: be resistant to change), even when there are better ways to do things. A more contemporary example of the dynamics in play in "Gunfire at Sea" is when employees resist new technology because they believe (accurately or not) that accepting the change means that they will work themselves out of a job.[3]

Change also brings about uncertainty, in which people have to tolerate ambiguity about, for example, what the new organization will look like and what their new role will be in it. From the school of thought that says "the devil you know is better than the devil you don't know," we can understand why people may resist. Having to do things differently also takes people out of their comfort zones. They may be competent at what they currently do, but because the change will require them to do new things they worry about their competence going forward.

Change also requires us to do more work. While learning to do something new you still have a lot of ongoing responsibilities. For example, think back to the last time that you took a business trip or a family vacation. What was life like for you, on the personal or professional front, during the day or two before you left? Very hectic, I bet. Why? You were managing change on a personal level. You had to do a bunch of things to get ready for the trip in addition to the usual work fare (e.g., getting a report done and advising your direct reports) and over and above the usual stuff at home such as working with your kids on their homework and ensuring that the family pet was taken care of. In like fashion, when change is introduced in the workplace the extra work it often entails can make employees' lives much more demanding. Thus if they don't like where the change is going, if they don't welcome uncertainty, if they don't appreciate being taken out of their comfort zones, and if on top of all that they are being asked to take on more work, we can begin to understand why people oppose change.

In short, people have multiple reasons to resist change. Upon encountering their resistance managers need to be curious about discovering where it is coming from. It is not "one size fits all." Astute change agents diagnose the root cause(s) of employees' resistance to change because doing so generates effective ways to deal with the resistance. As always, diagnosis precedes intervention. What managers do to deal with employees' resistance should take very different forms, depending upon the root cause of the resistance. For example, suppose a manager diagnosed that employees were being resistant because they questioned their competence to do the new things that the change required of them. If that were the basis of their resistance, then a manager should allow them to practice the new skills or perhaps send them to a training program so that they could acquire the new skills. On the other hand, people may be resistant not because they question their capabilities but because they do not want to do what the change will require of them. If a manager were to send such individuals to a training program it probably would not be very helpful; they already have the capability. What could do the trick here is a further drill-down to the root cause of why they don't want to do what the change requires of them. Perhaps they don't see what's in it for them; if so, the challenge is to show them what *is* in it for them. Or perhaps they are being resistant not so much because of the substance of the change but because of the way in which it was rolled out. For instance, the reasons for the change may not have been communicated well. If so, the reasons for the change need to be communicated immediately, even if they weren't communicated well previously; better late than never. The more general point is that we need to recognize that the restraining forces (or bases of employees' resistance to change) can take many forms. Managers need to pinpoint the bases of resistance and take action accordingly.

A high-quality change process that is likely to result in employees embracing rather than resisting change can be summarized as follows:

$$Change = (D \times V \times P) > C.$$

The letters in the parentheses represent the driving forces. D stands for surfacing *dissatisfaction* with the current situation. V stands for providing a *vision* of the future state. P stands for having a *process* in place that motivates and equips people to move from the dissatisfying current state to the better future state. C stands for the *costs* of change; it captures the restraining forces, or bases of resistance to change.[4] Employees will embrace change (manifesting itself in high employee productivity and morale) to the extent that the driving forces toward change outweigh the restraining forces against change. Note that the equation is conceptual, not mathematical. It offers a way to think about what a high-quality change process looks like. Quite intentionally, there is a multiplication sign between D and V, and between V and P. The multiplication signs symbolize that *all* of the driving forces need to be present for change to happen: 100 times 100 times 0 is still 0. Put differently, if any one of the driving forces is not handled well, change is unlikely to happen. Furthermore, the equation suggests that managers not put all of their eggs in the basket of driving forces. There are restraining forces or bases of resistance that need to be attended to as well.

Because so many things have to be in place for a change process to be done well it can feel overwhelming to any one would-be agent of change. Although trying to bring about change is not for the faint of heart, I do not mean to suggest that any one person has to be great at all of the things that go into a well-managed change process. I am simply saying that all aspects of the DVP > C framework need to be present, which is not the same thing as saying that a manager trying to make change happen has to be proficient at all aspects of D, V, P, and C. In a few moments we will discuss the specific behaviors that make up the framework, which will allow managers to further evaluate how well they do things as agents of change. Let's say, for example, that a manager is very good at some of the bigger-picture aspects of a well-managed change process, namely

D and V, but not as strong in some of the implementation details, namely P and C. This manager has two possible paths forward here, which are not mutually exclusive. On the one hand, he could focus on ways to improve in the areas in which he is less strong. I will offer specific advice on the kinds of things he needs to be doing more of or less of that may make him more effective in the aspects of process in which he is less strong. On the other hand, he could try to align himself with other people who bring the skill sets that complement his own. If he is strong in D and V, and if he can forge a collaborative relationship with other people who are strong in P and C, then all of the elements that go into a well-managed change process will be present, in which case there is an excellent chance for change to happen.

Doing Things Right, Specifically

Drawing on the work of John Kotter and others, Todd Jick offered a more specific way to think about a well-managed change process, which he dubbed "The Ten Commandments" of managing change.[5] I will build on Jick's recommendations in several important respects. First, since all of his ideas overlap in some way with Beer's DVP > C framework, I will connect the dots between the Jick commandments and the Beer framework. Indeed, Jick's commandments present the Beer framework in a more specific and therefore actionable form. Second, in the service of trying to make a well-managed change process even more actionable, I have devised a thirty-four-item checklist based upon many of Jick's commandments. Although I will not talk about *all* thirty-four items here, I will cover many of them; the complete instrument (the

Change Implementation Survey and its Scoring Guide) appears in appendixes A and B. The complete instrument is important for two reasons: it will portray a well-managed change process in a way that is both comprehensive and detailed, and it will provide a forum for managers to evaluate themselves as agents of change. As you read through the instrument, do some self-diagnosis. Which items reflect the things that you do a lot? Which ones reflect the things that you don't do as much? I will provide specific examples of how many of the items have been implemented by forward-thinking agents of change, along with supporting research evidence. I also will discuss the Jick commandments as they relate to each of the components of the Beer change framework, $(D \times V \times P) > C$.

Two of Jick's commandments fall squarely in the domain of D, which refers to surfacing dissatisfaction with the status quo: (1) analyzing the need for change, and (2) creating a sense of urgency. Let's discuss each of these, in turn.

Analyzing the Need for Change

Analyzing the need for change requires managers to have a very good grasp of how well the organization is doing, as well as a solid understanding of the root causes of the organization's performance. If a manager has a strong ability to analyze the need for change, it will put her in a good position to carry out item #1 from the Change Implementation Survey: "I clearly describe to people *why* the situation as it exists prior to the change is not acceptable." We touched on the importance of giving explanations in chapter 2; it is one of the components of a fair process. What we did not discuss in the previous chapter, however, is why giving explanations helps get people onboard. In other words, why is it important to explain why? For one thing, explaining why is important for substantive or informational reasons. Managers who are trying to make change happen sometimes lose track of the fact that their employees are not as up to speed on the reasons for the change as they are. In some ways this oversight is understandable. After all, managers may be closer to the information that makes the need to change clear, relative to the employees they are trying to convince. Managers also may be aware of the planned change for quite some time prior to rolling this information out to their direct reports. For example, they may know for a while that a downsizing or plant closing is in the works before this is made known to all members of the organization. What change agents need to do is put themselves back in time to the moment in which it was first explained to them why the current situation is not acceptable. Just as they likely found it helpful at that earlier point to be given information about the reasons for the change, so too are their employees likely to find such information useful.

A second reason why it is important to explain why is more symbolic than substantive. The explanation may symbolize a number of things that may make employees more willing to get onboard. For instance, the explanation communicates that managers care enough about their employees to give them reasons for the impending changes. It also shows that managers empathize with or at least are aware of the uncertainty that their employees may be experiencing, which they will appreciate. In such instances the substance of the explanation does not even have to be all that informative; it's the mere presence of the explanation that matters. A number of years ago my wife (Audrey) and I were sitting in the departure area at the airport waiting for our flight.

Under normal circumstances the airline announces the beginning of the boarding process thirty minutes prior to departure. We had a scheduled 1:00 PM departure, but 12:30 came and went, with no announcement. The same thing happened at 12:45 and then again at 1:00. At this point Audrey noticed that many people in the waiting area were growing fidgety. It was not as if there was no plane; it was parked right outside the boarding area. Audrey strode up to the gate agent and politely said, "Excuse me. I am a business psychologist, and I think it would be very helpful to all of us if you could give some sort of explanation of why we have not been asked to board the plane." Shortly thereafter, we heard the following announcement about our flight: "The departure time for the flight has been delayed." Although this was patently obvious, this "information" was enough to appease many of the waiting passengers. One of them muttered, "At least they said something!" Another one said, "At least we know that they are aware of what is going on."

A clever study done by Ellen Langer, Arthur Blank, and Benzion Chanowitz shows how people may be more willing to go along with the person giving an explanation even when the substance of the explanation is devoid of information. The participants in the study were at a photocopying machine, making copies and minding their own business, and unbeknownst to them were about to take part in a psychological study. In all cases they were approached by the researcher, who wanted to interrupt their photocopying so that she could go ahead of the participants. To some participants the researcher said, "Excuse me, I have five pages. May I use the photocopier?" whereas to other participants the researcher said, "Excuse me, I have five pages. May I use the photocopier, because I have to make copies?"

Although the second request was accompanied by an "explanation" ("Because I have to make copies"), it is pretty obvious that this explanation provided no new information to the participants. However, the participants who received this explanation were significantly more likely to step aside to let the researcher do her photocopying relative to those who did not receive any such "explanation." Langer and her colleagues suggested that people sometimes interact with each other in a mindless kind of way, in which they don't pay attention to the substance of what people are saying or doing. As long as others' behavior has the right form (in this case, requests *should* be accompanied by an explanation), we are willing to go along with it.[6] All of this is not to say that if you are trying to bring about change you need not provide substantive information as to why change is necessary and that any old explanation will do. Unlike the participants in the photocopying study, employees whose organizations have introduced change are likely to be very attentive to what they are being told. If so, it behooves change agents to provide explanations that are clear and reasonable. The results of the Langer, Blank, and Chanowitz study suggest, however, that one of the reasons why people are willing to get onboard when they are given a clear and reasonable explanation is the symbolic rather than the substantive value of the explanation.

Creating a Sense of Urgency

The silver lining in the cloud when organizations find themselves in dire straits is that there is little need to create a sense of urgency to change; the felt urgency is already present. Creating a sense of urgency refers to managers initiating change on a proactive rather than a reactive basis, in which the current state of the organization is at least satisfactory and maybe even a lot better than that. An example of an action that reflects creating a sense of urgency is item #3 from the Change Implementation Survey in appendix A: "I introduce change in anticipation of problems, not only in response to problems that have already surfaced." This raises the following question: How can change agents *credibly* create a sense of urgency if people believe that there is nothing particularly wrong with how things currently are? There are two answers to this question, and I will provide supporting evidence for each one. First, people can be told that although the current state is not bad, things are likely to turn south in the not too distant future. Let's call this "the burning platform" approach. Second, people can be told that although the organization's current state is satisfactory, it could very plausibly be so much better; therefore, to not try to improve amounts to leaving money on the table. I will call this the "the going for the gold" approach. Let's talk about both, in turn.

THE BURNING PLATFORM

A number of years ago I served on a strategic planning committee for Columbia University. Even though our task was rather straightforward (to develop a new strategic plan for the entire university for the next five years), it was rather daunting. Columbia University is a complex institution; therefore, generating a new strategic plan was going to be no small undertaking. At the first meeting, in which the provost of the university tried to make a compelling case for why we needed a new strategic plan, we (the members of the committee) listened politely, but many of us weren't buying it. After all, we thought to ourselves, Columbia is a premier academic institution. Were things really that bad that we needed a new strategic plan for the next five years? Couldn't we just go with what we had been doing up until that point? Complacency enveloped the room at that first meeting until we listened to a report from the university's chief financial officer (CFO) about the fiscal state of the university. The immediate picture was pretty good, he told us. Although the university had overspent its budget during the previous year it was not by an amount about which we should be worried. What shocked us, however, were his forward-looking projections. If the university failed to adopt a new strategic plan and instead continued to adhere to the one that was already in place, we would have a very sizable budget overrun in the next academic year, and an even more sizable budget overrun than that two years hence. Our sense of complacency evaporated almost instantaneously. We were now onboard to take the strategic planning process much more seriously. I can think of at least two reasons why the CFO's presentation was so effective in creating a sense of urgency. First, it was the presentation itself; he made a compelling and easily understandable case for change, replete with an impressive set of PowerPoint slides. Second, the fact that the presentation came from the CFO himself rather than from one of his underlings added to the credibility of the presentation. In any event, suffice it to say that we committee members were feeling a lot less smug after the CFO's presentation than we were before.

GOING FOR THE GOLD

An alternative way to create a sense of urgency is to show the audience that the satisfactory current state of the organization can plausibly be replaced by a much better alternative. Upon perceiving the discrepancy between where things stand and where they *could* stand, people should experience dissatisfaction with the current state. No one exemplified this particular way to create a sense of urgency better than Steve Jobs, the late cofounder of Apple Computer and its longtime chief executive officer. Most of us managed to make our way through life reasonably well before the introduction of some of Apple's popular products (e.g., iPod, iPhone, and iPad). The genius of Steve Jobs was to envision a world that would be so much better with these products than it was before and to make the compelling case for change to people inside and, perhaps more important, outside the organization. When questioned by a reporter about the market research preceding the launch of the iPad, Jobs famously replied, "None. It is not the consumers' job to know what they want." Jobs saw it as his (and Apple's) responsibility to show people a new world that was so much better than the current one.

Given these two ways to create a sense of urgency, which one would you say is the better way to go? Do you think people would be more motivated to depart from a satisfactory current state by the "burning platform" approach or by the "going for the gold" approach? When I pose this question to executive audiences most of them say that the former is more likely to create a sense of urgency than is the latter. Note that this answer reveals their theory of human nature, in that they are essentially saying that people are more motivated to avoid a bad situation than they are to approach a good situation. The Nobel laureate Daniel Kahneman and his late coauthor, Amos Tversky, put it this way: losses loom larger than gains. For instance, the pain of losing $100 is greater than the pleasure of winning $100.[7]

Research conducted by one of my colleagues at Columbia University, Tory Higgins, suggests, however, that the answer to the question of which method is a more effective way to create a sense of urgency is not that simple. As suggested by Higgins's influential regulatory focus theory, it depends on the people you are trying to reach. Let me explain. Taking as his point of departure the basic principle that people seek to approach pleasure and avoid pain, Higgins has suggested that there are important differences in the way that we go about trying to approach pleasure and avoid pain that have substantial effects on what we think, feel, and do. (Higgins's message is the same as the main one in this book: it's not only the result that matters but also the process we go through to get there.)

Higgins suggests that we can go about approaching pleasure and avoiding pain in a promotion-focused way or in a prevention-focused way. There are three noteworthy differences between being promotion focused and being prevention focused: the needs that we are trying to satisfy, the standards that we are trying to meet, and how we think about our outcomes in relation to the standards. When promotion focused, people are motivated by the desire to grow and develop. The salient standard for people when they are promotion focused is the "ideal self," which reflects dreams and aspirations. Promotion-focused persons think about outcomes in relation to the standard along the dimension of gains versus non-gains; when they have been successful in attaining their ideal self they experience the pleasure of a gain and when they have not been successful in attaining their ideal self they experience the pain of a non-gain.

In contrast, when people are prevention focused they are motivated by safety and security. The salient standard for prevention-focused people is the "ought self," which reflects duties, obligations, and responsibilities. Prevention-focused persons think about outcomes in relation to the standard along the dimension of loss versus non-loss; when they have been successful in reaching their "ought self" they experience the pleasure of a non-loss and when they have not been successful in reaching their "ought self" they experience the pain of a loss.[8]

Here's a perhaps simpler way to think about the difference between promotion and prevention focus: promotion-focused people "play to win" whereas prevention-focused people "play to not lose." Practically all people can be promotion focused or prevention focused, depending on the situation or context. Nevertheless, there are individual differences in people's tendencies to be more or less promotion focused and more or less prevention focused. An example of promotion-focused leadership was Martin Luther King in the March on Washington in 1963, in which he made his famous "I have a dream" speech calling for an end to racial discrimination. An example of prevention-focused leadership is Andy Grove, the cofounder of Intel (the maker of computer microprocessors), who wrote the best-selling management book *Only the Paranoid Survive*. King and Grove were both visionary leaders who wanted to bring about change, which underscores an important point about people's regulatory focus orientations. The tendency to be promotion focused or prevention focused is not inherent to the behavior itself. Virtually anything we do can be undertaken in a promotion-focused, play-to-win manner or in a prevention-focused, play-to-not-lose manner. However, it is how we go about our attempts to self-regulate (that is, the process) that makes a big difference.

Over and above individual differences in people's tendencies to be promotion or prevention focused, certain situations or environments influence people's regulatory focus orientation. For example, the corporate culture in an entrepreneurial start-up is likely to be promotion focused, especially in its early days. Members of a start-up organization often are highly motivated to achieve the aspirational vision of its founders. In contrast, the culture in an established utility company may be more prevention focused, in which a highly salient goal is to avoid power outages ("keep the meters running").

Having walked through the basics of regulatory focus theory, we now return to the question I asked earlier about which is the more effective way to create a sense of urgency: Are people more motivated to depart from a satisfactory current state by the "burning platform" approach or by the "going for the gold" approach? I am hopeful that at this point you are saying to yourself something like, "It depends upon whether people are promotion focused or prevention focused." When people are playing to not lose, the "burning platform" approach is more effective in creating a sense of urgency. When people are playing to win, however, the "going for the gold" approach is the better way to go.

A study by Lorraine Idson, Nira Liberman, and Tory Higgins shows that even subtle situational cues may affect people's tendencies to be promotion or prevention focused, which in turn affects the intensity with which they experience positive versus negative outcomes. In this study participants were asked to imagine that they were in a bookstore, buying a book that they needed. Slight differences in language were used to make them promotion or prevention focused. Those induced to be promotion focused were told, "The book's price is $65. As you wait in line to pay, you realize that the store offers a $5 discount for paying in cash, and you decide that you want to pay cash." In contrast, those induced to be prevention focused were told, "The book's price is $60. As you wait in line to pay, you realize that the store charges a $5 penalty for paying with a credit card, and you decide that you want to pay cash." Note the minor difference in language: the promotion frame emphasized the upside of gaining $5 by paying cash whereas the prevention frame emphasized the downside of losing $5 by paying with a credit card. People who care only about outcomes or results may look at these two scenarios and say, "six of one, half dozen of the other." After all, regardless of whether the wording is framed to emphasize promotion or prevention, people will spend $65 if they pay with a credit card and $60 if they pay with cash.

Participants also received outcome information. Those given the promotion frame were told either that "You look in your purse, and you realize that you actually have the cash, so you will be getting the discount" (gain condition) or that "You look in your purse, and you realize that you don't have the cash; you will have to use your credit card so you will not be getting the discount" (non-gain condition). Those given the prevention frame were told either that "You look in your purse, and you realize that you actually have the cash, so you will not be paying the penalty" (non-loss condition) or that "You look in your purse, and you realize that you don't have the cash; you will have to use the credit card, so you will be paying the penalty" (loss condition).

All participants then rated how good or bad they would feel if they were in the situation described to them. Naturally, people felt much better when the outcome was positive rather than negative; they felt much better in the gain than in the non-gain condition and they felt much better in the non-loss than in the loss condition. What is much more interesting is that whether people were promotion or prevention focused also influenced their experience. Promotion-focused people who experienced a gain felt a lot better than did prevention-focused people who experienced a non-loss. Note that both groups experienced the same positive outcome: paying $60 for the book in cash. However, promotion-focused people assign greater importance to positive outcomes than do prevention-focused people. As a result, promotion-focused people experienced more of the upside when the positive outcome came their way. On the other hand, prevention-focused people who experienced a loss felt a lot worse than did promotion-focused people who experienced a non-gain. Both of these groups experienced the same negative outcome of paying $65 for the book with a credit card. However, prevention-focused people assign more importance to negative outcomes than do promotion-focused people. Consequently, prevention-focused people experience the downside more strongly when a negative outcome comes their way.[9]

These results suggest at least three reasons why it may be useful to take into account whether people are promotion focused or prevention focused when presenting them with change. First, the findings offer an amendment to the generally well-accepted idea that "losses loom larger than gains." In fact, this seems to be more applicable to prevention-focused people than to promotion-focused people. Second, although I presented these findings to help us better understand which of two ways would work better in creating a sense of urgency to change, the distinction between promotion and prevention focus sheds light more generally on the kind of feedback that will induce people to put forth high levels of effort. Indeed, managers, educators, and parents have long wrestled with the question of whether positive feedback or negative feedback is more motivating. When Michael Jordan's Chicago Bulls won their first NBA championship it motivated him to win another, and another, and another. (He was a member of six championship teams.) Other people (e.g., Winston Churchill, Abraham Lincoln, and Ronald Reagan) were motivated to strive to reach great heights by earlier failures in their careers. So which is it? According to research by Dina Van-Dijk and Avraham Kluger, it depends on people's regulatory focus. Promotion-focused persons are more motivated by positive feedback than by negative feedback whereas just the opposite is true for prevention-focused persons.[10]

Third, the results refine our understanding about the most effective way to instill the urgency to change in other people. If we are trying to bring about change on a proactive rather than reactive basis, it will always be necessary to create a sense of urgency. The punch line, however, is that change agents need to do it in different ways for different audiences. For some people (e.g., promotion-focused types) it is the lure of the upside that will be particularly captivating. For others (e.g., prevention-focused types) it is the desire to avoid the downside that will be especially motivating.[11]

Among the questions raised by our discussion of promotion and prevention focuses is: Is there any way to know whether we tend to emphasize one orientation rather than the other? Here is one quick-and-dirty diagnostic that you can try out on yourself and your friends.

It turns out that the predominant nature of people's emotional experiences differs depending upon whether they are promotion or prevention focused. Promotion-focused persons live in a world characterized by happiness and exhilaration at one extreme and by sadness or dejection at the other. They play to win; when things are going well (that is, when they are winning) they feel excited and upbeat. On the other hand, when they are not winning, they feel dejected and downbeat.

Prevention-focused persons live in a world of calm at one extreme and agitation at the other. They play to not lose; when things are going well (that is, when they are not losing) they feel relieved. However, when they are losing they feel anxious and/or angry. Of course, all of us feel all of these emotions some of the time. But the question is, which emotional continuum do you live on *more*? If you believe that your emotions fluctuate between happiness and sadness more than they fluctuate between calm and agitation, you probably are more promotion focused. If, however, you believe that your emotions vary between calm and agitation more than they vary between happiness and sadness, you probably lean toward being prevention focused.[12]

My wife unwittingly revealed her regulatory focus orientation to me during the course of our initial conversation. We were fixed up on a blind date. I called her on the phone (this was 1979) to suggest a time and place for us to meet. We were having a friendly, getting to know one another chat on the phone during which I asked her, "How would you describe yourself?" Without hesitating for a moment, she good-naturedly said, "I would say that I am fun-loving and depressed." What my future wife was essentially telling me that very first night is that she is promotion focused (upbeat and lighthearted when things are going well and dejected when they are not).

Another interesting example of how people's reports of their emotions may reveal their regulatory focus may be seen in how the University of Chicago economics professor James J. Heckman reacted to the news that he had been selected to win the Nobel Prize in Economic Science. The story I am about to tell is also a particularly vivid reminder of how virtually anything we do or experience can be done or felt in a promotion- or prevention-focused way. How do you think you would react if you were told that you had been selected to receive the highest honor in your field? I think most of us would experience the promotion-focused emotions of elation or exhilaration after receiving such news. To win the highest honor in your field is something of which most people can only dream. To use the language of regulatory focus theory, if this isn't a clear marker of having attained the promotion-focused standard of the ideal self, I don't know what is. How did Professor Heckman respond? Positively, of course. However, his reaction suggests that he viewed the news through the lens of being prevention focused rather than promotion focused. He said, "I feel relieved to get a Nobel."

Relieved to win the Nobel Prize? How can that be? Well, at the time that he won the award, Professor Heckman was one of nine University of Chicago professors to have won the award in Economic Science; no other university had that many winners of that particular award. Perhaps he felt that as a University of Chicago economist it was his duty and responsibility to win a Nobel Prize in Economic Science. Recall that duty and responsibility go hand in hand with the "ought self," which is the standard that people are trying to attain when they are prevention focused.

Heckman's own words suggest this possibility. Referring to a point in his career prior to winning the Nobel Prize, Professor Heckman said, "I remember some reporter called me and asked, 'How does it feel to be at Chicago *without* a Nobel Prize?' After a while it starts to hurt" (emphasis added).[13]

Here's another quick-and-dirty test you can do on yourself or others to assess regulatory focus, which is based on the fact that positive feedback is more motivating for promotion types and negative feedback is more motivating for prevention types. The question to consider is this: Which type of feedback energizes you more? If you find positive feedback gets you to try hard more than does negative feedback, then you probably are more promotion focused. On the other hand, if you find negative feedback more energizing than positive feedback, then you probably are more prevention focused.

Psychologists have developed a number of measures of people's tendencies to be promotion or prevention focused. Several of these measures are presented in appendixes C and D. The one in appendix C is a more general measure whereas the one in appendix D (called the "Work Regulatory Focus" scale) looks at people's typical tendencies to be promotion or prevention focused in the workplace.

Vision of the Future

Analyzing the need for change and creating a sense of urgency are two pillars of "D," which is surfacing dissatisfaction with the way things are. However, a high-quality change process doesn't simply point out what's wrong with the current situation; it also shows people how things can be better. This better way is captured by the vision, which refers to an appealing image of the future state. Doing the visioning aspects of a change process in a high-quality way entails three things: (1) ensuring that the vision has the necessary ingredients ("All the Right Stuff"); (2) ensuring that everyone understands the vision ("All on the Same Page"); and (3) ensuring that everyone buys into the vision ("All Rowing in the Same Direction").

All the Right Stuff

To bring about change, visions have to be clear, achievable, and inspirational. If the vision is not clear then we can't really talk about making change happen in any meaningful way. "Achievable" is not the same thing as "easy"—far from it. The best visions stretch people. However, they can't stretch people too much or they will give up in a state of hopelessness and despair. Finally, it takes energy to change, which may be supplied by a vision that is motivational or inspirational.

Visions are one of a number of entities that provide direction and focus, and in so doing show people a better alternative. Others include the mission (the organization's basic purpose), the strategy (how the organization plans to bring about the vision), and the goals (specific performance indicators of how much the vision has been reached). Furthermore, whereas values are not inherently future oriented (in the way that the vision is), values need to inform the vision to make it inspirational.

Vision statements are important because they reflect the "public face" of the organization. They vary considerably along the dimensions of how clear, achievable, and inspiring they are. All else being equal, shorter statements tend to be clearer. For example, the Gillette Company's Vision is:

> To build Total Brand Value by innovating to deliver consumer value and customer leadership faster, better and more completely than our competition. This Vision is supported by two fundamental principles that provide the foundation for all of our activities: Organizational Excellence and Core Values. Attaining our Vision requires superior and continually improving performance in every area and at every level of the organization. Our performance will be guided by a clear and concise strategic statement for each business unit and by an ongoing Quest for Excellence within all operational and staff functions. This Quest for Excellence requires hiring, developing and retaining a diverse workforce of the highest caliber. To support this Quest, each function employs metrics to define, and implements processes to achieve, world-class status.

In contrast, the vision of the Ken Blanchard Company (founded by the leadership training expert Ken Blanchard) is "To be the number one advocate in the world for human worth in organizations." Based on sheer length alone the vision at Blanchard is clearer than the one at Gillette.

Inspirational vision statements typically go beyond striving for financial profitability goals to some grander purpose that such profitability would promote. For example, DuPont's vision is "To be the world's most dynamic science company, creating sustainable solutions essential to a better, safer and healthier life for people everywhere." Making the world a safer and healthier place are values about which most of us can get excited.

The dimension with which architects of vision statements struggle the most is achievability. Sometimes the future state is portrayed as so lofty as to be unreachable. For example, similar to Henry Ford's vision of "a car in every garage," Microsoft claims that "There will be a personal computer on every desk running Microsoft software." If employees were to take such a vision statement literally they likely would feel overwhelmed and give up. Of course, perhaps both Henry Ford and Bill Gates at Microsoft meant their visions figuratively rather than literally. If so, then employees may use information about strategy and goals to make more informed judgments about the achievability of their employer's vision of the future state.

One thing great visions do not have to have is originality. Sometimes change agents spend too much time trying to think about how their vision needs to be different from that of their competitors. Originality is one way to be inspiring, but there are other ways to be inspiring without being original. Let me share with you a personal example. I have been a faculty member at Columbia Business School since 1984. Four years later, *Business Week* came out with its first ranking of MBA programs. We didn't fare too well, coming in at #14. We weren't very happy about this; no one was walking around the halls of Columbia Business School chanting, "We're #14, we're #14!!" The very next year a new dean, Meyer Feldberg, was appointed. His vision for Columbia Business School was to be a preeminent business school ("quintessential" was one of his favorite words), that is, to be among the very top schools along any of the dimensions that our key stakeholders (students, recruiters, and the academic management community) cared about.

To be among the very top schools; how original is that? Not very. After all, all of the best business schools are trying to be among the very top schools. But how inspirational is that? Highly. Dean Feldberg and his successor, Glenn Hubbard, have successfully shown that it is well within our reach to be so much better than we were.

Where does Columbia Business School stand now, more than twenty-five years after the first *Business Week* ranking? Let me provide some hard statistical data as well as some soft anecdotal evidence. Since the original *Business Week* survey other media outlets have joined the fray (e.g., *Financial Times* and *US News and World Report*); indeed, the ranking of business education programs has become a cottage industry of sorts. Columbia Business School usually comes out in the top ten in the various surveys, and our overall ranking in early 2012 (which is a composite based upon many different polls) put us at #5. Not bad! The softer evidence? In my opinion as a longtime faculty member, without question we are offering much better programs to our students. We are on the road to achieving the inspirational (but not particularly original) vision of our former and present deans.

All on the Same Page

The vision also needs to be one that everyone understands. Although much of this depends on whether the vision has the right stuff, namely whether it is clear, it also depends on the way the vision is communicated. An example of what I mean is item #6 from the Change Implementation Survey: "I remind people of our common vision, throughout the change effort." The important word in item #6 is "remind." If people are regularly told the vision it is more likely to be salient in their minds. From the perspective of change agents, it may feel a little tedious to have to remind their employees about the common vision, but they need to be told the vision on a regular basis. One way to make the communication of the vision more engaging (to those on both the delivering and receiving end) is by sending the same message in different forums, such as in annual reports and monthly newsletters, in town hall meetings, and in more informal encounters between employees and their immediate managers. The communication of the vision also needs to be a two-way one. For employees to arrive at a common understanding of the future direction of their company, they also need to be able to ask questions about the future direction.

All Rowing in the Same Direction

Getting everyone on the same page in terms of understanding is necessary but not sufficient to ensure that they are actively engaged in seeing the vision come to fruition. There is a subtle difference between everyone understanding the vision and everyone being actively engaged with the vision, as reflected in the following riddle: "What's the difference between ignorance and apathy?" Answer: "I don't know, and I don't care." Hence the distinction between understanding and engagement: a lack of common understanding (not being on the same page) connotes ignorance whereas a lack of common engagement (not rowing in the same direction) reflects apathy. Here again, the extent to which everyone is rowing in the same direction depends on how the vision- or direction-setting activities are managed. For employees to be engaged with the vision, three things have to happen: (1) change agents have to show their employees what's in it for them if the vision were to be realized; (2) assuming that people see what's in it for them, change agents should involve their employees in developing the implementation plan, that is, the many who, what, where, when, and how details; and (3) *while the journey is in process* change agents need to remind their employees of how what they do and how well they do it are directly related to the attainment of the vision. This final point suggests that it's not enough to emphasize what's in it for employees if the vision were to be achieved; it also is important to emphasize what's in it for the attainment of the vision if employees were to do their jobs well.

Thus change agents need to be "dot connectors." On the one hand, there is the work that employees have to do to bring about change. On the other hand, the change effort should bring with it a grander sense of purpose so as to be inspiring. The dot-connecting change agent helps people see how the work that they do is directly linked to the grander sense of purpose associated with the change. Nobody illustrates the dot-connecting role more clearly than Mary Kay Ash, the founder of Mary Kay Cosmetics. If you were to ask any outsider to describe the purpose of Mary Kay Cosmetics, the simple answer would be that the organization is in the business of selling cosmetics. But that's not how it looks to those on the inside. Mary Kay Ash has gone on record as saying that the purpose of her organization is to help women become the beautiful creatures that God intended them to be. Suppose you were working at Mary Kay Cosmetics, and you bought into Mary Kay Ash's view of the organization's mission. Would you define your work as simply selling cosmetics? And, if not, how would you define your work? My guess is that if you bought into Mary Kay

Ash's perspective you would be more likely to see your-self as doing God's work than as just selling cosmetics. Many people would be highly motivated if they saw the fulfillment of their work activities as akin to doing God's work rather than as simply selling cosmetics. In short, the challenge and opportunity for change agents is not only to craft an inspirational vision but also to remind people of the reciprocal relationship between themselves and the attainment of the vision: just as attaining the vision will bring with it rewards they find personally meaningful, so too should it be clear to them how they have a significant role to play in bringing about the vision.

Process: Getting There from Here

Although surfacing dissatisfaction with the way things are ("D") and showing people a better alternative through an alluring vision of the future ("V") are necessary to bring about change, they are not sufficient. The journey from dis-satisfying Point A to a better Point B doesn't just happen. Change agents have to do many other things to engage and equip their employees to make the trip. Each of these elements maps onto one of Jick's Ten Commandments for managing change: (1) help people separate from the past; (2) develop a strong leader role; (3) line up political and social sponsorship; (4) craft an implementation plan; (5) develop engaging and enabling structures; (6) monitor and refine; and (7) communicate, involve, and be honest.[14] To repeat, do not expect yourself to be highly skilled in all of these elements; it takes a collective to enact the "P" part of change management (process) in a high-quality way. I will illustrate each of these elements with items from the Change Implementation Survey, with specific examples from the rough-and-tumble real world in which managers are trying to make change happen, and with the results of empirical research.

Help People Separate from the Past

One reason why people have a hard time letting go of the old way of doing things is because of what they infer the change to mean: that their previous efforts were inadequate or invalid. If people have grown accustomed to doing certain things, or to doing things in a certain way, it may become a part of who they are. For example, if Charlie is known as the "go-to guy" for getting things done with one form of technology, and the organization introduces a new technology for which Charlie is no longer the expert, then the introduction of the new technology could throw Charlie into a bit of an identity crisis. Or if Tom plays a major role in developing the strategic planning process that has been in use for many years and the organization switches to a new type of process, he may feel like his baby is being taken away from him. Moreover, depending on how the transition is handled he may believe that not only is his baby being taken away but also that the organization is telling him that his baby is defective.

In short, people may interpret change to mean that their previous efforts are no longer effective (after all, why else would the organization introduce change), which may cause them to feel invalidated and disrespected. Just because they *may* feel invalidated and disrespected, however, does not mean that they *will*. It all depends on how the process is handled. Item #10 from the Change Implementation Survey directly addresses this point: "When telling people about the need to change our current practices, show respect toward those practices that have served us well in the past."

If people believe that previous ways of doing things have been shown respect, they find it easier to separate from doing them. This is particularly true regarding practices that are relevant to their sense of identity, such as those they have been doing well for a long time or those they had some say in developing. One of the most effective ways to show respect for the old and thereby help people embrace the new is through the use of ceremony. For example, consider the case of a midlevel manager in a manufacturing plant that is introducing several changes all at once (layoffs, relocation, and new technology). She has been told by senior management that there is no time to dwell on how things used to be; it is very important for her team to "move on." Try as she might, however, she just cannot get her employees to move on. The team is disoriented, similar to what happens when people are experiencing grief. Rather than working harder in what would have been a vain attempt to get her team to move on, she works smarter. She calls an all-hands meeting of the group (about twelve people) and asks them to write down on a piece of paper their reactions to the myriad changes that the organization is going through. They are free to write down anything: their hopes, fears, and fantasies, in short, any thoughts they have or emotions they are experiencing with regard to the changes. One by one, the manager goes around the table and asks people to read aloud what they have written. After this venting session, the group talks for approximately an hour about the common themes in their reactions to the changes. The manager then collects all of their written comments, puts them in a shoebox, and ushers the group to a lot adjacent to the plant. Collectively, they bury the shoebox; they give their remembrances of the old organization a proper funeral. Upon returning to work after lunch, the group feels as if a major cloud has been lifted. In a few short hours, they have become psychologically freed up to move on in the way that senior management wants.

I am not suggesting that when change agents are trying to get people to separate from the past they necessarily have to use this manager's particular form of ceremony; you may find her method too "schmaltzy" or "touchy-feely." I am suggesting, however, that change agents consider the use of *some* form of ceremony. Interestingly enough, by acknowledging transition, ceremonies *facilitate* transition. We readily recognize this in our personal lives. It is no accident that ceremonies often accompany life-changing events. There are birth ceremonies, confirmation ceremonies, bar mitzvah and bat mitzvah ceremonies, graduation ceremonies, wedding ceremonies, and funeral ceremonies. By acknowledging the change in the form of a ceremony, we somehow find the change easier to make. For example, although funerals are *about* a deceased person, they are really *for* the living, to help them deal with the loss of that person. If we recognize the value of ceremony during times of change in our personal lives, change agents may do well to use them more frequently during times of organizational change to help people separate from the past.

Develop a Strong Leader Role

Psychologists have long been interested in the processes that cause people to change their behavior. Behaviorists such as B. F. Skinner have argued that it's all about consequences. People are more likely to do something different if they are rewarded for it.[15] For example, if the change entails more interdependent work in which people have to work more collaboratively than they had in the past, then the reward system needs to be based on the performance of the collective rather than on the performance of individuals or subunits. In a classic management article aptly titled "On the Folly of Rewarding A While Hoping for B," Steven Kerr has suggested that organizations often get their reward systems wrong.[16] Social learning theorists such as Albert Bandura, however, have suggested that people do not necessarily have to experience consequences to change their behavior. Learning to do new things may result from watching others role-model the behavior.[17]

These two processes are not mutually exclusive. In fact, as John Kotter and James Heskett have suggested, strong leaders do both.[18] Several items from the Change Implementation Survey illustrate this point. Two of the items (#12 and #14) pertain to how role models may bring about change. Item #12 is "When introducing change, I 'walk the talk'; that is, I serve as a role model for the new behaviors that are needed." In this instance it is the change agent himself who is serving as the role model. When Meyer Feldberg took over as the dean of Columbia Business School with the not very original but very inspirational vision of wanting Columbia to become a preeminent business school, he knew that he was going to have to raise a lot of money. Indeed, the year he took over coincided with when the faculty were asked to contribute money to the school's annual fund-raising campaign. Some of my recently hired colleagues found such a request a bit odd; one mentioned that he viewed the request as being asked to take a pay cut of sorts, in that he essentially was being asked to give some of his pay back to his employer. They were on the fence about whether to contribute until they learned that Dean Feldberg had contributed many thousands of dollars of his own money to the fund-raising campaign. Seeing him "walk the talk" so convincingly made their decision to contribute a no-brainer.

Item #14 is "I positively publicize the activities of people that are supportive of the change effort." In this instance change agents shine the spotlight on other people doing the right thing (vis-à-vis the change) and thereby make them role models for all to see. So if the change requires people to work more collaboratively with others in different parts of the organization, those who do so should be singled out for others to emulate. For example, at faculty meetings at Columbia Business School, our dean makes it a regular practice to discuss the ways in which certain faculty members have done things to move us down the road toward preeminence and to thank them for doing so. It's a win-win: those being thanked appreciate having their good work recognized, and everyone else gets a clearer picture of what we can do to help move the institution in a more positive direction.

Thus far I have been talking about positive role models who help bring about change by showing others around them what to do. We also learn new things from watching negative role models who demonstrate what *not* to do. In a thought-provoking exercise (known as "The Lifeline") that we use in executive leadership development programs at Columbia Business School, participants are asked to describe their leadership style and to explain how certain of their life experiences may have contributed to their style. The life experiences they choose to talk about may come from outside the workplace (for example, people often talk about their family dynamics, such as the conflict-avoidant executive who spent her adolescent years trying to smooth her parents' tempestuous relationship) or they may come from inside the workplace. A common theme in their narratives is the importance of role models. I have noticed that some participants choose to talk about the impact of positive role models, such as the boss who showed confidence in them or who helped them find their own voice. Others talk about how negative role models showed them what not to do, such as the micromanaging boss who was constantly breathing down everyone's neck. The fact that some participants speak of positive role models whereas others speak of negative role models raises a number of interesting questions: Are certain kinds of people more influenced by a positive role model while others are more affected by a negative role model? If so, in what ways do these two kinds of people differ?

A series of studies by Penelope Lockwood, Charles Jordan, and Ziva Kunda address these questions directly. They found that positive role models are more motivating for promotion-focused individuals whereas negative role models are more motivating for prevention-focused persons. Participants in one study completed the measure of regulatory focus appearing in appendix C. They were then asked to write a brief description of an instance in which they were motivated by a role model. All of them were given the option of describing how they were affected by a positive role model ("You may have found another person's success motivating because when you found out that this person had excelled at an activity that you cared about, this made you hopeful that you too could do really well at that activity, and motivated you to work harder to achieve excellence yourself") or by a negative role model ("You may have found another person's failure motivating because when you found out that this person performed really poorly at an activity that you cared about, this made you worry that you too might do really poorly at that activity, and motivated you to try harder to avoid failing yourself"). Although participants generally elected to write about the influence of a positive rather than negative role model, this was especially true for people who were promotion focused rather than prevention focused. Thus when thinking about the kinds of role models who have influenced their leadership style, promotion-focused persons are more likely than prevention-focused persons to spontaneously call to mind positive role models.

Lockwood and her colleagues also showed that subtle cues inducing people into a promotion- or prevention-focused state also influenced the motivational power of positive versus negative role models. The participants in the study were undergraduate students who were asked to sort thirty-six words into three different categories. Of the thirty-six words, twenty-four were filler words related to cooking and children. For half of the participants, the remaining twelve words pertained to promotion: strive, seek, pursue, gain, win, succeed, ambition, achieve, thrive, triumph, accomplish, and ambition. For the other half, the remaining twelve words pertained to prevention: avoid, prevent, avert, rejection, mistake, fiasco, flounder, flunk, defeat, disappointing, setback, and fail. Because the study was allegedly concerned with "life transitions" after college, all participants were then asked to read a passage written by a recent graduate of their university.

Some participants read a passage that portrayed the writer as a positive role model: "I just found out I won a major scholarship for postgraduate study. Two major companies also contacted me about great positions. Right now, I'm extremely happy with my life. I feel like I know where I am going and what I want. I never imagined that my future could be so amazing." Other participants read a passage that portrayed the writer as a negative role model. It said, "I haven't been able to find a good job. I have spent a lot of time working in fast-food places, and doing some pretty boring stuff. Right now I'm pretty down about things. I am not sure where I am going to go from here. I can't afford to go back to school but I also can't find a good job. This is not where I expected to be at this point in my life." A third group of participants did not read any passage (the control condition).

All of the participants then completed a measure of their academic motivation, indicating how much they agreed with statements such as "I plan to put more time into my schoolwork." As predicted, promotion-focused individuals were more motivated by the positive role model than were promotion-focused individuals who read the negative role model passage or those in the control condition. Prevention-focused persons were more motivated by the negative role model condition than were prevention-focused individuals who read the positive role model passage or those in the control condition. In other words, exposure to "goal-congruent" role models (positive in the case of promotion-focused individuals and negative in the case of prevention-focused persons) had a positive effect on participants' motivation.

Perhaps what is even more interesting is that this particular study showed that exposure to "goal-incongruent" role models (negative role models in the case of promotion-focused individuals and positive ones in the case of prevention-focused persons) was not in the least bit motivating or even neutral; it actually was demotivating.

Promotion-focused persons who read about a negative role model reported being less motivated than promotion-focused persons in the control condition (who were not exposed to a role model), and prevention-focused persons who read about a positive role model were less motivated than prevention-focused persons in the control condition.[19] Participants' reactions to goal-incongruent role models are yet another reminder that a high-quality change management process needs to be tailored to its audience. If change agents do not take into account the psychological profile of the employees they are trying to influence, then the generally good rules for change agents to live by, in this case, exposing employees to role models to motivate change, may not work and might actually backfire.

Strong leaders do more than draw on themselves or others as role models to pave the way for change. They also make good use of rewards to motivate change. Change-motivating rewards can be extrinsic, as in our earlier example of the organization that tried to foster greater collaboration and teamwork by tying employees' compensation to the performance of the collective rather than to the performance of their respective subunits. Change-motivating rewards also can be intrinsic, in which the very doing of the new behaviors called for by the change serves as its own source of reward. For example, one of people's primary bases of intrinsic motivation is to feel competent, as Robert White pointed out in his classic article on "effectance" motivation.[20] However, the problem is that when employees do the new things called for by the change, they often feel anything but competent, at least in the short term.

Given that employees like to feel competent and given that they don't feel competent in the early stages of an organizational change, there is something that change agents can do to ensure that the transition will go more smoothly, as illustrated in item #13 from the Change Implementation Survey: "In the change process, I make efforts to ensure that people will be working on at least some tasks at which they are likely to succeed." A high-quality change process gives people a chance to experience at least *some sense* of competence, which is much needed during times of change. In their insightful book titled *The Progress Principle*, Teresa Amabile and Steven Kramer write that one of the main drivers of employees' motivation is whether they believe they are making progress in some significant activity in the workplace. The progress and associated sense of competence do not have to be dramatic. They do have to be perceptible and they do have to be in an area that people care about.

In an extremely ambitious and impressive attempt to determine why certain groups in the workplace flourish while others do not, Amabile and Kramer observed nearly 250 people from a wide variety of organizations over a four-month period *every workday*. The study examined the relationships between employees' "inner work lives" and various indicators of performance including creativity, productivity, commitment, and collegiality. Inner work lives was a combination of employees' perceptions of the work environment (e.g., how open their leaders were to new ideas), of their emotions (e.g., frustrated, happy), and of their motivations (e.g., how much they were intrinsically interested to work). The results showed that when people experienced more positive inner work lives they responded better on all measures of performance. By way of explanation, the authors suggested, "When inner work life is good, people are more likely to pay attention to the work itself, become deeply engrossed in their team's project, and hold fast to the goal of doing a great job." The biggest determinant of whether people experienced positive inner work lives was their sense that they were *making progress*.[21]

Ensuring some form of progress is particularly important in times of change in at least two ways. First, change often requires people to do very different things from what they have done before. It is good to be stretched, but not to be stretched to the point that success feels downright impossible. If people experience *some* sense of progress in taking on the new behaviors, the ensuing feeling of competence may be just what they need to stay the course. People often don't feel comfortable taking giant leaps in the direction of change; quite appropriately, they fear failure. They may, however, be much more willing to take baby steps. Astute change agents create the space for those baby steps to happen.

Second, even if the change does not require people to do anything new, the broader context in which the change is taking place often is very stressful. Change threatens people's sense of power, status, and control. Progress may be a powerful antidote to the stress that accompanies change in a couple of ways. For one thing, the process of trying to make progress is a great distractor. If you focus on what you need to do to make progress on a meaningful task, you are less likely to dwell on the unpleasantness of the situation. But the positive effect of making progress is probably not due to distraction alone. A second reason why progress is a great antidote to stress is that it replaces feelings of self-threat with feelings of efficacy and control.

In their study Amabile and Kramer provided a particularly compelling example of how progress helped employees deal with the stress of change. A group of them were asked to work on a project in an eight-day period that would help their organization fend off a potentially costly lawsuit. It was bad enough that the eight-day period coincided with a national holiday, and therefore that many of them had been planning to take a vacation. They also had witnessed repeated layoffs in their organization in the prior weeks and months. Indeed, it was not at all obvious that they would be able to keep their jobs *even if* the project they were working on were successful. And yet what kept the group going was the belief that they were making progress on obviously meaningful work. One group member who reported six weeks earlier that the organization had treated her like an abused spouse wrote, "Today our entire office worked like a real team again. It was wonderful. We all forgot the current stressful situation and have all worked around the clock to get a big project done. I have been here about 15 hours, but it has been one of the best days I've had in months!!"[22]

It turned out that the team did a very good job on the project, thereby enabling the organization to save $145 million. But that's not the main point. The main point is that *during* the eight-day period in which they worked on the project, it was the perception that they were making progress that kept them engaged, to the point that they were willing to work very long hours at a time when they previously expected to be on vacation, in a firm that was not even guaranteeing that they would be able to keep their jobs.

In short, Amabile and Kramer's progress principle helps explain why it is important for change agents to ensure that their employees "are working on at least some tasks at which they are likely to succeed." Furthermore, for the experience of progress to fuel motivation on a self-sustaining basis, it (1) can't come too easily, and (2) has to be seen as meaningful. If the success comes too easily it may be seen as cheap. When my kids were young I used to play checkers with them. Sometimes I would let them win, but I couldn't do it in too obvious a way lest they conclude that they didn't win but that I had "arranged" for them to win. In trying to create success experiences change agents need to find the sweet spot between an activity in which it is easy enough to be successful but not so easy that the success feels hollow.

Let's go back to our example of the organization that was trying to break down silos and foster greater collaboration between the different subunits. Senior executives pulled the groups together and worked with them to hold an offsite, figuring that if people from the different units got to know one another and did some team-building activities away from work they would start to act more like a team. Just as important as what they did at the offsite, the mere fact that the different groups worked collaboratively to *plan* the offsite was helpful in bringing them together. The offsite was not a completely unifying experience. But it certainly helped. The disparate groups took baby steps in the direction of being more aligned. Planning a constructive offsite together captured the sweet spot. It was certainly within reach for the groups to be able to plan the offsite. However, it was not too easy; prior to planning the offsite together (with senior managers lending a helping hand) the groups had rarely given each other the right time of day.

Planning the offsite together also cleared the meaningfulness hurdle. It said a lot that these heretofore disjointed groups were able to work together on *something* of mutual interest. There are lots of ways in which an activity may be meaningful, but it usually comes down to doing something of value for a cause or for people you care about. Working well together in planning the offsite was one step along the significant journey of the groups forging a better relationship with one another.

I do not mean to suggest that it's simply a matter of change agents selecting the "right" task in which success will be meaningful and attainable (but not too attainable). Change agents can and should do other things to facilitate progress, such as helping procure necessary resources, helping minimize possible roadblocks, and being interpersonally supportive. To return to the team that worked for eight days to ward off a lawsuit against their firm and thereby save $145 million, senior management reassured the team members that they did not have to worry about the other pressing tasks they were working on while they were focusing on this particular project. Although senior managers lacked the expertise to work on the project itself, they stayed onsite while the team was working, even bringing them fancy bottled water and pizza. The physical presence of the senior managers and their offer of water and pizza were hugely symbolically important. Together, these steps reinforced to the team members that they were working on a very important task and that senior managers appreciated their heroic efforts.[23] In sum, it's not simply a matter of change agents choosing a task in which meaningful success is likely and then getting out of the way.

Finally, although progress is a great motivator, it also is important to help people set realistic expectations about the journey. People usually don't get better at new behaviors day by day. This is not to say that behavior change (or progress) is not gradual, only that it is not *linearly* gradual. In most instances, it's a matter of taking "two steps forward and one backward." As long as there are more steps forward than backward, progress is happening. There will be better days and (hopefully fewer) worse days. The important thing is for people to undertake the journey with their eyes wide open to this likelihood. If they are operating under the mistaken assumption that progress is going to be linear, they can get discouraged by the bad days that they inevitably are going to have. If, however, they see the steps backward as going with the turf of progress, then they are likely to be far more resilient and thereby sow the seeds for them to take even more steps forward.

A good example of setting expectations about the nature of progress takes place at the conclusion of an executive leadership development program I help run at Columbia Business School. As the program is wrapping up we ask participants to identify a small number of behaviors they want to change in their managerial style. We remind them at this point not to expect their change to be linear and that they are likely to make more progress on some days than on others. We tell them that we will contact them three months later to see how they are doing. The appropriate judgment for them to make at that point is how they have done *on average* over the three months. That is, would they say that relative to where they stood prior to the program they have made significant changes in their behavior over the three-month period as a whole, rather than on a day-to-day basis.

Line Up Political and Social Sponsorship

We often take cues from other people about what to think, feel, and do. One of the most dramatic illustrations of this tendency is the research done by Solomon Asch, who studied conformity among a sample of Princeton under-

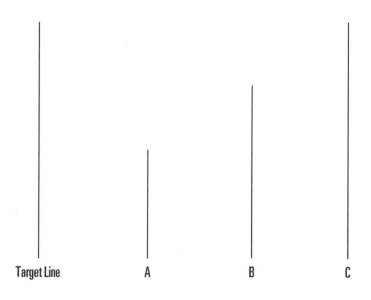

Figure 3.1. Asch Conformity Study
Participants were asked to indicate which of the three lines (A, B, or C) was the same length as the Target Line.

graduates. Groups of five people were seated around a table and were led to believe that they were partaking in a study on visual perception. They were shown the information in figure 3.1 and were asked to indicate which of the three lines (A, B, or C) was equal in length to the Target Line. This was not a trick question; participants could clearly see that the correct answer was Line C. Of the five people seated around the table, only one was an actual participant. The other four people were confederates, working in cahoots with Asch although the actual participant did not know this. The exercise was choreographed such that each of the four confederates stated his opinion before the actual participant was asked for his. One by one, each of the confederates said aloud that he thought the correct answer was Line A. As you can imagine this came as quite a shock to the actual participant, whose eyes were telling him that the right answer was Line C. What do you think happened in this situation? What percentage of people would follow the crowd and say Line A and what percentage would go with what their eyes were telling them and say Line C?

The rugged individualists among you may be reassured to know that the majority of people went with their eyes rather than with the crowd. However, only about 60 percent responded correctly. Nearly 40 percent of the participants gave an answer that they knew to be wrong, with almost all of them selecting the one that everyone else selected: Line A. (A very small percentage of people [about 5 percent] chose Line B. It was as if they were saying to themselves, "I know the answer is C, but everyone else is saying A, so let's split the difference and call it B.")[24]

If people go along with the opinion of others that they clearly know is wrong, imagine how much people are influenced by others in situations in which the right answer is more uncertain. Indeed, social psychologists such as Leon Festinger have shown that people are especially prone to social influence under conditions of uncertainty.[25] Employees' experience of organizational change is nothing if not filled with uncertainty. Questions abound with few answers, leading to a "water cooler effect," in which employees informally hover together to make sense of what is going on. For example, if word of a layoff is in the air, employees want to know, among other things, why it is happening, when it will happen, who will go and who will stay, and what life will be like afterward. Indeed, in one study my colleagues and I found that a major determinant of the organizational commitment of employees who survived a downsizing was their beliefs about the commitment level of their fellow survivors. Employees who believed that their fellow survivors were committed (whether correctly so or not) were willing to work harder on behalf of the organization relative to their counterparts who believed that their fellow survivors had pretty much checked out.[26]

The fact that organizational change promotes uncertainty and that people take cues from others especially in the face of uncertainty suggests that a high-quality change process is one that marshals the power of social influence. It's kind of like a snowball rolling downhill. If you can get some people onboard with the change early on then others are more likely to follow suit; before too long you will have generated social momentum for the change. Our previous discussion of how you can serve as a role model for change (or call attention to others who have done so) speaks to this point. What we will discuss next suggests that you need to pay attention to *whom* you select as the role model and that there are other ways to generate social momentum for change beyond using yourself or others as role models.

In every group of people the views and actions of certain individuals are more influential than those of others; the more influential ones are the "opinion leaders." We naturally think of people as opinion leaders based on their position in the formal hierarchy. That is certainly true, but how high up people are on the organizational chart is not the only determinant of their status as opinion leaders. Their personal characteristics, in particular their *credibility*, matter a lot as well. The two main bases of credibility are expertise and trustworthiness. We follow the lead of people (1) who know what they are talking about, and (2) who have shown that they have our best interests at heart or have a strong sense of personal integrity.

Situational factors also affect people's likelihood of being an opinion leader. You may have heard the saying that in real estate the three most important things are location, location, and location. Similarly, the location of people in a communication network influences their likelihood of becoming an opinion leader; the greater their centrality the more likely they are to become opinion leaders. For example, major league baseball players whose position on the field puts them in the thick of the action (e.g., catchers) are more likely to become managers after their playing days are over, relative to players whose positions are in the outfield. In the communication network shown in figure 3.2, the person who occupies position C is the one most likely to emerge as the opinion leader.[27] There is even evidence that employees whose offices are located next to the washroom are more likely to become opinion leaders. After all, employees who have an office near the washroom will have more of a chance to see their coworkers passing by on a regular basis and, with that, have more of an opportunity to develop a relationship with them. Of course, having the opportunity to develop a relationship with many people does not ensure that someone will become an opinion leader. For instance, someone with low personal credibility whose office happens to be next to the bathroom is not necessarily destined to become an opinion leader. In any event, to generate social momentum for change you first need to know who your opinion leaders are. Recognize that they come in a variety of shapes and sizes, sometimes as a result of personal attributes such as their credibility and sometimes as a result of situational factors such as where their office is located.

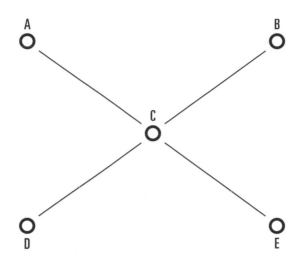

Figure 3.2. How Location in a Communication Network Affects Leadership

Each letter refers to a person. Solid lines refer to the presence of a direct line of communication. Hence in this network Person C has a direct line of communication with everyone else, and everyone else only has a direct line of communication with Person C.

Having identified your opinion leaders, you need to figure out where they stand. Are they with you, against you, or on the fence? The need to do this assessment is captured by item #15 from the Change Implementation Survey: "I find out the opinions of key parties about the change, that is, whether the parties are likely to favor it or oppose it." If they are against you or on the fence, you need to try to win them over. Consider item #18 from the survey: "I devote extra attention to 'opinion leaders' to gain their support of the change effort." Try asking them, perhaps in different ways, *why* they are against you or are on the fence. ("Can you tell me a little more about that?" or "Help me understand where you are coming from.") In the language of negotiations experts, see if you can move the conversation from their *positions* of non-support to their underlying *interests*, which are the reasons why they are being non-supportive. If you don't know why they are not with you, there is very little chance that you will be able to win them over. For example, they may not be supporting you because they don't believe in the change; it has to do with the outcome. If so, drill down further to find out just what it is that they don't believe in. Or they may not be supporting you because they don't like the way the change has been rolled out; it has to do with the process. Once again, determine which aspects of the process they are not happy about, and see if you can address their concerns. Dealing with opinion leaders requires extra time and effort. However, it is time and effort that are well spent: if the opinion leaders are onboard with the change they will help you spread the gospel. And if they are not onboard they have a lot of power to block you in your efforts.

Finally, once the opinion leaders are onboard, publicize their support. Making visible the support of people who have credibility in the eyes of those you are trying to influence can go a long way. I saw this principle come to life a number of years ago when I was trying to persuade my colleagues at Columbia Business School to hire a faculty member from another university. Quite appropriately, they asked me to explain why I thought we should do so. The three main dimensions along which university faculty are evaluated are teaching, research, and service. So I put together what I thought would be a really persuasive case. First, I provided evidence that this individual was a star in the classroom. I then regaled them with hard evidence of this person's research record; he had publications galore, in all of the best journals, and on very interesting and important topics. I next proceeded to describe his impressive record of service to both his university and the profession as a whole. My colleagues were very intrigued by this point, but what truly helped seal the deal was when I told them that he had recently been awarded tenure by Stanford University. Once my colleagues at Columbia heard that Stanford wanted him, they wanted him all the more. Why? I believe it was because those with credibility (Stanford University) in the eyes of my audience supported my view. I am delighted to say that the individual I am describing has been a member of our faculty for more than ten years.

Craft an Implementation Plan

To ensure that the plan remains connected to the vision, it is useful for managers to periodically talk with their employees about the plan at a broad conceptual level. However, for the plan to be actionable it needs to be discussed at a specific operational level, that is, the details of who, what, where, when, and how. For example, as part of a broader growth initiative a privately owned retailer with more than a hundred local stores recently moved away from its previous business model in which key strategic decisions were made at its corporate headquarters and then farmed out for implementation at the store level. Recognizing that the store managers and their associates are much closer to local customers, the retailer's CEO and his senior management team chose to give much more decision-making authority to the individual store managers, essentially encouraging them to see themselves as the CEO of their own store. Of course, it is one thing for the senior team to say that it wants to empower those at a lower level of the organization. It is quite another, however, to actually implement such empowerment. For example, rather than business plans for the respective stores being initiated at the senior management level, it was up to the store managers to develop their own business plans and present them to senior management, which, in turn, led to a healthy give-and-take between the two sides. Furthermore, once store managers and senior management reached agreement in principle on their respective business plans, senior management played the important role of helping store managers procure the resources necessary to achieve their business plans and removing possible obstacles to achieving the plans. As Rosabeth Moss Kanter has put it, the delegation of decision-making authority does not mean abdication.[28] While empowering those at lower levels of the organization, senior management continues to play a very important role, albeit different from its previous one of command-and-control.

There are a few key things to keep in mind vis-à-vis the crafting of implementation plans. First, such plans don't just happen; they require dedicated resources such as people and time. For example, the retailer put together a steering committee whose job it was to come up with an implementation plan that was clear, comprehensive, and achievable. Second, the information needed to develop a clear, comprehensive, and achievable implementation plan is typically located in different parts of the organization. Hence the retailer's steering committee consisted of people from diverse functions and regions. The spirit of this idea is captured by item #19 from the Change Implementation Survey: "In crafting the plan, I seek input from numerous others on how to best implement the plan." All members of the steering committee, in turn, did a few things to ensure that their input into the plan was informed by the people they represented, such as conducting focus groups and holding regular town hall meetings. By involving their respective communities, members of the steering committee provided input into the implementation planning process that was not only on target but also had the buy-in of the people ultimately responsible for bringing the plans to life. Crafting implementation plans takes time and effort, but it's well worth it in the end. As the old expression goes, if you fail to plan, plan to fail.

Develop Engaging and Enabling Structures

"Structures" refers to formal organizational arrangements, such as policies, programs, and systems pertaining to how people are selected, trained, appraised, and rewarded; "structures" also refers to how the organization is designed, that is, the bases on which groups are differentiated as well as integrated. The key is to ensure alignment between the vision/ strategy of the change effort and the various elements of structure. Whereas implementation plans provide guidelines to *launch* a change effort, proper structures need to be in place to *sustain* it. In keeping with the motto that a high-quality process engages and equips people, structures need to motivate people to go in new directions and to provide them with the knowledge and skills to do so. For example, the retailer that gave greater decision-making authority to its store managers changed its reward system in the hopes of motivating behavior change. Prior to the implementation of the change, store managers' pay was largely based on a fixed salary; they also could earn a bit more depending upon how well their store performed. The new pay system reversed things: now, most of the store managers' pay depends on their stores' performance and only a small portion consists of a fixed salary. The retailer also went to great lengths to enable store managers to change their behavior. For example, all of them took part in a rigorous, multiweek training program designed to enhance their capabilities not only in leadership and strategy but also in the functional areas (e.g., finance, marketing, and accounting) needed to run their own businesses.

Engaging and enabling structures provide support for change both substantively and symbolically. For example, the retailer provided substantive support to motivate behavior change by shifting the ways in which managers were compensated, and it enabled behavior change by enhancing managers' skill set through training and development. Perhaps just as important, there was an important symbolic message associated with the change in reward system and the introduction of the training program: both reflected the retailer's deep commitment to seeing store managers succeed in their new roles. As a number of store managers told me, the fact that the organization showed authentic commitment to their being successful in their new roles was motivationally significant to them over and above any effect due to the change in the reward system. The importance of attending to the symbolic value of structural changes is reflected in item #22 in the Change Implementation Survey: "I communicate how changes in the enabling structures symbolize the direction of the intended change."

Monitor and Refine

Even the best laid-out change process is likely to produce unforeseen consequences. Therefore, rather than introducing change and hoping for the best, astute change agents "expect the unexpected." They actively monitor how the change is going, and they are not afraid to make adjustments based upon what they learn. This healthy way to proceed is reflected in item #30 in the Change Implementation Survey: "I make adjustments in response to the feedback received about the change effort." The empowering retailer who changed store managers' compensation so that it was based primarily on the performance of their respective stores discovered that the new reward system was producing an unintended negative consequence: store managers were growing increasingly myopic in their focus. Rather than concerning themselves with the performance of the collective, they were now almost exclusively focused on how their own individual stores were performing. The retailer decided to tinker even further with its reward system, making it worthwhile for store managers to be concerned not only about the performance of their own stores but also about the performance of other stores in their region and about the company as a whole.

Even the physical positions people take during meetings devoted to monitoring and refining can make a difference. Meetings often take place in rooms in which group members are seated around a table with the leader at the head. Some groups, however, meet standing up rather than sitting around tables in chairs. Such was the case for the group called in to rescue the failed launch of the Affordable Health Care Act in late 2013. "Obamacare," as it has come to be known, was introduced amid great fanfare and controversy. Intended to drive down health costs for millions of Americans, it ran into a major glitch when the website on which people had to enroll crashed. Mikey Dickerson, a website reliability engineer from Google, was called in to lead the team responsible for fixing the problem. According to *Time* magazine, what saved the day were Dickerson's "stand-ups." Stand-ups are meetings in which everyone works through a problem while standing rather than sitting. Dickerson held stand-ups with his team at the beginning of the day and at the end. To foster productivity, Dickerson introduced three rules: (1) The purpose of the stand-ups was to solve problems. As he put it, "There are plenty of other venues where people devote their creative energies to shifting blame." (2) The people doing the talking should be the ones with the most knowledge, not necessarily the highest rank. (3) The greatest focus should be on the most urgent matters, that is, problems likely to arise in the ensuing twenty-four to forty-eight hours.[29]

The success story of Dickerson's team has been borne out in research that compares meetings in which the group stands versus sits. Dickerson's rule that the most knowledgeable should do the most talking was designed to get the most useful information into the conversation. But according to recent research by Andrew Knight and Markus Baer, there is another reason why having the meeting standing up rather than sitting down enhances the quality of the exchange of information: standing up promotes greater openness of group members to each other's ideas. In this study undergraduate students had to develop a recruitment video for their university. Half of the groups held their discussion in a conventional way, sitting around a table. The other half had their discussions in the same room, from which the chairs had been removed. Sitting around a table in chairs fosters people's territoriality about their physical space. In contrast, eliminating chairs shifts people away from their individual spaces to a broader space that is occupied by the group as a whole. Working in a less individually territorial space, those who had their meeting standing up were less territorial about their own ideas as well. They listened to each other, built upon each other's ideas, and generated videos that were rated as more creative and polished than those of their counterparts, who did the exact same task sitting down.[30]

Communicate, Involve, and Be Honest

Everyone agrees that great communication is an essential part of leadership in general and a high-quality change process in particular. What you say and how you say it go a long way toward determining how successful you will be in influencing people to move from Point A to Point B. For example, there are more versus less compelling ways to communicate why people should be dissatisfied with the current state, and the same holds for showing them a better alternative in the form of the vision of the future state. When we think of how great leaders communicate, what usually comes to mind is the expressive part. We conjure up images of people who speak well, inspire passion, and have "presence." However, communication is a two-way street. Just as it is important to get the "sending out" or *expressive* part of communication right, it is essential to do likewise for the "taking in" or *receptive* part. You need to know how the change is experienced by those affected by it. At the end of the day, no matter how eloquent your communication about change may be, it is not simply what you said or how you said it that matters. What drives people is what they *heard*, which means that you have to know not only what they heard but also how they are responding to what they heard.

Of course, it is generally a good idea for managers to have access to their employees' experience of the workplace.

The need to be in touch with employees' experience, however, is particularly acute during times of change. In an ideal world, employees will hear the message intended by their managers and be onboard with it. In the midst of change, however, there is a very high likelihood that employees either will not hear the intended message or will not be onboard with it. Change introduces uncertainty, confusion, and anxiety, making it harder for the intended message to come through loud and clear. Moreover, even if they understand the message, they may not like it and hence seek to deny or otherwise distance themselves from it. Indeed, in the absence of feedback indicating that employees accurately perceived the intended message of the change and are onboard with it, it is probably more likely that they did not hear the message, are not onboard with it, or both.

And if they do not hear the intended message or are not onboard with it you need to find that out. I once spoke to an executive after he had announced a major change to his team; I asked him how the team took to the announcement. He said, "I thought it went pretty well. I mean, nobody raised any questions or objections." Just because people do not raise questions or objections, however, does not mean that they do not have them. People vote with their feet. So if there are lurking misperceptions or underlying bases of resistance, it is far better for change agents to find these things out sooner rather than later. The implications for doing the receptive aspects of communication are clear: change agents need to open or create lines of communication so that they can truly be in touch with what their employees believe and feel about the change. One way to do this is by making it easy for employees to approach their managers, as reflected in item #25 in the

Change Implementation Survey: "I give people the opportunity to initiate communications about the change effort (e.g., through an open-door policy, management by walking around, question-and-answer sessions at meetings, etc.)."

In addition to making it easy for employees to approach their managers, managers also should go to them, as suggested by item #24 in the survey: "After communicating information [about the change] to people, I assess how they have interpreted the information." In fact, out of all thirty-four items in the survey, item #24 is among those that are done the least often. The item suggests that it's not enough to craft the communications change agents send out; they also need to follow up with their employees to find out how they have interpreted the message and whether they are in agreement with it. This requires extra work, but as with many aspects of a high-quality change process, it is better to pay now than to pay later. The amount of time and effort needed to unearth people's misperceptions about or resistance to the change early on is probably far less than that which would be needed at a later point in time when they already have acted on their misperceptions and resistance.

LISTEN ACTIVELY

Regardless of whether they come to you or you go to them, you need to listen actively to your employees' perceptions and possible bases of resistance to the change. What does active listening mean? It is not simply being quiet and giving others the floor; those are the table stakes. Active listening is a combination of mental activity (internally, you *truly consider* what others are saying) and behavior (externally, you show others that their views are being truly considered). Furthermore, showing others that their views are being truly considered takes place at two points in time: during the conversation and afterward. During the conversation, you can show people that their views are being truly considered through a variety of verbal and nonverbal behaviors. For example, the verbals include paraphrasing, asking for further explanation or clarification, and talking about your own experience without hijacking the conversation (e.g., "I had the same experience, so I can really understand what you are going through right now"). The nonverbals refer to the various ways in which people are shown that your attention is squarely on them. Unfortunately, modern technology impedes undivided attention; computers, tablets, and smartphones distract us. A friend of mine went into her boss's office to voice concerns about a recently announced change. Without once looking up from his computer the boss said to her, "Keep talking, I am listening." I suggested to my friend that what her boss was more likely telling her was, "You can keep talking, but I'm not really listening."

In some ways the better indicator of whether active listening truly took place is what happens *after* the conversation. Suppose that your direct reports made specific recommendations about how the details of the change should be implemented. The most persuasive evidence that you listened would be if, afterward, you actually implemented their suggestions. Therefore, do not hold their suggestions to the standard of having to be better than what you would have done or better than what is already in place. Instead, lower the bar: their suggestions simply have to be *not worse* than what you would have done or what is already in place. By holding their suggestions to the higher standard of having to be better, you make it less likely that their suggestions will be implemented, and with that, you are forgoing the opportunity to show them that you truly listened.

Of course, sometimes their suggestions will be worse, in which case it would not make sense to implement them. However, they still need to know that their suggestions were seriously considered. By sincerely thanking them, giving them a reasonable explanation of how it would not be advisable to implement the suggestion, and delivering the explanation in a nondismissive way you will let people know that their views were indeed taken into account. As a result, they are likely to be engaged with the current change effort, and because they know their views are taken seriously, they will likely provide input into future organizational matters.

In short, a high-quality change process entails attending to both sides of the two-way street of communication, the expressive and the receptive. Daniel Ames, Lily Benjamin, and I recently examined how influential managers were as a function of how well they carried out the expressive and receptive aspects of communication. Managers in this study were rated by people familiar with their methods of communication. How well they expressed themselves was measured with items such as "S/he is able to use vivid images and compelling logic and facts to support an argument" and "When communicating with others, s/he is honest, open, and candid." Sample items reflecting managers' receptive or listening skills were "After listening, s/he builds on what s/he has heard, incorporating it into the conversation" and "S/he listens effectively to criticism and alternative points of view." As might be expected, managers were rated as influential if they expressed themselves well. Furthermore, over and above the effect of their expressive communication skills, managers were rated as influential if they had good listening skills. Interestingly enough, the two types of communication skills also interacted with each other to determine managers' influence power. Managers who combined strong expressive skills with strong listening skills were particularly influential. In other words, this was not a case of 2 + 2 = 4; rather, it was 2 + 2 = 5.[31]

ARE YOU AN OPENER?

A significant part of the interpersonal work of listening is getting other people to open up. Lynn Miller, John Berg, and Richard Archer developed a scale that assesses people's ability to get others to open up, aptly named the "Openers" scale (see appendix E). You may want to rate yourself on this measure or have others familiar with your managerial style rate you. It could provide insight into how good a listener you are.[32]

Chapter Summary

Change initiatives fail more often than not either because their substance or content is off the mark ("not doing the right thing") or because the process of planning or implementing them is misguided ("not doing things right"). Of these two broad reasons for the failure of change initiatives, the latter is more likely to be the culprit than the former. Indeed, John Kotter has suggested that nearly three-fourths of change management failures are due to one or more shortcomings in the process. In chapter 2 we considered the importance of fairness in the change process. In chapter 3 we incorporated fairness into a more general model of a high-quality change management process.

Moreover, we discussed what is meant by a high-quality change management process at two levels. Initially we considered the "big picture" view. Borrowing from Kurt Lewin, the founder of social psychology, Mike Beer suggested that for a change initiative to be successful the driving forces in the process that engage and equip people to change have to outweigh the restraining forces in the process that impede change. As he put it: Change = $(D \times V \times P) > C$. The change equation is useful in at least three ways. First, it provides change agents with a comprehensive set of the four process considerations that need to be present whenever change is being planned or implemented. Second, it reminds managers that all four elements of the process need to be handled well; this is an example of "the chain only being as strong as its weakest link." Third, an important implication of the equation is that all four elements need to be supplied but any individual manager does not have to be great at all four elements. Change management requires a team effort, not simply because there is so much to do but also because it is not realistic to expect most managers to be highly skilled in all four aspects of a high-quality change process.

In attempting to make the big-picture framework more user-friendly, we then discussed specific action items. John Kotter has an eight-step process, whereas Todd Jick offered specific advice in the form of "Ten Commandments." The overlap between Kotter and Jick far outweighs their differences. Both offered a great deal of specificity in what goes into a high-quality change process, which is an amalgam of engaging people (that is, ensuring that they are running in the right direction with a high degree of energy) and equipping people (that is, ensuring that they have the resources needed to bring about the change, as well as helping remove the obstacles that may stand in their way).

Another key point in the chapter is that even the best practices in a change management process need to be adjusted, in two senses. First, this very idea is the essence of one of Jick's commandments, namely, the need to "monitor and refine." A second way we talked about the adjustment of best practices is ensuring that they are congruent with the audience that the change agent is trying to influence. For example, whether to motivate employees via positive role models or negative role models, or whether to create a sense of urgency by "going for the gold" or by using the "burning platform" method, may depend on whether employees' psychological state is more promotion focused or prevention focused.

Finally, I included several instruments along with the chapter material for two reasons. One was to provide greater insight into key dimensions. For instance, the thirty-four-item Change Implementation Survey offers many details about what goes into a high-quality change management process. It is designed to move the writings of Kotter and Jick further along the continuum of "actionability" for would-be agents of change. A second reason to include the instruments was to allow managers to learn about themselves as agents of change. I encourage you to not only complete the instruments yourselves but also ask people who are willing and able to rate you on the same instruments. You are likely to be enlightened.

4 → Taking the Process Personally

Steve is the owner of a small business that has been in decline for many years. Trying to turn things around is taking up a lot of his time and emotional energy. He works more than seventy hours a week and feels beaten up by the whole experience. He has a family to support, so a lot is riding on his success. And yet in the midst of all of this professional turmoil he decides to volunteer five hours a week in his community, teaching illiterate adults to read. Surprised by this additional commitment, I asked him how he could afford to take on yet another responsibility when he already had so much on his plate. His answer was simple: "With what's going on in my life right now I can't afford *not* to do this."

Peter is a midlevel manager in a large financial services organization. He is incredibly motivated to be successful. There is one problem, however. Sometimes his dogged determination and perseverance get the better of him. Once he starts on a particular path he is oblivious to cues suggesting the need to take a different direction. For example, upon learning that the project he had taken the lead on was performing way below par, he redoubled his efforts to try to make things work. Most rational outside observers would have said that it was time to pull the plug on the project; not Peter, however.

One day, his boss asked him if he would be willing to serve as a mentor in a program that was about to be launched in his organization. Peter signed on and to his delight discovered that he really enjoyed mentoring. For one thing, seeing his protégé's improvement was very rewarding. Furthermore, serving as a mentor appealed to his deeply held values to "give back." His coworkers noticed something else about Peter. After becoming a mentor he was much less rigid in the face of information that challenged his initial decisions. Unlike beforehand, he took the information in, considered it, and sometimes even changed his initial decision as a result. Why did becoming a mentor make Peter more open-minded, even to information that had nothing to do with mentoring?

These two examples shed additional light on what goes into a high-quality process. In chapter 2 we discussed how the fairness of a process is one determinant of its quality. In chapter 3 we considered a more encompassing set of factors that shape the quality of virtually any change management process, large or small. Throughout, we have suggested that the essence of a high-quality process is that it equips people (makes them more capable of doing what needs to get done) and engages people (makes them more motivated to do what needs to get done).

Of course, to engage people it is necessary to know what they *want*. Although a complete analysis of what people want is beyond the scope of this book, one thing seems pretty clear: we want to see ourselves in certain ways. The eminent social psychologist Claude Steele put it well: he suggested that people seek "to maintain a phenomenal experience of themselves—self-conceptions and images—as adaptively and morally adequate, that is, as competent, good, coherent, unitary, stable, capable of free choice, [and] capable of controlling important outcomes."[1] These various self-conceptions comprise what Steele calls "self-integrity," and they consist of three different pillars: esteem, identity, and control. Esteem refers to how much people see themselves positively; it is reflected in seeing oneself as competent and good. Identity refers to people seeing themselves as having a fundamental core; it is captured by seeing oneself as coherent, unitary, and stable. Control refers to people seeing themselves as agentic and influential. It is reflected in people seeing themselves as capable of free choice (agentic) and as capable of controlling important outcomes (influential).[2]

Self-Affirmation Theory: A Brief Tutorial

Based on the idea that people seek self-integrity, that is, to see themselves as having esteem, identity, and control, Claude Steele developed self-affirmation theory. One of the intellectually exciting aspects of the theory is that it offers a common explanation of what may at first appear to be different social psychological phenomena. For example, dating back to Leon Festinger's path-breaking research on cognitive dissonance in the 1950s, social psychologists have suggested that people seek consistency between their beliefs and their behaviors.[3] Thus if we do something contrary to what we believe, we may change our attitudes to be consistent with our behavior, especially when there is no obvious external reason for the behavior. For example, in one study people did something that was in all likelihood contrary to their underlying attitudes: they ate fried grasshoppers. Half of them did so for a researcher who was friendly in his demeanor whereas the other half was induced to eat the grasshopper by an unfriendly researcher. Afterward, all of the participants were asked about their attitudes toward eating fried grasshoppers. Those who did it for the friendly researcher continued to feel negatively about eating fried grasshoppers, whereas those who did it for the unfriendly experimenter were much more positive about eating fried grasshoppers.[4] Why? If the researcher was friendly participants had a handy external reason for why they ate the fried grasshoppers: they did it to help the guy out. If the researcher was unfriendly, however, participants had to come up with some other reason for eating the grasshoppers; one such reason is that maybe eating fried grasshoppers is not so bad after all.

Rather than simply taking people's need to maintain consistency between their beliefs and behaviors as a given, Claude Steele asked the important question: *Why* do people seek consistency? One answer is that inconsistency threatens people's self-integrity. For example, if I say or do one thing but privately believe another, it hardly enables me to see myself as "coherent, unitary, and stable." In other words, it is not the inconsistency per se that upsets us but the negative implications of the inconsistency for how we view ourselves. One way to evaluate this explanation is by giving people who have done something contrary to what they believe an opportunity to affirm their self-integrity. Furthermore, the self-affirmation opportunity need not have anything to do with the inconsistency between their beliefs and their behavior. As long as the self-affirmation activity allows people to experience esteem or identity or control they should feel less of a need to change their attitudes in the direction of their behavior, relative to a control group of people who are not given the opportunity to self-affirm.

Steele tested this idea by doing a study in which all participants did something contrary to what they believed (much like eating fried grasshoppers). Half of them were then given an opportunity to self-affirm: they completed a survey measuring values that were personally important to them (such as their political values, economic values, or aesthetic values, whatever was important to them). In the course of answering questions reflecting deeply held values people had the experience of reminding themselves of their substantiality, which is quite self-affirming. The other half were not given this opportunity to self-affirm. The results showed that people were much less likely to change their attitudes in the direction of their behavior if they had been given the opportunity to self-affirm relative to the control group, which was not given the opportunity to self-affirm.[5]

Whereas eating grasshoppers is pretty irrelevant to most of us, self-affirmation processes have proven helpful in maintaining employees' productivity and morale in the aftermath of layoffs. Batia Wiesenfeld, Chris Martin, and I conducted a study in which participants witnessed a procedurally unfair layoff, which has been shown to adversely affect the people who remain (known as the "survivors"). Once again, it is worth asking the question: *Why* do layoffs that are procedurally unfair have a negative effect on the people who remain? One possibility is that survivors experience procedurally unfair layoffs as a threat to their sense of self. The symbolic message that employers send when they are procedurally unfair is that they do not value or respect their employees, which could be damaging to the esteem of not only the people who leave but also those who remain. Procedurally unfair layoffs also may threaten survivors' sense of predictability and with that their sense of control.

If procedurally unfair layoffs negatively affect survivors by threatening their sense of self, then giving survivors the opportunity to self-affirm should significantly reduce the adverse impact of procedurally unfair layoffs. To test this idea, one group of participants in our study who had witnessed a procedurally unfair layoff subsequently completed the survey measuring values of personal importance, whereas another group of participants witnessing the same layoff did not complete the values survey. The results showed that people given an opportunity to self-affirm responded much more positively; they were much more willing to do extra work for the experimenter, and they were much less emotionally upset compared to the people who did not self-affirm. In fact, those who witnessed the procedurally unfair layoffs and had self-affirmed reacted just as favorably as another group of participants who witnessed a procedurally fair layoff.[6] These results suggest that it's not the unfairness of the layoffs alone that causes survivors to react badly. Rather, it's the negative implication of the unfairness for survivors' sense of self that matters.

On the surface, behaving inconsistently with one's underlying attitudes has little to do with being the survivor of a procedurally unfair layoff. At a psychologically deeper level, however, they have a lot in common: both threaten people's self-integrity. We know this because giving people the opportunity to self-affirm, even in a way that was unrelated to the specifics of the self-threatening experiences, counteracted the effects that these experiences produced: in the former case, people who self-affirmed did not change their attitudes in the direction of the behavior, and in the latter case people who self-affirmed did not react badly to procedurally unfair layoffs.

Having discussed the benefits of self-affirmation, we now are in a better position to explain the behavior of the two people described at the outset of the chapter. Why did Steve take on the extra responsibility of doing volunteer work in the community when his job situation took up practically all of his waking hours and emotional energy? And why did Peter become more open to alternative points of view after he became a mentor in his organization? The affirmation of self-integrity provides an answer to both questions. Steve's job situation was a constant threat to his sense of esteem, identity, and control. He needed to do *something* self-affirming. Doing some good in his community was a great antidote. Truth be told, he was much more effective helping illiterate adults learn to read than he was in turning around his business. For those few hours a week when he was volunteering he felt competent and in control. He even mentioned that although there was no objective relationship between trying to run his business and the volunteer work he was doing, somehow the stress he was experiencing at work became much more tolerable because of his volunteering experience. The self-affirming quality of his volunteer activity took away a lot of the sting of running the business.

The change in Peter is understandable once we understand the reasons why he was not especially open to new information. It turned out that Peter generally felt quite insecure about his competence as a decision maker. From his perspective, not sticking with his original decision was tantamount to admitting that it was wrong. What better way to show others that his initial decision was correct than by persisting with it? Rather than viewing changing gears in light of new information as a sign of flexibility, Peter saw it as an indicator of being "wishy-washy" or weak. His experience as a mentor changed all of this. It turned out that Peter had always wanted to be a teacher but decided to go the corporate route for more pragmatic reasons. The mentoring role enabled him to express important values, and his success in helping others develop was a great source of esteem. The self-affirmation he experienced from being a mentor freed him up to take a different approach when doing his regular work, particularly when he encountered information suggesting that his initial decision may have been incorrect. Rather than viewing such information as self-threatening and therefore something to be dismissed, he was more able to evaluate the new information on its own merits. By being a more open-minded decision maker he became a much more effective leader.

Applying the Theory

Knowing that people want self-integrity provides a somewhat different lens through which to evaluate the quality of a process. Rather than focus on attributes of the process (such as its fairness, as discussed in chapter 2, or the various elements of the $(D \times V \times P) > C$ model, as described in chapter 3),[7] we can evaluate the quality of a process based on the *experience* it triggers in those on the receiving end. The more self-affirming the process, meaning, the more it gives people a sense of esteem or identity or control, the higher the quality.

From the time that people first become members of organizations to the time that they leave (and at many points in between), they are treated in ways that may affect their sense of self, for better or worse. Consider the various stages in employees' tenure as organization members. First they are brought in, during which time they are expected to learn the ropes about what they are expected to do and, more generally, the culture of the organization. Starting out is a critical period for employees; it is therefore important for employers to get their people off on the right foot. Once employees are onboard, organizations need to find ways to motivate them to do the best job possible. Moreover, forward-thinking organizations know that it is not enough to motivate their employees for the short term; they need to find ways to help their people grow and develop for the longer term. Overlaid on these natural stages of employees' tenure is the stark reality of constant change in the external environment. Therefore, regardless of where employees are in their tenure as organization members, they may be asked to do different things or the same things in a different way. The way in which organizations handle each of these aspects of employees' tenure matters greatly. Indeed, as we will see, small differences in how the various aspects are handled may affect employees' experience of self-affirmation and, as a result, have significant effects on their productivity, morale, and overall sense of well-being. Let's look at the evidence, while simultaneously considering how you may be able to put it to good use.

GETTING OFF ON THE RIGHT FOOT

Think back to the first few days and weeks at your current job. My guess is that that time period was anything but dull. You probably felt excited, apprehensive, and, perhaps most of all, uncertain—uncertain about the best ways to do the job, uncertain about how you were expected to behave, uncertain about whether you made the right decision to join the organization, and so on. Most organizations know that new employees feel uncertain, which is why organizations often devote a lot of energy and resources to orienting people. Orienting new employees is both a responsibility and an opportunity for employers. It is a responsibility in that people need help dealing with uncertainty. It is an opportunity in that when people are uncertain they are especially susceptible to influence. The way that management treats employees experiencing uncertainty can make a huge difference. Indeed, when employees are uncertain management is likely to get a bigger bang for its buck than it would in a more steady-state environment, in which employees are less uncertain. Therefore, what management does at this early stage to socialize their employees and, just as important, how they do it may have a lasting effect on employees' productivity, morale, and well-being.

Consider the starting-up experience for new hires. A typical method of socializing new employees consists of training them for the specific work they will be doing and, more generally, acculturating them to the values of the organization and how they are expected to behave. When people are new they are told about the traditions of the organization, what the organization stands for, and why they should be happy with their decision to become a part of the team. The main goal is to ensure a perceived fit between the people and the place. What if, in addition to telling new people about the place, what it stands for, and so forth the organization went about socializing people in a somewhat different way? What if employers asked their new people to identify their "signature strengths," that is, what *they* stand for, what *they* are good at, and how *they* could enact their signature strengths within the confines of their work?

A recent study by Dan Cable, Francesca Gino, and Brad Staats addressed this question by comparing three different methods of socialization at Wipro, an India-based company that is a leader in the business process outsourcing industry. For example, if you are having trouble buying an airline ticket or configuring your printer and call for tech support, you might be connected to an employee in a Wipro call center. Most jobs in Indian call centers are stressful. Employees often have to deal with frustrated callers. Furthermore, employees are expected to mask their Indian identity, such as by taking on Western accents and ways of interacting. It is no wonder that the annual turnover rate in Indian call centers hovers around 50–70 percent. One of the three methods of socialization (the control group) consisted of Wipro's typical method, which focused on skills training and making newcomers generally aware of the firm's purpose. A second method of socialization consisted of everything done in the control condition along with activities emphasizing the organization's identity (organizational identity condition). These included (1) hearing presentations from a senior leader as well as a star performer about Wipro's values and why it is a great place to work; (2) after hearing the presentations, the new recruits answering such questions as "What did you hear about Wipro that makes you proud to be part of this organization?"; and (3) discussing with one another their answers to these questions. Afterward, the new employees were given two sweatshirts and a badge with the company name on it, which they were asked to wear during the training session.

The third method of socialization also entailed everything that was done in the control condition, along with a series of self-affirming activities focusing on employees' individual identity (individual identity condition). For example, the presentation from the senior leader emphasized how working at Wipro would enable the new recruits to express themselves and to develop their own opportunities. They then took part in an exercise ("Lost at Sea") that was conducted in an individually oriented way. The exercise requires participants to imagine that they are stranded on a life raft at sea and to rank order the usefulness of fifteen items in that situation. They also were asked to think about how their responses compared to those of the other participants. They then were asked to respond to the following four questions pertaining to their "best selves": (1) What three words best describe you as an individual? (2) What is unique about you that leads to your happiest times and best performance at work? (3) Can you please describe a time (perhaps on a job, perhaps at home) when you were acting the way you were "born to act?" (4) How can you repeat that behavior on the job? They then introduced their best selves to the people they would be working with in the future and described their own approach to the "Lost at Sea" exercise. They also received two sweatshirts and a badge to wear during the training sessions, but this time the name on them was their own rather than that of the company.

The results of the study were dramatic. Employee turnover *for the next six months* was significantly lower in the individual identity condition than it was in the control condition and in the organizational identity condition. Moreover, customer satisfaction was significantly higher in the individual identity condition than it was in the control condition.[8] In spite of these very positive consequences of socializing people by appealing to their individual identity, the skeptical reader may not be convinced. For instance, skeptics may see the method used in the individual identity condition as giving (away) too much responsibility for the onboarding process to the new employees rather than keeping it under the employer's control. Not necessarily. In the individual identity condition the responsibility for getting people off on the right foot is *shared* by the employer and the new employees. Employees are asked to reveal their signature strengths and how to enact them on the job. Employers, for their part, maintain control of the socialization process in at least two ways. First, participants in the individual identity condition continued to be exposed to the company's traditional socialization process prior to being asked to indicate their signature strengths and how to enact them. Second, it is not as if participants were free to implement their signature strengths in *any* way that they chose; the employer still had to approve ideas that employees generated on how to enact their signature strengths in the workplace.

Another possible reason for employers to be skeptical about the applicability of the results of this study is that they do not have the time to tailor socialization processes to include the unique features of the individual identity condition. But the entire procedure took only about an hour, with fifteen minutes devoted to each of four events: (1) the senior leaders at Wipro describing how working there "would give each new employee the opportunity to express him or herself"; (2) having participants complete the "Lost at Sea" exercise in a way that made their individuality salient; (3) having participants reflect on how their responses to the "Lost at Sea" exercise compared with those of their professional colleagues; and (4) having participants complete the series of questions associated with their signature strengths. Even though the procedure took only an hour, the individual identity induction reduced employee turnover and improved customer satisfaction for the next six months. Given this impressive cost-benefit relationship, it is perhaps more appropriate to ask whether companies can afford *not* to experiment with socializing their employees along the lines of the process used in the individual identity condition.

KEEP IT GOING

The study by Cable and his colleagues shows that small procedural differences in how employees are brought into the organization can help them get off on the right foot. Just as important is to keep them moving in a positive direction. Fortunately management processes that create the experience of self-affirmation are not limited to the time period when employees enter organizations; they can happen later as well. And that is a good thing because now perhaps more than ever, people want more than just a paycheck from their work. They also want their work to be intrinsically rewarding. Organizational psychologists Richard Hackman and Greg Oldham have raised two very important questions about intrinsic motivation. First, what is it specifically that people experience when they are intrinsically motivated? Second, how can organizations shape their work environments so that people have such experiences? For instance, people are intrinsically motivated when they perceive their work to be meaningful. They experience meaningfulness, in turn, when the work they are doing allows them to use or develop a variety of skills (rather than just one), when they perform a task from beginning to end (rather than just being a "cog in the wheel"), and when they are informed about the significance of their work.[9]

In like fashion, people are intrinsically motivated when they experience a sense of esteem (e.g., "I did the job well"), control (e.g., "Doing my job well made a difference"), and identity (e.g., "Doing the job well made a difference in an arena that is central to how I see myself"). The challenge for organizations is to create work environments in which people experience esteem, control, and identity in the course of doing their work. One way that managers try to elicit intrinsic motivation is by pointing out the fundamental value of the organization's mission and by showing people how the work they are doing helps the organization achieve its worthwhile mission.

The recent work of Adam Grant and his colleagues demonstrates a particularly effective way to do this: by having the ultimate end users of the organization's product or service tell employees how their efforts made an important difference in their lives. For example, consider the work of a university fund-raiser. The job typically entails calling alumni to ask for contributions. The work is repetitive and dull, and the word that fund-raisers probably hear more than any other is "no." Grant discovered that "a brief visit from a student who had received a scholarship motivated the fund-raisers to increase their efforts." By "brief visit" I mean five minutes. And by "increase their efforts" I mean a 400 percent boost in fund-raisers' weekly productivity![10]

In a related context, many doctors say that one of the most rewarding aspects of their job is to see improvement in their patients' health as a result of their efforts. However, certain doctors, such as radiologists and pathologists, miss out on these opportunities because they often do not interact directly with their patients. Doctors whose work introduces psychological distance between them and their patients may especially benefit from interventions that enable them to see the fruits of their labor. A recent study found support for a related idea: merely showing radiologists a photograph of their patient significantly increased the radiologists' productivity (the accuracy of their findings improved by nearly 50 percent) and morale (they reported feeling "more like physicians"), relative to those who had not been shown a photograph.[11]

Adam Grant suggests that positive feedback from end users inspires more effectively than if the same feedback were to be provided by, say, managers because it has greater credibility when it comes from the end users. For one thing, feedback from end users has the advantage of being direct. End users are more likely to provide the unvarnished truth, relative to managers who are (a) one step removed from the benefit and hence less able to tell the truth or (b) more likely to have a personal agenda in describing the benefits and therefore less willing to tell the truth.[12]

Organizations have found a variety of ways for employees to be on the receiving end of praise from end users. For example, Wells Fargo shows employees videos of customers describing how the bank's low-interest loans helped them manage high levels of debt. Another method is letters. In Let's Go Publications, an organization that updates travel books, managers share with staff grateful letters from readers who used the company's books to navigate their way through dicey situations in foreign countries and cultures.

I have observed firsthand the motivating effects of disseminating letters from satisfied customers. As faculty director of the Columbia Business School executive education program, High Impact Leadership (HIL), I often receive letters from participants after the program in which they describe how they benefited from it. For example, consider the letters of these four different participants.

1. (Three months later.) I have to say that without the experience of the HIL program, I'm not sure that I would have ever been able to see things as clearly as I do now. The quality of the presentations was key in getting through to me. Suffice to say the program changed me and I am forever grateful.

2. (Five months later.) My experience in HIL will forever stay in my thoughts. It continues to create significant change in how I lead and live my life. I just had my annual feedback meeting with my boss and the feedback was AWESOME!

3. (Six months later.) I totally enjoyed the program. The 360 feedback that I received helped me chart a course toward truly making a difference. Last week I received the ultimate compliment when, on separate occasions, my boss and one of my direct reports told me that they had noticed a big improvement in my managerial style since I returned from the HIL course.

4. (One year later.) I recently got promoted to the Global VP role after an extensive search by my company. What really helped was the huge improvement in self-awareness of my leadership skills. I have the HIL program to thank for this level of progress.

Receiving these letters is very gratifying looking backward and very motivating looking forward. The letters are powerful reminders of the great responsibility and opportunity we have in delivering a first-rate program. The word "we" is important. I am blessed to be working in HIL with an extremely talented team of faculty colleagues (Caryn Block, Bob Hurley, and Mark Kiefaber). As soon as I receive these letters I quickly pass them along to Caryn, Bob, and Mark. They all say that the letters help fuel their already high level of engagement with the program.

As motivating as videos and letters may be, there is nothing quite like getting positive feedback from real live end users. The medical device company Medtronics practices this idea in several ways. One is by bringing end users to employees. Perhaps the most poignant moment of the company's annual holiday party is when patients describe how the company's products made enormous differences in their lives. Another way is by bringing employees to the end users. A common practice at Medtronics is for engineers, salespeople, and technicians to attend procedures in which the company's medical devices are used. This enables employees whose work removes them from end users to see the fruits of their labors in a very palpable way.

TAKING THE NEXT STEPS

The idea that intrinsically motivated employees show greater productivity and morale is certainly not new. The bigger challenge for employers is putting this idea into actual practice. Consistent with the overarching theme of this book, studies suggest that *how* employers go about trying to put an idea into actual practice can make a world of difference. Certain ways of doing things are more self-affirming to employees than are others. As the study at the

Indian call center showed, onboarding employees by asking them to identify their signature strengths and how to enact them in their jobs is a good way to go. And as Adam Grant and his colleagues have found, being told by end users that their work made a difference is much more inspiring to employees than if the exact same message were delivered by their bosses.

Typically the impetus for introducing changes in the workplace, such as how to make the nature of the work more intrinsically motivating, comes from those in management positions. If employees are intrinsically motivated when they have autonomy, or when they are able to work on a task from beginning to end (known as "task identity"), management should structure employees' work to include autonomy and task identity. For example, task identity is achieved when the same nurse has responsibility for the care of certain patients from the time they check into the hospital to the time they leave.

Although management-initiated changes in job design can improve employees' productivity and morale, these positive effects often don't last very long. Unfortunately, within a few weeks or months employees' productivity and morale revert to baseline. What if the process of job redesign was done in a different way, such that the impetus for it came from the employees themselves? Employee-initiated changes in job design are known as "job crafting," and there are at least two reasons why job crafting enables people to feel more self-affirmed, relative to more conventional, employer-initiated methods of job redesign. First, when employees initiate job redesign the changes introduced are especially likely to be personally relevant. As Amy Wrzesniewski and her colleagues put it, "By *customizing* their jobs to suit their *unique needs, motives, and values*, employees may experience a lasting positive reaction to the improved nature of the work itself, rather than only a temporary response to the novelty of a job re-designed by managers" (emphasis added). In other words, the *content* of the change brought about by job crafting is likely to reinforce people's sense of identity. Second, the very fact that the change is employee initiated suggests that the *process* of job crafting allows people to experience a sense of control, in addition to the self-affirmation they may experience as a result of substantive changes to the job itself.[13] (Remember the nursing home study that showed that residents who watered their own plants or chose the night a movie would be shown were more alert than were residents who were told by management when to water their plants or when the movie would be shown.)[14]

In their thoughtful analysis of job crafting, Amy Wrzesniewski and Jane Dutton showed that practically any type of job lends itself to crafting. Furthermore, craft-ing can take at least three different forms: (1) a change in task boundaries, which refers to the number or types of tasks that people take on; (2) a change in cognitive task boundaries, which refers to how employees think about or define their work; and (3) a change in relational bound-aries, which refers to the number and types of others with whom employees interact in the course of doing their job. For example, even low-skilled jobs such as hospital cleaning may be taken up in a more or less crafted way. In one study hospital cleaners who crafted their jobs took on tasks in addition to those mentioned in their formal job description; they also timed when they did their work so as to be more coordinated with other work in their units (change in task boundaries). These high crafters also did not view their work as a series of discrete activities, such as cleaning patients' rooms, cleaning the hallways, and so forth but as an integrated whole designed to improve the patient experience (change in cognitive task boundaries). Furthermore, high crafters behaved proactively in ways that made for a more pleasant work environment, such as by being friendly to patients, helping visitors find their way, and coordinating with the nurses on their units (change in relational boundaries).[15]

A recent study by Wrzesniewski, Grant, and their colleagues examined how employees were affected by job crafting. Having extolled the virtues of job crafting, I bet you are expecting me to say that it had positive effects on employees' productivity and morale. It did, but the results were actually more complex and interesting than that. Participants were drawn from the sales and general administrative functions of a Fortune 500 technology firm with headquarters on the West Coast of the United States. They took part in a short (90–120 minute) workshop on career development conducted on company time. All of the workshops were designed to stimulate participants to see their job situations as malleable and as a result motivate them to engage in crafting. However, there were three different versions of the topics covered during the workshops. In one (job crafting only), participants described the tasks in their current job in a "before diagram" and then indicated the tasks they would like their job to consist of in an "after diagram." In a second (skill development only), participants described their current levels of job-relevant knowledge, skills, and abilities in the "before diagram" and then depicted in an "after diagram" the knowledge, skills, and abilities they wished to develop in order to perform better at their jobs. In a third version of the workshop (dual crafting), participants constructed before and after diagrams for *both* the crafting of their jobs and the development of their skills. In all three versions of the workshops participants also were asked to write the steps they would take over the following few weeks to translate their intended changes in jobs and/or skills into reality. Moreover, in all three versions participants were asked to strike a balance between idealism and realism when describing their "after diagrams." Participants' job performance and morale were assessed at two points in time after the workshop: six weeks later (the shorter-term measure) and six months later (the longer-term measure).

Taking part in the crafting exercise had no effect on those who took part in the skill development only workshop, in either the shorter term or the longer term. Furthermore, consistent with previous research on the effects of management-initiated changes in job design, those who took part in the job crafting only workshop showed positive effects in the shorter term but not in the longer term; performance and morale were significantly higher six weeks after the workshop, but by the time six months rolled around performance and morale levels were back to where they had been prior to the workshop. The more lasting changes were shown by those who had taken part in the dual crafting workshop. For this group, morale was no different six weeks later but was significantly higher six months later. Moreover, their performance actually dipped significantly in the shorter term; however, six months later their performance was slightly higher than it had been prior to the workshop.[16]

Why is it that those who did job crafting without skill crafting showed a boost in their productivity and morale, but only for a short period of time? And why is it that dual crafting (that is, the combination of job crafting and skill crafting) failed to produce any benefits in the shorter term but did so over the longer haul? And why did those who only did skill development fail to show any benefit, in either the shorter term or the longer term? In contemplating how they would like to change their jobs, those who did job crafting without skill crafting took less initiative than their counterparts who did dual crafting. In other words, the magnitude of the changes that participants envisioned for themselves (as represented by comparing their before diagrams with their after diagrams) was significantly lower when they did job crafting rather than dual crafting. And yet it is taking the initiative that enables people to experience identity and control, the very ingredients that fuel motivation and satisfaction. Those who only did job crafting generated modest enhancements for themselves, which were beneficial in the shorter term but not in the longer term.

Perhaps because they took greater initiative, those who did dual crafting also may have experienced self-threat upon realizing the discrepancy between their current state (as reflected in the before diagram) and their future state (as reflected in the after diagram). Those who did dual crafting may have had the following thoughts: (1) "I would like for my job to be expanded or enhanced in certain ambitious ways"; (2) "To be successful in my newly crafted job, I am going to need to develop certain skills"; and (3) "Uh-oh, I have a long way to go before my skill set is up to what the newly crafted job will require." Thus in the short term the sense of identity or control that those who did dual crafting experienced in response to the job crafting part of the exercise may have been counteracted by feelings of incompetence in reaction to the skill development part of the activity. No wonder that, in the short term, those who did dual crafting failed to show improvement in their productivity and morale.

Several factors, however, may have enabled those who did dual crafting to do better over the longer term. As we know, performance depends on motivation and ability. Whereas six weeks may not have been enough time to develop the capabilities dual crafters identified in the skill development part of the exercise, six months may have been. Hence, six months after the workshop dual crafters likely had more ability to perform. For that matter, they may even have become more motivated to perform in that their previously felt sense of incompetence may have given way to feelings of competence and self-assurance; quite often we are more motivated to do something as we see ourselves becoming more competent. Furthermore, dual crafters may have been the beneficiaries of a virtuous cycle. Just as, over time, they developed the skills needed to be successful at their crafted jobs, their enhanced skill levels may have motivated them to consider additional ways to craft their jobs, and so on.

By encouraging employees to expand their psychological horizons via dual crafting, do organizations run the risk of losing good people? One skeptical view is that a natural outcome of the virtuous cycle elicited by dual crafting is for people to start looking for opportunities elsewhere. In fact, those who engaged in dual crafting were twice as likely to transition to a new role within eight months after the workshop, relative to those who did job crafting only or skill development only. However, the vast majority of those transitions (more than 90 percent) occurred within the organization in the form of lateral or upward moves rather than employees taking positions elsewhere.[17] My hunch is that organizations need not worry about mass defections to other employers if they use processes such as dual crafting that enable their people to experience self-affirmation. Quite the contrary: processes that promote the experience of esteem, identity, and control are likely to be a source of competitive advantage in the quest for employee retention. Some good employees may leave because their horizons have been expanded by processes such as dual crafting, but it is not likely that a *disproportionate* number of people will leave. Furthermore, the cost of some good people leaving is more than offset by the benefits of greater productivity and morale among the much larger group of employees who choose to stay.

Wrzesniewski and Grant also speculated about why those who took part in just the skill development workshop failed to show any positive effects. Their reasoning is entirely consistent with the thrust of this chapter: they reasoned that skill crafting that is not accompanied by job crafting makes people focus on personal weaknesses and ways they need to improve, which may be experienced as self-threatening. Thus, rather than promoting a positive experience of the self, the workshop emphasizing skill development alone may have had the exact opposite effect in certain ways, which may explain why it did not lead to improved productivity and morale in either the shorter or the longer term.[18]

The emerging theme from several studies, then, is that small differences in *how* organizations implement their human resource practices can have large effects on productivity and morale by positively affecting employees' sense of esteem or identity or control. Recent research in educational settings makes an analogous point: relatively minor tweaks in how students are treated have dramatic effects on important attitudes (e.g., life happiness) and behaviors (e.g., performance in school), also by affecting their sense of esteem or identity or control. In one study, Sohyeon Shim, Alia Crum, and Adam Galinsky asked college students to take just a few minutes every other day over a two-week period to briefly write about several things in their lives that they could control; this was the high control condition. Another group wrote about things they could not control; this was the low control condition. For example, one person in the high control condition wrote:

> I have changed people's opinions of me in the past. For example, my vice president for a student organization that I was president of openly said to me that he wouldn't listen to me and disagreed with the election because I am female. But throughout the year, I worked closely with him and gave him larger responsibilities and eventually he learned to trust my judgment and leadership skills. At the end of this year, he sent me an e-mail saying that he was sorry for what he said at the beginning of the year and that he thought that I was one of the best presidents of any club that he was a part of. I think depending on what type of attitude I have and how I interact with others, their reaction and thoughts can be changed.

In contrast, a participant in the low control condition wrote:

> I thought about things involving my boyfriend. We've been dating for about six years and things are really serious between us. Like, engagement serious. But, what his mom thinks of me are things that I can't change. His mom has done some mean things to me. Like,

hiding my wallet so that I have to stay longer or yelling at me so much that I've run out of my boyfriend's house crying. And then she guilt trips me when I can't make family functions. I just feel like she never gave me a chance. I mean, I consider myself a pretty normal, sweet person. But no matter how much I try to extend the olive branch sometimes, it seems like she doesn't notice and I don't think I can change her actions/thoughts toward me.

One day after the two-week period ended, all participants rated their happiness in life, which is known in research parlance as "subjective well-being." Sample items include "In most ways my life is close to my ideal" and "I am satisfied with my life." The results showed that people who focused on things they could control had higher life satisfaction than did those who focused on things they could not control.[19]

Keep in mind that the differences between how participants were treated in the high control condition versus the low control condition were not large. It was not as if they were put in situations in which they actually had different levels of control. Rather, they merely *thought about* aspects of their lives over which they felt more versus less control. Also, it was not as if they were required to think about either having control or not having control for prolonged periods; instead, the treatment consisted of six brief experiences, every other day for two weeks. Furthermore, the dimension affected by the treatment, life satisfaction, is quite important. Thus what we have here is a relatively small difference in process having a statistically significant effect in a domain of obvious psychological significance: life satisfaction.

A skeptic might say that these positive effects on life satisfaction brought on by differences in perceived control were fleeting. After all, life satisfaction was measured only a day after the two-week intervention. Could it possibly be that taking part in this study had longer-term effects on well-being? Remarkably, it did. Seven months later, the same participants completed a standard measure of well-being used by the U.S. Centers for Disease Control and Prevention. For instance, participants reported the number of days per month since taking part in the study that their physical and mental health had not been good. Those asked to think about things they could control seven months earlier reported having fewer bad days per month than did their counterparts who had been asked to contemplate things that they could not control. It is not too surprising that immediately after the study those who thought about things they could control felt more optimistic than those who thought about things they could not control. What was much more surprising, however, was that the optimism experienced during the study somehow influenced participants' physical and mental well-being seven months later.

Recent research in the middle school classroom provides further evidence that objectively small differences in how people are treated influence their experience of esteem or identity or control, which in turn makes a big difference, in an important domain, that persists over time. Here is the backdrop. It has been well documented that the academic achievement of African Americans has lagged behind that of their European American counterparts. One explanation is Claude Steele's notion of *stereotype threat*, which refers to the somewhat paradoxical tendency for a negatively stereotyped group to perform poorly, precisely because of the anxiety they feel about performing in a way that confirms the negative stereotype. People who are members of groups that are negatively stereotyped are all too aware of the stereotypes. Furthermore, they abhor the thought of performing at a level consistent with the stereotype. Hence when they find themselves in situations in which the stereotype is relevant, they experience the anxiety-provoking burden of trying hard not to live up to (or rather down to) the stereotype. Unfortunately, their anxiety detracts from their ability to perform, thereby bringing about the low level of performance they are trying so hard to avoid.

One example of such a stereotype is that African Americans are academically inferior. Many people, including African Americans, know about this stereotype; indeed, some of them are consumed by it. One of my former MBA students at Columbia Business School, an African American, commented that he feels constantly on guard about his intellectual capabilities. He said that about the only time he is not concerned about how well he is performing is when he is alone in his apartment, doing something like surfing the web or pursuing a hobby. It is not too hard to imagine how worrying about intellectual capabilities detracts from much-needed attention to perform. Steele and his colleagues found that when black undergraduate students from prestigious universities worked on what they thought was an intelligence task they performed much worse than white students from the same universities. However, when the exact same task was portrayed as not being a measure of intelligence, the black students performed much better, in this instance just as well as the white students.[20]

The harmful effects of stereotype threat on intellectual functioning are not limited to African Americans. The performance of members of any negatively stereotyped group on intellectually challenging tasks may suffer when their worry about confirming the stereotype prevents them from fully focusing on the task at hand. For instance, some believe that women are less talented than men in math and the hard sciences. When intellectually talented undergraduates worked on a math test that they were told was known to produce gender differences, women performed a lot worse than men. However, when they took the same test under conditions in which nothing was said about gender differences, the women did a lot better, this time performing at the same level as the men.[21]

Let's go back to the middle school classroom, in which Geoff Cohen and his colleagues at Stanford evaluated whether self-affirmation would improve the academic performance of students prone to experience stereotype threat. Stereotype threat, by its very nature, assaults people's sense of esteem or identity or control; it's no wonder that students perform poorly when they experience it. If so, then doing something self-affirming may be particularly helpful to them. Cohen and his colleagues started small. They figured that if the threat-prone students did something self-affirming while taking a particular class, say, social studies, their performance in that class might improve. Early in the school year African American students took part in a self-affirmation activity during one of their social studies classes. The activity was modeled on the one used by Claude Steele in his early laboratory experiments. Students rank ordered the importance of different values relevant to their age group, such as their relationships with friends or family members and being good at certain subjects (e.g., art). Two different conditions were created. Those in the self-affirmation condition then chose their most highly ranked value and wrote a paragraph about why that value was important to them. Those in the control condition chose their least highly ranked value and wrote a paragraph on why that value might be important to someone else.

Three months later, those in the self-affirmation condition earned higher grades in social studies than did those in the control condition. Given that the self-affirmation exercise lasted for all of fifteen minutes, it is astounding that it led to higher grades in social studies three months later. But that's not all. Students who did the self-affirmation exercise didn't simply do better in social studies; they did better in *all* of their classes over the next three months, relative to those in the control condition. Buoyed by these findings, Cohen and his colleagues evaluated whether these positive effects might last even longer. In fact they did: a full two years after the African American middle school students completed that initial fifteen-minute self-affirmation exercise (along with a few "booster shots" along the way over the next year, in which they basically repeated the self-affirmation exercise), they earned higher grades than their counterparts in the control condition in *all* of their major school subjects.[22]

Why did this happen? How could taking part in a few brief self-affirmation exercises produce such long-lasting positive effects? Recall that the study on dual crafting showed that having employees craft both their jobs and their skill development had positive long-term effects on their productivity and morale. This may have happened because dual crafting put in motion a recursive process that made employees the beneficiaries of a virtuous cycle: job crafting may have motivated people to develop the skills needed to perform the jobs that they crafted for themselves, and developing skills may have generated new ideas for employees on how to craft their jobs even further.

Similarly, perhaps taking part in a short self-affirmation exercise affected another type of recursive process with long-term effects. Rather than activating a virtuous cycle as in the case of dual crafting, however, the self-affirmation activity may have helped students prone to stereotype threat to not be victimized by a vicious cycle. That is, stereotype threat interferes with the performance of challenging intellectual tasks, and performing poorly on challenging intellectual tasks further reinforces stereotype threat, and the cycle continues. Early in the school year, students prone to stereotype threat are likely to perform poorly on at least some of their tests and assignments. Such negative feedback is likely to reinforce doubts about their competence, which could lead to continued poor performance, and so on. This is why taking part in the self-affirmation exercise may have been so helpful to them. As we saw earlier in the chapter, doing something self-affirming need not be in the same arena that threatened people's esteem, identity, or control in the first place. As long as the activity meaningfully reaffirms people's overall sense of self-integrity, it can undercut the potentially damaging effects of the original source of self-threat. Giving students prone to stereotype threat an opportunity to reflect on and write about their important values does not take away from the fact that they may have performed poorly. However, the self-affirmation exercise may lower the negative implications of their poor performance for their overall sense of self and, in so doing, slow the momentum of the vicious cycle.

As further evidence that students prone to stereotype threat were trapped in a vicious cycle, Cohen and his colleagues found that the academic performance of those who did not take part in the self-affirmation exercise steadily declined over the entire two years of the study. The performance of the students who did the self-affirmation exercise also declined over the two years of the study, but a lot less so; in other words, for the latter group, the cycle wasn't nearly as vicious.

There is even evidence that taking part in a brief self-affirmation exercise may help people's longer-term functioning in the social arena. People who are insecure in their relationships with their friends, families, and lovers tend to give off awkward vibes, which is likely to invite criticism and rejection, which in turn reinforce their insecurity; it is a social form of vicious cycle. If self-affirmation can help break the vicious cycle of stereotype threat and thereby bolster the academic performance of African Americans, perhaps it could do likewise for the "social performance" of people who are insecure in their relationships.

Danu Anthony Stinson and her colleagues identified a group of undergraduates who reported being uncomfortable in their social relationships. For instance, they tended to agree with statements such as "I often worry that my family will stop loving me" and to disagree with statements like "My friends regard me as very important in their lives." Half of them did the brief self-affirmation exercise in which they identified an important personal value and wrote a few paragraphs about why the value was important to them; the other half did not. Two months later, participants completed the same measure of how uncomfortable they felt in their social relationships. Those who had done the self-affirmation exercise two months earlier reported being significantly less socially uncomfortable than did their counterparts who had not self-affirmed.

Furthermore, the group that self-affirmed *behaved* more calmly in the interview than those who did not.[23]

A MATTER OF WHEN

People are most likely to benefit from self-affirming processes when they feel self-threatened. For example, it is probably no accident that asking new employees to identify and express their signature strengths was particularly helpful in getting them off to a good start. After all, being new to an organization is inherently threatening to people's sense of esteem or identity or control. Therefore, doing something self-affirming may be just what they need at that moment in time. Additional findings from the middle school study also suggest that self-affirmation is particularly helpful when people feel self-threatened. The African American students who benefited the most from the self-affirmation exercise were the ones who, beforehand, had the lowest level of academic performance and therefore were the most likely to be feeling self-threatened. Furthermore, the affirmation exercise had no effect on the performance of European Americans, for whom the experience of stereotype threat (and hence self-threat) is a lot less relevant.

The beginning of the academic year in middle school is not the only educational context in which students are prone to experience self-threat. Whenever students are in transition, such as upon starting high school or college, uncertainty about whether they belong or whether they have the ability to succeed makes them susceptible to self-threat. Imagine how upon starting out, students with a shaky sense of whether they belong or whether they have the ability necessary to succeed encounter some form of negative feedback; it need not be severe. For instance, suppose that during the first week of school a student from an ethnic minority is not invited to join a lunch group of people from the ethnic majority. At first blush, this is not necessarily the end of the world. Perhaps the group from the ethnic majority was feeling uptight themselves about starting out, causing them to seek out people like themselves. As members of the majority group settled in themselves, they may have had every intention of including people from the ethnic minority. By then, however, it may be too late for the minority group member, who may be hypersensitive to evidence suggesting that s/he does not belong. Moreover, once people infer that they do not belong, they start to think and act in ways that virtually assure that they will continue to not be included.

Interventions that affirm people's sense of belonging, which map onto a social basis of self-esteem, may be especially helpful to those sensitive to feelings of exclusion. To test this idea, Greg Walton and Geoff Cohen studied first-year college students at the beginning of the academic year. Half of them were told that it is perfectly normal to feel at least somewhat apprehensive or worried at the beginning about whether they belong and that over time these feelings largely go away. To buttress the intervention, students wrote a short essay that would be shown to the next year's incoming class about how they had actually experienced a growing sense of belonging in their time at college. The other half took part in a control condition in which nothing was done to allay their worries about belonging. Although white students did not benefit from the intervention, black students did, and for a full three years. In fact, the belongingness intervention cut the achievement gap between whites and blacks in half. The belongingness intervention required all of an hour of the students' time. Walton and Cohen found analogous results in research examining students who had just started high school. Those who experienced an even briefer belongingness intervention (this one took only twenty-five minutes) were much less likely to show an increase in depression for the entire school year, relative to those in a control group.[24]

Another type of intervention that likely influences esteem and control, and, in so doing, students' odds of academic success, focuses on their beliefs about intelligence. In her path-breaking book *Mindset*, Carol Dweck suggests that people maintain two different belief systems or implicit theories about intelligence. Entity theorists think that intelligence is a fixed trait; you either have it or you don't, and the amount you have cannot be easily altered. Incremental theorists, in contrast, believe that intelligence is malleable. Of course some people have more of it than others, but incremental theorists believe that almost all people can improve their intelligence, particularly if they are willing to put forth the necessary effort to do so. A key difference between entity and incremental theorists is in how they react to negative feedback. Entity theorists tend to give up; after all, they believe, they don't have what it takes. Incremental theorists tend to redouble their efforts. Obviously the latter are far more adaptive than the former in responding to the academic setbacks that will inevitably come their way, some much more quickly than others. Studies have shown that interventions extolling the virtues of an incremental mind-set have positive *long-term* effects on students' academic performance and their progress in school, particularly among those who are more prone to doubt their ability to succeed. The interventions can be as brief as an hour, during which time students not only learn the benefits of adopting an incremental theory but also write a letter to be shown to the next year's students about what they have just learned.[25]

In summary, the common theme emerging from studies in the workplace and various educational settings is that processes that enable people to experience esteem, identity, or control positively affect their performance, their sense of well-being, and their comfort with others. This is hardly a new idea, but what is new is how eminently feasible it may be to make this happen. Time and again, we see that interventions costing little in terms of time and money can have beneficial, long-lasting effects on obviously important outcomes, such as productivity and morale in the workplace, performance and academic progress in a variety of educational settings, and social comfort on the college campus.

ORGANIZATIONAL CHANGE AND SELF-THREAT

It is when people feel self-threatened that they may most benefit from processes that enable them to affirm their sense of esteem or identity or control. The experience of change is a prime candidate for eliciting self-threat, such as when students start high school or college, or when people first join an organization. Of course, the experience of change in an organization is not limited to when people join it. As we saw in chapter 3, it also happens when the organization rather than the individual is the impetus for the change, such as when there is a shift in strategy, culture, procedures, technology, and the like. The following reaction of a midlevel manager whose organization was going through myriad changes such as downsizing and restructuring is a virtual poster child for how organizational change threatens people's sense of self: "I knew the old organization, its mission, its operation, its people, its culture. In that knowledge, I had a sense of identity and confidence about my company and myself. Now, I work for a new company, one-fourth its former size. I find myself asking, who are we, and who am I?"

Sounds grim; this is hardly the stuff of a happy, engaged, and productive employee. Indeed, it has been suggested that one basis of employees' resistance to organizational change is the experience of self-threat. As the noted change management expert William Bridges put it, "At bottom, it is a person's identity that he or she has trouble letting go of (during organizational change), and it is that identity that stands in the way of the change producing its desired result."[26] But there is a way out. If employees made to feel self-threatened by change do *something* self-affirming, they are much less likely to exhibit the negative reactions emblematic of resistance. Furthermore, the venue in which they self-affirm need not be the same as the one in which they were made to feel self-threatened in the first place; virtually any meaningful self-affirmation experience will do.

There are different types of self-affirmation experiences that may counteract feelings of self-threat and thereby reduce employees' resistance to organizational change. Two dimensions help organize myriad possible self-affirmation experiences: (1) the party who initiated them, and (2) the location in which the experiences took place. Some experiences of self-affirmation may be the impetus of employees themselves whereas others may be initiated by employers. And some of these experiences transpire in the workplace whereas others take place after-hours, on employees' own time. All of them, however, can serve as welcome antidotes to the experience of self-threat brought on

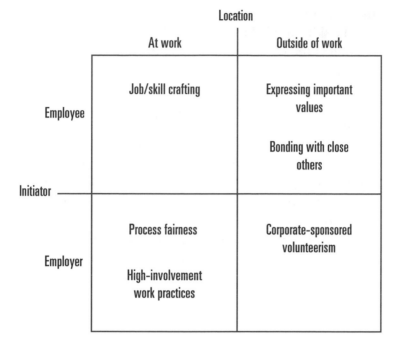

Figure 4.1. Experiences Promoting Self-Affirmation

Examples cited within each quadrant reflect sources of self-affirmation.

by organizational change. In considering some examples, we will sample from each of the quadrants created by the 2 × 2 matrix shown in figure 4.1.

Employee/At Work. A good example of how employees can be the impetus for self-affirmation in the workplace is reflected in our earlier discussion of crafting. For practically any job employees have latitude to change the substance of what they do or how they go about doing it. The study by Wrzesniewski, Grant, and their colleagues showed that the positive effects of crafting on productivity and morale were most enduring when employees took it upon themselves to alter the job (job crafting) as well as to identify the skills needed to do their jobs and to develop (skill crafting). One obvious implication of these results is that employees should engage in dual crafting (job and skill).[27]

Relative to a more steady-state environment, in which routines are well established, there actually may be more room for employees to engage in dual crafting during times of change. In other words, in the face of change not only *should* they do dual crafting but also they *can* do dual crafting. For example, a former student of mine (Sarah) who now works as a midlevel manager at a bank had long wanted to have more voice in how her department's work would be done. Prior to an organizational downsizing, however, she had been unable to persuade her boss to allow her much input. The downsizing changed all that. With fewer people available to do the work, she and all of her colleagues now had much more room to craft their jobs.

Furthermore, recognizing that fulfilling her career goals required her to improve her leadership skills, Sarah had long wanted to attend a leadership training program held offsite. Prior to the downsizing, her boss did not support her attending the program; somehow, every year, he told her that the timing to attend the program "wasn't right." After the downsizing, however, her boss recognized that with fewer employees a leadership vacuum threatened the group's long-term viability. So, when at the beginning of the year Sarah put in her usual request to attend the training program, she was pleasantly surprised to learn that her boss approved it. In sum, dual crafting elicits self-affirmation, which in turn leads to positive long-term effects on employees' productivity and morale. Here I am suggesting that the onset of change makes it a particularly opportune time for employees to engage in dual crafting, in that the system may be more receptive to the idea than it would be in a static environment.

Employee/Outside of Work. Remember our chapter-opening example of Steve, the small business owner who started doing volunteer work on his own time as a way to deal with the self-threat brought on by the decline in his business? Volunteerism is a great antidote to self-threat because it enables people to affirm themselves. For one thing, the perception of making a meaningful difference through volunteerism enhances esteem and control. Furthermore, for some people volunteering affirms their identity as caring and concerned individuals. Of course, volunteering is not the only activity that people can do on their own time that is self-affirming. Taking part in activities that reflect deeply held personal values, whatever those activities and values happen to be, reinforces people's sense of identity.

In a typical self-affirmation study participants are asked to rank order the importance of different types of values: theoretical, economic, aesthetic, social, political, and religious (see appendix F for more information on each of these values). Those in the experimental condition are then asked to write a short essay pertinent to their most important values, indicating why these values are important to them or specific instances in which they were able to express these values, whereas those in the control condition are asked to write about their least important values or about a different topic altogether. The results of numerous studies have shown that people handle a wide variety of self-threats much more effectively in the experimental condition than in the control condition.

In dealing with the self-threat brought on by organizational change, people may take their lead from the method used in the experimental condition of a typical self-affirmation study. First, they need to clarify the values that are most important to them and, once having done so, find ways to do things that enable them to experience those values. For example, one way to satisfy the social value is by doing something good for others, such as engaging in volunteerism. One way to satisfy the aesthetics value is by making time to hone one's artistic abilities; another way is by helping to create conditions for others to hone their artistic abilities, which also may be a good way to satisfy the political value. One way to satisfy the theoretical value is by taking part in some significant learning experience (e.g., taking a course).

Note that all of these examples of self-affirmation are based on people's conceptions of themselves as independent actors, in which they define themselves based upon their internal attributes that include not only values but also traits, abilities, and preferences. However, most people to some degree (and some people to a very large degree) *define* themselves based on their relationships with the people they are close to, such as family or select friends. This is known as having a relational-interdependent self-construal (RISC). People high in RISC strongly agree with statements such as "My close relationships are an important reflection of who I am" and "I usually feel a strong sense of pride when someone close to me has an important accomplishment." Serena Chen and Helen Boucher found that after experiencing self-threat, such as learning that they did poorly on a measure of intellectual capability, those higher in RISC described themselves in more relational terms ("I am Jen's best friend" and "I am my parents' second son"), as a form of self-affirmation; indeed, describing themselves more relationally led to higher self-esteem. One implication of these findings is that people may be able to counteract the self-threat brought on by organizational change by doing something to affirm their "relational self," for example, doing something constructive for an important relationship.[28] In her book on happiness, Sonya Lyubomirsky suggests that one way spouses can increase marital satisfaction is by taking a few minutes each day to identify ways to make their partner's life better.[29] Given that most married people (even those generally low in RISC) define themselves on the basis of their relationship with their spouse, it stands to reason that such simple acts of marital kindness may do more than just good things for the marriage; they also may counteract the self-threat people feel when their organization introduces change, thereby enabling them to deal with it more constructively.

Employer/At Work. When an organizational change takes the form of downsizing it generally has negative effects on the productivity and morale of the people who remain. But this is not always the case; it depends on how well the downsizing process is handled. In chapter 3 we discussed the various elements that go into a well-handled change process, regardless of the nature of the change. Here I build on chapter 3 by suggesting that a well-managed change process is one that enables the "survivors" to experience esteem or identity or control. For instance, in the days and weeks leading up to the downsizing it is important for employees to believe that the processes used to plan and implement the layoffs are fair. In chapter 2 we discussed the many elements that go into a fair process, for example, whether advance notice is provided, whether the decision is based on accurate information, and whether the reasons for the decision are clearly explained. The symbolic value of process fairness also should not be underestimated. When organizations plan and implement decisions with fair processes the implicit statement they are making is that they value and respect their employees. The sense of feeling valued and respected by the organization, in turn, positively affects people's self-esteem.

But it is not only high fairness in the change process that allows employees to experience self-affirmation. Once the change is in place, what people covet over the longer haul is a sense of control. The perception of control could counteract or even eliminate any adverse effects that the change may have produced. In one study my colleagues and I examined the organizational commitment of two groups of employees from the same division of an aerospace organization headquartered in Southern California. One of the groups witnessed significant layoffs; a month earlier 10 percent of all contract workers had been let go. The other group did not experience layoffs. Participants in both groups also indicated the extent to which they felt in control, as measured by items such as "I have significant autonomy in determining how I do my job" and "My impact on what happens in my department is large." Among the people who reported feeling relatively little control, people in the group that experienced layoffs had much lower organizational commitment than did their counterparts in the no layoff group. However, the negative effect of layoffs on organizational commitment disappeared entirely among those who felt high levels of control. Put another way, perceiving high control warded off any adverse effects of the layoffs on employees' organizational commitment; as far as their organizational commitment was concerned, it was as if the layoffs hadn't happened.[30]

If perceived control, a pillar of self-affirmation, reduces the adverse effects of layoffs on survivors' productivity and morale, it is important to identify what downsizing organizations can do to engender a sense of control among the remaining employees. In fact, a slew of things are possible, under the rubric of "high-involvement work practices." High-involvement work practices transfer control to employees by giving them the authority to make decisions as well as the resources needed to do so. Examples of high-involvement work practices include semi-autonomous work groups, in which team members and not managers play the major role in determining how the work should be done, and gainsharing (the Scanlon Plan), in which employees financially share in the rewards attributable to having done their jobs well. If control refers to people believing that their behavior makes a difference, then gainsharing promotes perceived control not only by showing people the effect that doing their jobs well has on their pocketbooks but also by giving people a deeper appreciation of how doing their jobs well affects the success of the company.

In a particularly ambitious study of how layoffs affect organizational productivity, Christopher Zatzick and Roderick Iverson surveyed senior executives from more than three thousand Canadian firms. They asked the executives to report the layoff rates in their organizations as well as whether the organization used six specific high-involvement work practices (such as semi-autonomous teams and gainsharing). The respondents also provided information about revenues, expenditures, and the number of employees, which allowed the researchers to compute an objective measure of company productivity: revenues minus expenditures, divided by the number of employees. The results were striking. Companies with high layoff rates that went from using high-involvement work practices to not using them saw a huge decline in productivity, relative to that of comparable companies with low layoff rates. More optimistically, however, companies with high layoff rates that continued using high-involvement work practices did not witness any decline at all in productivity; if anything, these companies performed somewhat *better* than comparable companies with low layoff rates. Thus, as reflected in company productivity, it was as if layoffs at higher rates had not happened *provided that* the company continued to use high-involvement work practices.[31]

Employer/Outside of Work. People feel self-affirmed when they take on volunteer activities, which in turn help them deal with self-threats at work. Therein lies a good argument for corporations to sponsor volunteerism done outside the workplace. Corporate-sponsored volunteerism helps people experience self-affirmation for at least two reasons. First, just as when people take it upon themselves to volunteer, the very act of contributing to a worthy cause sponsored by their employers allows them to experience esteem or control or identity. Second, corporate volunteerism enables employees to experience self-affirmation "by association." People like to belong to groups that do the right thing, in part because their belonging shines favorably upon themselves. In fact, the notion of self-affirmation by association suggests that it may not even be necessary for people to *do* the volunteer activity to experience esteem or identity or control; merely seeing oneself as belonging to a collective that does the right thing may be sufficient. Just as the "relational self" refers to how people define themselves based on their relationships with the people to whom they are close, people's identity is also based on the "collective self," that is, the groups to which they belong. Essentially people are reasoning, "If the group does the admirable thing and I am a member, then I am admirable as well."

Deanna Senior, Will Welch, and I found that corporate volunteerism leads to self-affirmation through both of these routes. We asked employees of a major pharmaceutical company how often they took part in corporate-sponsored volunteer programs during the previous year, such as the United Way Campaign or the American Heart Association Heart Walk. Employees also rated how much they experienced esteem in the workplace (e.g., as measured by "I feel like I am a competent person at work"), identity in the workplace (e.g., as measured by "I feel that I have a clear sense of who I am at work"), and control in the workplace (e.g., as measured by "I feel that I have the opportunity to make a difference at work"). We assessed employees' commitment to the organization as a proxy for their productivity and morale, and we also measured how much they saw their employer as committed to its corporate volunteer programs. The more employees volunteered, the more likely they were to experience self-affirmation, and the more they experienced self-affirmation, the higher their organizational commitment. Furthermore, over and above how much they took part in corporate volunteer activity, the more they saw *their employer* as committed to its volunteer programs, the more they experienced self-affirmation, which, again, led to higher organizational commitment.[32]

Some organizations may be reluctant to facilitate their employees' participation in volunteer activities. They may believe it's none of their business: if employees want to do volunteer activity, they can make their own arrangements and do so on their own time. Corporations also may be concerned about allocating the resources needed to set up such programs, or perhaps they fear that facilitating employees' engagement elsewhere may detract from their commitment to the organization or their jobs. Not to worry on that last point: research shows that participating in corporate volunteer activity heightens rather than detracts from employees' organizational commitment, in part because people feel self-affirmed when they do the good deeds that their organizations made it easier for them to do.

As important as people's work is, it is merely a part of their lives. People want job engagement and job satisfaction to be sure, but probably even more than that they want *life* engagement and *life* satisfaction. Some organizations take it upon themselves to help employees think through their career growth and development path. Forward-thinking organizations take things one step further: they take the initiative to help employees clarify their path for life growth and development. It's a win-win for employees and employers. Employees benefit in that they have a greater sense of direction. Employers benefit in that employees are more productive and have higher morale. This is precisely the approach that a utility company took as part of a massive change management effort designed to turn around the company's woeful performance. What follows are the words of the company's CEO, delivered in an address at the annual conference of the Academy of Management:

> For years, companies asked people to leave their personal lives and dreams at the door—to have a work self

and a personal self. That's not realistic! We want to help employees find a balance. We want them to become more integrated, whole persons. Only by doing that can they meet their fullest human potential. We are trying, first, to help people reach their own potential and demand more of themselves than they ever thought possible. Second, we're trying to teach people to use that potential to help our company compete at warp speed. For example, we're encouraging people to develop a strategic plan for their own lives, not just their work. Because when competition really heats up, we want people focused. We want them thinking, learning and operating at their peak, not worrying about problems at home. I believe these are the kinds of things that will separate the winners from the also-rans.[33]

This company met its turnaround goals a full two years ahead of schedule. As with many organizational change initiatives, this one had a lot of aspects to it, so it is difficult to identify which ones were most responsible for its success. Based on everything in this chapter, however, I believe that one of the main reasons why employees embraced the initiative is that the way in which it was implemented enabled them to feel self-affirmed.

Translating Self-Affirmation Theory into Practice: Some Caveats

Research inspired by self-affirmation theory yields results that may appear too good to be true. Self-affirmation has positive effects on obviously important outcomes such as employees' productivity and morale and students' academic performance. Moreover, these positive effects persist.

Employees brought into an organization in self-affirming ways performed better for six months, and underperforming students who wrote about personally meaningful values did better at school for years to come. The expression "you get what you pay for" suggests that it should be very expensive to bring about such effects. This is not true in the case of self-affirmation. Activities costing *very* little in time or money, such as an extra hour during employee orientation, a two-hour seminar on dual crafting, or, in the middle school classroom, a couple of fifteen-minute writing exercises sprinkled throughout the academic year, lead to significant effects with staying power. Indeed, a little bit of self-affirmation can go a long way, suggesting that people should self-affirm particularly when they experience a threat to their esteem or identity or control.

Translating self-affirmation theory into actual practice is easier said than done, however, for reasons having to do with the central theme of this book. It is not enough simply to do something self-affirming. Rather, it is the way in which that something is done that determines how self-affirming and therefore how beneficial it will be. For the most part, the activities and events described in figure 4.1, such as job crafting and volunteerism, are all about content; they represent *what* people and organizations can do to facilitate self-affirmation. Just as important as the content, however, is the process or the *how*. Regardless of whether self-affirmation is initiated by employees or employers and regardless of whether self-affirmation occurs in the workplace or outside, it has to be done in a way that enables people to experience intrinsic rather than extrinsic motivation.

There are two ways to differentiate between people's experience of intrinsic versus extrinsic motivation. One way refers to the initiation of behavior whereas the other refers to the consequence of behavior. First, when people see themselves as responsible for initiating a behavior they experience intrinsic motivation, whereas when they see themselves behaving in response to factors outside of themselves they experience extrinsic motivation. Second, when doing the activity serves as its own source of reward they experience intrinsic motivation; it is an end in its own right. When doing the activity is not an end in its own right but is a means to an end, they experience extrinsic motivation. Research suggests that activities like those mentioned in figure 4.1 are likely to be more self-affirming and therefore beneficial when the way in which they are done allows people to experience more intrinsic than extrinsic motivation. There are also several "dos and don'ts" in *how* employees and employers may best go about implementing these activities.

COMING FROM WITHIN

Employers can elicit employee self-affirmation based on what they do, such as by sponsoring volunteer programs, and how they do it, such as making decisions with high process fairness. Whatever organizations do is likely to be more self-affirming for employees when the action is seen as coming from within, that is, when it is *authentic*, rather than motivated by external factors. For example, as reported earlier, employees were more self-affirmed and consequently more organizationally committed when they believed their employers were more genuinely interested in sponsoring volunteer activity. In a related study, Kate Roloff, Batia Wiesenfeld, and I found that people experienced the benefits of being treated with high process fairness more when the managers behaved fairly out of their own free will than when the managers behaved fairly in response to an external mandate.[34]

We also discussed how subsequent to organizational downsizings high-involvement work practices can be a source of self-affirmation and therefore fuel employee productivity and morale (see the Zatzick and Iverson study mentioned earlier). Consistent with the idea that the activity is more self-affirming if it is seen as coming from within, organizations with a history of involving employees in decisions maintain their commitment if the organizations continue to utilize high-involvement work practices in the aftermath of downsizing. In contrast, organizations that do not previously involve their employees in decision making but begin to do so following a downsizing are less likely to foster high employee commitment.[35] This is not to say that downsizing organizations that do not use high-involvement work practices beforehand should not even bother trying to use high-involvement work practices after the layoffs. Rather, it may take a while for such practices to be seen as intrinsically motivated and therefore self-affirming; old reputations die hard.

AN END IN ITS OWN RIGHT, NOT A MEANS TO AN END

Several recent studies suggest that people experience self-affirmation more when the activity is inherently rewarding in its own right rather than a means toward experiencing another, more extrinsic type of reward. In a study cleverly titled "Not All Self-Affirmations Were Created Equal," Jeff Schimel and his colleagues compared two different forms of self-affirmation: intrinsic versus extrinsic. As we saw in our chapter-opening example of Peter, the manager who became more open to challenging information once he had the self-affirming experience of mentoring, self-affirmation makes people less defensive to information that goes against their beliefs or attitudes. And as we have seen in a host of studies, self-affirmation has a positive effect on how well people perform, particularly when they have experienced self-threat. Schimel examined the effects of two different types of self-affirmation on people's openness to threatening information and on their task performance. Undergraduate students were first asked to rank order the importance of different ways of defining themselves, such as artist, athlete, student, doctor, funny person, and entrepreneur. They were then asked to insert their most important self-definition into the blank portion of the first part of six sentences and then to complete the blank part of the remainder of the sentences. For half of the participants, the sentences were phrased such that completing them would have the effect of highlighting intrinsically self-affirming thoughts. For example, "Being a _____ makes me feel _____" could have been answered: "Being an entrepreneur makes me feel creative and resourceful," and "Being a _____ reflects my true _____" could have been completed as follows: "Being a doctor reflects my true personal values."

For the remaining half, the sentences were written such that completing them would call to mind extrinsically self-affirming thoughts, with sentences such as "When I am a successful _____ I will receive _____" (e.g., "When I am a successful entrepreneur I will receive a lot of money") and "If I perform at a high level in _____ then other people will _____" (e.g., "If I perform at a high level as a doctor then other people will admire me").

In the first case the sentences make people focus on how important self-definitions are rewarding in their own right, whereas in the second case the sentences prime people to consider how important self-definitions may be a means toward the end of other benefits such as money or others' admiration. All participants then performed a task. Just beforehand, they rated how much their performance would be due to external reasons such as time pressure or the difficulty of the task. For people worried about how well they will do at the task, the defensive or self-protective thing to do is to say, beforehand, that performance is due to these external reasons. The results showed that a subtle difference in how people were treated (that is, whether they completed sentences that made them think about self-affirmation intrinsically or extrinsically) had a big effect on both their defensiveness and task performance. Those who completed the sentences referencing intrinsic self-affirmation were less likely to attribute their upcoming task performance to external factors; furthermore, they also performed a lot better on the task relative to those who completed sentences that made them think about self-affirmation extrinsically.[36]

When a potentially self-affirming experience is done in a way that smacks of being a means to an end, it loses something. Remember Stuart Smalley, the character from *Saturday Night Live* played by Al Franken? He used to do a sketch called "Daily Affirmation," in which he would look in the mirror and mutter out loud, "I'm good enough, I'm smart enough, and doggone it, people like me." Part of what made the routine so funny is that Stuart Smalley was so obviously doing the "affirmation" to feel better about himself that it was hard to imagine how it could be successful; it wasn't very natural, authentic, or intrinsic. In fact, research suggests that when people contemplate how the activity is a means toward the end of feeling better about oneself, rather than engaging with the activity as an end in its own right, they do not experience nearly as much self-affirmation. In one study, David Sherman, Geoff Cohen, and their colleagues looked at how open people were to information that contradicted their views. More specifically, people who strongly identified themselves as fans of the San Francisco Giants baseball team read an editorial that was very critical of its then star player, Barry Bonds. The editorial argued that because Bonds was a likely user of performance-enhancing drugs his accomplishments as a baseball player should not be celebrated. Prior to reading the editorial participants were randomly assigned to one of three groups. One group took part in the self-affirming activity of rank ordering several personal values and then writing about why their most highly rated value was important to them and a specific situation in which the value proved to be important. A second group wrote about why one of their lowest-rated values might be important to someone else, along with an accompanying example.

The third group did the same thing as the first group. However, to highlight the "means to an end" aspect of the self-affirmation exercise, participants in this group had been told beforehand that "the writing activity is designed to make you feel better about yourself and to increase your self-esteem." The results showed that those who did the self-affirmation exercise were less defensive or more open to the editorial relative to those who did not do the self-affirmation exercise. What about the group that did the self-affirmation exercise that was designed to make them feel better about themselves? They were more open to the editorial than the group that did not self-affirm but were less open to it relative to the first group, which did the standard self-affirmation exercise.[37] Somewhat ironically, then, deliberately doing something to boost self-esteem can detract from how much it will actually do that.

DOS AND DON'TS

A corollary of the notion that the process matters is that "the devil is in the detail." Translating the promise of self-affirmation theory into practice requires attending to how things are done, in particular, for self-affirmation to be done in a way that fosters the experience of intrinsic rather than extrinsic motivation. This is true regardless of whether the self-affirming experience is employee or employer initiated and whether it takes place in the workplace or elsewhere. An important "Do" for employees if they want the self-affirmation process to be intrinsic is to clarify their self-aspects that are particularly important. It requires answering such questions as "What defines me? What is really important to my sense of who I am and what I stand for?" Admittedly, answering these questions is a lifelong journey. One way to think about these questions is this: How would I want people to answer them at my funeral? The clearer we can be about what is important to us, the more the stage is set for the self-affirmation process to be intrinsic. If we are clear about who we are and what motivates us, the more likely we are to go down paths that are true to us. Consequently, the more likely it will be for us to experience both pillars of intrinsic motivation: (1) to see ourselves rather than external forces as the initiators of what we do, and (2) to experience what we are doing as rewarding in its own right rather than as a means toward experiencing some extrinsic reward.

An important "Don't," therefore, is to not jump on the bandwagon. Don't do something that may at first appear self-affirming simply because others are doing it or because doing it may lead to some other type of reward. A case in point is taking part in a corporate-sponsored volunteer program. Previously I described a study showing that employees who did more corporate volunteerism felt more self-affirmed, which in turn led them to be more committed to their organizations. However, it's not simply *how much* corporate volunteerism employees do that influences how self-affirmed they feel. What also matters are *their motivations* for volunteering in the first place. Gil Clary and Mark Snyder and their colleagues found that people volunteer for many different reasons. In some instances the act of volunteering serves as its own source of reward. Employees who volunteer for such "value-expressive" reasons strongly agree with statements like "I feel that it is important to help others in need" and "I can do something for a cause that is important to me." Other employees volunteer as a means to an end. For example, they strongly agree with statements such as "Volunteering can help me to advance in the workplace" and "Volunteering can help me get my foot in the door at a place where I'd like to work."[38]

My study with Deanna Senior and Will Welch showed that employees experienced greater self-affirmation when they volunteered for more intrinsic or value-expressive reasons. We also found that volunteering for more extrinsic reasons such as wanting to get ahead in their careers did not elicit self-affirmation. Of course, it is appropriate for people to want to get ahead in their careers. And it may even be reasonable for people to volunteer as a way to help their careers. However, when people volunteer *in order to* help their careers they are less likely to experience the volunteerism as self-affirming. More generally, when we do something that has the *potential* to be self-affirming, it is how we go about it, which includes our reasons for doing it, that will determine just how self-affirmed we *actually* feel.[39]

The same can be said when the event, activity, or experience is employer rather than employee initiated. When organizations provide opportunities for their employees to feel self-affirmed, an important "Do" is to show that they are genuinely committed to whatever it was that allowed their employees to feel self-affirmed. For example, one way for employers to demonstrate genuine commitment to their volunteer programs is by indicating how such programs are but one example of a pattern of socially responsible behavior. Whereas the intended beneficiary of many corporate volunteer programs is the broader community in which the organization is located, other potential beneficiaries of socially responsible organizations include the natural environment and consumers. What employers can and should do is help their employees "connect the dots" between the various activities in their corporate social responsibility portfolio. Just as my colleagues and I found that employees felt more self-affirmed when they saw their employers as more committed to their corporate volunteer program, my hunch is that employees are likely to feel self-affirmed whenever they see their employers as committed to their portfolio of socially responsible activities. For employees, it just *feels right* to be a member of an organization whose heart is in the right place, regardless of the activity that indicates that its heart is in the right place.

Another important "Don't" for employers is to not overly emphasize the expected psychological benefits of employees taking part in potentially self-affirming activities. For example, research has shown that when people self-affirm they experience less stress, even physiologically.

David Sherman and his colleagues found that undergraduates who wrote about personally important values in the two weeks prior to taking an exam in the class that they previously defined as the "most stressful" showed lower levels of bodily indicators of strain (as reflected in catecholamine excretions in their urine), relative to a control group of students who did not write about personally important values.[40] Even though self-affirmation lowers stress, I would not recommend advertising a self-affirming activity as a "stress reducer" or a "self-esteem booster." If the self-affirming activity is framed in terms of its expected positive consequences it may lose its effectiveness, as found in the study of San Francisco Giants baseball fans who did not benefit as much when they were told before taking part in a self-affirming exercise that its purpose was to bolster their self-esteem. On the one hand, it is advisable to "connect the dots" in the sense of getting employees to see the relationship between various employer-initiated sources of self-affirmation. On the other hand, it is less advisable to "connect the dots" when doing so consists of getting employees to see the relationship between employer-initiated self-affirmation activities and the psychological benefits expected to result from taking part in those activities.

Chapter Summary

In this chapter we considered a different way to determine whether a decision-making process was handled well. Rather than focusing on attributes of the process such as its fairness or adherence to various change management prescriptions, I suggested that we need to look at the psychology of those on the receiving end. A high-quality process is one that causes people to feel self-affirmed. From the time that employees enter the organization to the time that they leave, and at many points in between, the way that decisions are handled affects their sense of esteem or identity or control. The more they feel self-affirmed by the process, the higher their productivity and morale. And in the middle school classroom and other educational settings, the academic achievement of those prone to experience self-threats is heightened when they experience self-affirmation. What is particularly encouraging is that the positive effects of self-affirmation in the workplace and in educational settings can last for months and even years, without requiring much in the way of money, time, or human energy.

Given the highly favorable cost-benefit relationship of self-affirmation, it is important to consider how self-affirmation can be made to happen. Self-affirmation may be initiated by employees or by employers, and it may transpire in the workplace or outside of it. Not only can it have positive effects in the situation in which it is experienced, but it can also spill over to have positive influences in other important areas of people's lives. For example, the self-affirmation experience that minority middle school students had in their history class led to improved performance not only in that class but in all of their courses, and for years to come. Experimental research has shown that affirming important personal values enables people to deal with self-threats that have nothing to do with their personal values. In the workplace, meaningful self-affirmation experienced in one venue can carry over to have positive effects in other work domains. Indeed, it is even possible for self-affirmation experienced outside of work to cycle back to favorably affect employees' productivity and morale.

Given the highly favorable cost-benefit relationship, the decision to manage in ways that allow people to feel self-affirmed couldn't be simpler. However, as the overarching message of this book reminds us, people are affected very much by *how* things are done, not merely by what is done. Managing for self-affirmation is no different. David Sherman, one of the world's most influential self-affirmation researchers, puts it well: "Although affirmation interventions can have large-scale effectiveness, we propose that they should adhere to small-scale subtlety."[41] Sherman is suggesting that translating self-affirmation theory into actual practice requires careful attention to the "how." To facilitate such translation, I have tried to specify the features needed for a self-affirmation experience to attain small-scale subtlety. At its core, employers or employees need to be intrinsically motivated in two ways. First, the activity has to come from within. For example, employers must provide opportunities for corporate volunteerism, or treat its people with high process fairness, because they believe it is the right thing to do and not merely to be in compliance with some external mandate. Second, when engaged in the activity, people need to perceive it as rewarding in its own right and not as a means toward some other end. It is for this reason, for example, that potentially self-affirming activities should not be labeled on the basis of the positive effects that they may be expected to produce, such as "stress-buster" or "self-esteem-pick-me-up." Stuart Smalley, our "Daily Affirmation" character from *Saturday Night Live*, had it all wrong.

5 → For Ethicality, the Process Also Matters

As you have seen by now good things happen when managers handle the process well, and bad things happen when they don't. Regardless of whether the process refers to attributes such as fairness or to the experience of those on the receiving end, employees' productivity and morale very much depend on how well things are handled. If that isn't enough to convince you of the importance of a high-quality process, let's discuss one more important consideration: ethicality. The way events and decisions are handled also affects employees' tendencies to do the right thing ethically. I have been suggesting throughout that a high-quality process engages and equips people to do their jobs. Being engaged and equipped does not ensure, however, that people will behave ethically when doing their jobs. For example, during their company's heyday Enron employees may have been engaged and equipped, but the behavior of at least some of them was anything but ethical.

In rousing their troops, managers often convey outcome-oriented messages such as "I don't care how you get there, just get there" or "The ends justify the means."

Of course, it is great to be a results-oriented manager; you won't be in business very long otherwise. One potential downside of the ends-justify-the-means message, however, is that employees may lose track of their moral compass. They may infer that it is okay to lie, cheat, and steal *as long as* doing so contributes positively to the bottom line. This is precisely what happened at the well-known professional services firm that Barbara Toffler describes in *Final Accounting: Ambition, Greed, and the Fall of Arthur Andersen.*[1] (Arthur Andersen, by the way, was Enron's auditor.)

It wasn't always that way at Arthur Andersen, a firm known in the early years for its unwavering commitment to ethics. One of the company's legendary narratives entails a young Arthur Andersen (age twenty-eight) telling a senior executive at a company he was auditing that he would not approve the company's books if doing so required him to lie. Although it cost him the account, Andersen told the executive, "There's not enough money in the city of Chicago to induce me to change that report." In an article written about a decade ago, Linda Treviño and Michael Brown provide a compelling synopsis of how the ethics culture at Arthur Andersen fell from its initially lofty perch to one that ultimately led to the company's demise. Citing Toffler, Treviño and Brown write that much of the decline resulted from "the fact that the firm's profits increasingly came from management consulting rather than auditing. The leadership's earlier commitment to ethics came to be drowned out by the firm's increasing laser-like focus on revenues.... Serving the client began to be defined as keeping the client happy and getting return business. And tradition [which had meant doing business in ethically correct ways] became translated into unquestioning obedience to the partner, *no matter what one was asked to do*. For example, managers and partners were expected to pad their prices. Reasonable estimates for consulting work were simply doubled . . . as consultants were told to back into the numbers"[2] (emphasis added).

If the process affects ethicality, it is worth examining which elements of the process influence ethicality. In fact, some of the process dimensions that affect employees' productivity and morale also affect how ethically they behave. For instance, chapter 2 considered the importance of process fairness, while chapter 4 discussed processes in the workplace that influence the way that employees think about themselves, with respect to esteem, identity, and control. As we will soon see, these and other aspects of process also influence employees' ethicality.

In extreme instances, the unethical behavior elicited by a poorly handled process can be severe. Whereas some employees sue for wrongful termination when they believe the process by which they were laid off was not handled well, a smaller minority take the law into their own hands by behaving violently, even attempting to murder their former bosses or coworkers. More typically and fortunately so, most unethical behaviors are not as dramatic. For example, I know of an employee working in a billing department who was unhappy about being laid off without any forewarning; he spent his last week on the job inserting notes into customers' bills telling them "they were idiots" for doing business with his organization. While most forms of unethical behavior are not as extreme as workplace violence, their cumulative consequences are quite significant nonetheless.

Remember Tom, the employee in the manufacturing plant whom we talked about at the beginning of chapter 2? Tom had no thoughts of leaving his firm until he was asked to endure a pay cut for several months. Research has shown that people like Tom base their decision on whether to remain with the company on, among other things, the process accompanying the pay cut. When the CEO of the company took the time to explain why the pay cuts were necessary and expressed regret about having to introduce them, it led to a much lower rate of voluntary turnover than when a less senior executive carried out the exact same pay cut in a more cursory way. More important for our present discussion, that same study also showed that process considerations affected employees' ethicality: they were much less likely to steal from their employer when the process accompanying the pay cut was handled better.[3]

In a larger-scale study of four different organizations and thousands of participants, Linda Treviño and Gary Weaver found that employees' perceptions of fairness were a strong predictor of how much they engaged in a wide range of unethical activities as well as in an important ethical activity. The unethical activities included unauthorized personal use of company resources, padding an expense account, and calling in sick to take a day off, while the ethical activity consisted of reporting any wrongdoings they had seen to their manager. Employees who believed that supervisors treated them with more dignity and respect were less prone to behave unethically and more likely to report ethical violations.[4]

Process factors not directly related to fairness also affect how ethically employees behave. Some organizations give employees feedback with a 360-degree performance appraisal process. When done well, a 360-degree feedback process may improve not only managers' effectiveness but also their ethicality, for two reasons. First, 360-degree feedback emphasizes *how* people lead and manage. Hence when an organization takes its 360-degree exercise seriously, for example, when managers know that their compensation will be affected by their 360-degree feedback, the message is unmistakable: the process matters. And when managers know that their employers care not only about results but also about how they got results, ethical breaches are less likely to occur.

Second, receiving feedback has the potential to draw people's attention to themselves, for example, how their behavior is less than what is expected of them. Receiving feedback from multiple sources at the same time, which is part and parcel of a 360-degree process, may be all the more self-focusing, especially when the different sources convey the same message. It's like looking into a mirror. When we look into a mirror, we don't focus on just one thing about ourselves. For instance, even though 360-degree feedback may initially focus attention on ways our behavior is less than what is expected, we may also begin to consider other things about ourselves, including our own standards for appropriate behavior. Since most people value being ethical, a likely effect of self-focused attention is to behave ethically. Indeed, one tried-and-true way to evaluate the ethicality of behavior is to subject it to the "mirror test." Looking back at previous behavior or looking forward to the future, we need to ask ourselves, "Will I be able to look at myself in the mirror and respect the person I see there?"

Yet another process dimension that affects ethicality is *when* a decision is made. For instance, the time of day at which employees make decisions can influence their likelihood of behaving ethically. Do you think employees are more likely to behave ethically earlier in the day or later in the day? We'll answer that question a bit later. For now, let's talk about how some of the process dimensions known to influence employees' productivity and morale also affect their tendency to behave ethically.

Process Fairness Influences Ethicality

Philosophers and psychologists have long noted how much ethicality and process fairness have in common. Some even have argued that a process cannot be fair if it violates standards of ethicality, just as it cannot be fair if decisions are made on the basis of inaccurate information or without the views of the relevant parties being represented.[5] Other research has shown that people's desire to affirm ethical values is one of the reasons why they prefer to be treated with high process fairness.[6]

To be sure, some explanations of why people prefer to be treated with high process fairness do not bear on ethics directly. Such explanations posit that being treated with high process fairness is a means toward other important ends. For instance, people may prefer high process fairness because they believe they will be more likely to receive their fair share of tangible outcomes over time.[7] Or they may prefer high process fairness to be reassured that they are held in high regard.[8] However, according to the deontological approach to ethics, high process fairness is not preferred because it is a means to an end; it is an end in its own right.

High process fairness, in short, is ethically correct. Consistent with the deontological approach, the importance people assign to their morality affects their reactions to how fairly they are treated. The more central people's moral identity is to how they define themselves, the more likely they are to react positively when they are treated with high rather than low process fairness.[9] In short, process fairness overlaps with ethics in several ways. How much people want fairness is an indicator of how much they want ethicality. Moreover, how much they behave fairly is an indicator of how much they have acted ethically.

Fairness also is socially contagious. In a variety of contexts, the process fairness with which people are treated affects how much they treat others with process fairness.[10] Given that their own process fairness behavior reflects their ethicality, it is therefore appropriate to say that the fairness with which employees are treated affects their own ethicality.

Paying It Back

In some instances, the fairness behavior of the person on the receiving end of more or less fair treatment is directed back toward the party who behaved more or less fairly in the first place. This was the case in the Treviño and Weaver study, which showed that employees behaved more ethically toward their employers when they saw their employers displaying higher process fairness toward them.

Another example of paying it back is the recent research by Daniel Skarlicki and his colleagues, which showed that the fairness with which *customers* treat employees affects how fairly employees treat the customers. In their study, the more that customers were disrespectful to telephone customer service employees, for example, by yelling at them or using condescending language (e.g., "You are an idiot"), the more employees showed disrespect in return, such as by hanging up on the customers, putting them on hold for a long period of time, or intentionally transferring them to the wrong department.[11] The next time that as a customer you find yourself on the verge of treating the provider disrespectfully, you may be well served (quite literally) to remember these findings.

Passing It Down

On other occasions, the person on the receiving end of process fairness is not simply directing fairness back to the original actor but is expressing it toward someone else. For example, midlevel managers are at once on the receiving end of process fairness from their bosses and on the dispensing end to their direct reports. Typically the level of process fairness midlevel managers receive from their bosses is what they pass along to their own subordinates; this is known as the "trickle-down effect."

Maureen Ambrose, Marshall Schminke, and David Mayer recently provided evidence of a process fairness trickle-down effect. Supervisors from numerous industries rated how fairly they had been treated by their bosses. When the subordinates of those supervisors rated the fairness climate in their teams, they rated it in ways similar to that of their own bosses, illustrating that supervisors passed down to their subordinates the process fairness with which they had been treated. Subordinates' perceptions of the fairness climate, in turn, also affected how ethically they behaved toward their coworkers and the organization. For instance, subordinates who judged the team climate as more fair were more likely to do ethically correct things, such as giving advance notice when they were unable to come to work. They also were less likely to behave unethically toward their coworkers and employers. For example, those who viewed the climate as more fair were less inclined to publicly embarrass their colleagues or take property from the workplace without permission.[12] Given the significant stakes associated with fairness/ethicality trickle-down effects, it is theoretically and practically important to consider why they occur. Like all behavior, fairness/ethicality trickle-down effects depend on people's motivation and ability. In particular, fairness/ethicality trickle-down effects are motivated by reciprocity and enabled by learning.

MOTIVATED BY RECIPROCITY

The norm of reciprocity is the expectation that people will treat others, for better or worse, in the ways that they are treated. It is beyond our scope to consider the many reasons why people are motivated to reciprocate. Sociologists such as Alvin Gouldner have suggested that the reciprocity norm lends stability to social systems, whereas evolutionary psychologists have argued that reciprocity has survival value for the species.[13] In any event, there is wide agreement that reciprocity is one of the most powerful norms governing social interaction. Thus the process fairness with which employees are treated motivates them to reciprocate. It is easy to see how this would happen in the case of "paying it back." For example, it is not surprising that the respect with which customers treat employees has an effect on how respectfully employees treat customers.

Interestingly enough, the motivation to reciprocate even applies when the person on the receiving end is not simply paying it back to the person on the giving end but is passing his behavior along to a different third party. David Wo and Maureen Ambrose suggested that supervisors treated fairly by their bosses feel obligated to treat their own employees fairly. Here is one reason why: supervisors see their bosses as agents of the organization, hence when their bosses exhibit fair treatment it is as though it is coming from the organization. One way supervisors can reciprocate to the organization is to treat their own subordinates fairly, because such treatment is likely to elicit organizationally supportive reactions from subordinates. The principle of reciprocity also applies when supervisors judge their boss to have treated them unfairly. Supervisors may try to *even the score* with their bosses by treating their own subordinates unfairly. Treating their own subordinates with low process fairness is likely to demotivate subordinates and thereby make them less likely to behave in organizationally supportive ways. This will serve to punish their bosses, whom they view as representatives of the organization.[14]

ENABLED BY LEARNING

Given that authority figures serve as models to the people who report to them, fairness/ethicality trickle-down effects also are the result of a learning process. Albert Bandura has suggested that most behavior is not learned from direct experience but from observing the actions of models. Supervisors learn the degree to which they should treat their employees with process fairness based on how they are treated by their bosses.[15] Particularly intriguing is the fact that even negative behaviors tend to be adopted by subordinates. In the workplace, the subordinates of more hostile and aggressive bosses are more likely to behave unethically themselves. Negative role models are a double-edged sword. On the one hand, they can serve as powerful reminders of how *not* to behave, motivating observers to go in a different direction. On the other hand, their behavior provides cues of how one *could* (note: not necessarily should) behave, thereby enabling observers to follow suit. For people with less life experience who have had few role models, these negative behaviors may become the default.

MORE THAN TRICKLING DOWN

The process fairness managers receive from their bosses is also likely to influence how fairly and ethically they treat those other than their subordinates, such as peers or customers. As Ambrose and colleagues showed, bosses' fairness behavior influences the climate for fairness in the team, which provides members with a blueprint for how fairly to behave toward coworkers in general, not simply their direct reports. Similarly, the Corporate Executive Board recently conducted a multiorganizational study of the factors that helped establish a culture of integrity. Out of the seven main drivers, such as clarity of expectations and openness of communication, the one that far and away had the biggest effect was organizational justice, which referred to how consistently and quickly the organization responded to unethical behavior. The more employees saw their employers responding to ethical breaches with organizational justice, the more it established a culture of integrity. As a result, employees were less likely to engage in misconduct themselves and even were more likely to report others who were engaging in misconduct. In short, process fairness does much more than trickle *down* to how managers treat their subordinates; it also "carries over" to influence how they behave toward other parties, such as their peers and customers, to name a few.[16]

Global Self-Integrity Influences Ethicality

In chapter 4 we discussed how employees' productivity and morale were positively affected by processes that enhance their global self-integrity, which refers to people seeing themselves as having identity, esteem, and control. Here we will discuss how workplace processes that affect employees' global self-integrity also influence their ethicality. Research suggests that people behave less ethically when they are treated in ways that make them less likely to see themselves as having identity, esteem, or control. In one study Francesca Gino and her colleagues measured participants' tendencies to lie about their performance when it was financially advantageous for them to do so. Lying was directly related to how much people felt disconnected from their true selves, as reflected in how much they agreed with statements such as "Right now, I feel really out of touch with the real me."

The way in which people were led to feel disconnected from their true selves was interesting in its own right. All participants in the study were asked to wear upscale sunglasses made by the fashion designer Chloe. Under the guise of examining people's reactions to wearing counterfeit products, the researchers told half of the participants that the sunglasses were knock-offs, whereas the others were told that the sunglasses were genuine. Even though everyone was wearing real designer sunglasses, those led to believe they were fake reported feeling more disconnected from their true selves, which in turn led them to lie more. As the researchers put it, "we suspect that feeling like a fraud makes people more likely to commit fraud."[17]

In another study in which people's self-esteem rather than their sense of identity was the main self-perception, participants were given feedback about their responses to a personality inventory. Half of them were given negative feedback (e.g., "you have a rather unstable personality, an inability to remain calm and level-headed in circumstances involving tension and pressure, and are very selfish"), whereas the other half were told positive things about themselves; presumably, those given negative feedback felt worse about themselves than those given positive feedback. When given an opportunity to cheat in a subsequent part of the study, the people led to see themselves negatively did so to a much greater degree.[18]

Just as self-perceptions of identity and esteem have been shown to influence ethicality, so too do people's beliefs about their control. Many of us believe deeply in the concept of free will, the idea that behavior comes from our own volition. And yet even that fundamental belief can be situationally altered and as a result can influence our tendency to cheat. In one study Kathleen Vohs and Jonathan Schooler asked people to ponder statements that emphasized free will or its opposite, determinism. For example, one of the free will statements was "I am able to override the genetic and environmental factors that sometimes influence my behavior," whereas one of the determinism statements was "A belief in free will contradicts the known fact that the universe is governed by lawful principles of science." Both groups then worked on a task, after which they rated their free will (i.e., how much they agreed with statements such as "People have complete control over life's decisions"). They also indicated how well they had performed at the task; by falsely inflating reports of their performance they could earn more money. People given the determinism statements reported feeling less free will and were more likely to lie about their performance, relative to their counterparts who thought about the free will statements.[19] Based on their findings, the authors speculated that one reason for the rampant increase in student cheating from the 1960s to the 1990s was a corresponding rise during that period in the number of people who believed that they lacked control over the outcomes of their behavior. Complementing the laboratory findings on how free will beliefs influence ethicality, a field study of employees in the financial services industry in South Africa by E. Boshoff and Ebben van Zyl showed that those who saw themselves as not having autonomy over their behavior or who saw their behavior as having little influence over their outcomes were more likely to report behaving unethically.[20]

Why might processes that influence people's sense of identity, esteem, and control influence their ethicality? The answers may be somewhat different for each. For instance, when people's attention is directed away from their identity or who they are, they have less access to and thus are less affected by the personal standards guiding their behavior. Most people have a strong sense of what is right and what is wrong, and for some being ethical even may be a fundamental part of how they define themselves. (At the beginning of the next section I will describe a measure you may want to complete that assesses how much morality is important to your sense of identity.)

How much people's attention is self-directed affects their reliance on personal standards for behavior, including those pertaining to ethicality. Interestingly enough, even subtle environmental factors may influence how much people's attention is self-directed and thereby affects their ethicality. In one study undergraduate students were asked to write down their SAT scores on a piece of paper. Half of them did so in front of a mirror that just happened to be lying around for use in an "unrelated" study whereas the other half wrote down their scores while the mirror was not visible. Those who did the exercise in front of a mirror were significantly more likely to answer honestly than those in the no mirror group, particularly if their scores were relatively low.[21]

Another study examined in a different way how making people focus on themselves influences their ethicality. After filling out documents such as tax forms people typically are asked to sign their name, indicating that they *have* completed the forms accurately. Lisa Shu and her colleagues recently evaluated whether having people sign their names at the outset—indicating that they *will* answer accurately—would lead to less misrepresentation. One experiment was analogous to signing tax forms, in which some participants signed their name at the beginning and others did so at the end. Those who signed their names at the beginning cheated less than those who signed at the end. Furthermore, the authors cleverly examined whether this result was due to the possibility that signing early made ethicality a more salient consideration. Participants were given a list of incomplete words that they had to complete. Some of the words could be completed in ways related to ethicality or in a more neutral fashion. For example, "_ _ RAL" could be completed as "moral" or "viral," whereas "_ I _ _ U _" could be completed as "virtue" or "tissue." Early signers "saw" more ethics-related words than did late signers, which in turn was associated with the fact that early signers cheated less on their taxes.[22]

Why would threats to people's sense of self-esteem lead them to behave less ethically? When people evaluate themselves negatively they may behave immorally to maintain a sense of self-consistency or identity. In the language of self-affirmation theory, people who are down on themselves may behave negatively/immorally to maintain a sense of self that is "coherent, unitary, and stable." Self-verification theory similarly suggests that people wish to see themselves consistently. What would happen if people who viewed themselves negatively were to receive positive feedback about themselves? On the one hand, if all they cared about was to feel good about themselves they might be expected to react favorably, and this would be especially true for people with low self-esteem who are in more need of positive feedback. On the other hand, research by Bill Swann and his colleagues has shown that people with low self-esteem often reject positive feedback about themselves, especially when their negative self-opinions are firmly held or when they expect to have an ongoing relationship with the evaluator.[23]

A somewhat different mechanism may be needed to explain why people's sense of control is positively related to their ethicality. An important consequence of seeing oneself as in control is to perceive greater personal responsibility for one's outcomes. Consequently, good outcomes for which people feel personally responsible cause them to feel really good about themselves, whereas bad outcomes for which they feel personally responsible lead them to feel really bad about themselves. Therefore, how much people feel bad about themselves in response to negative experiences such as behaving unethically depends on how much they see themselves as personally responsible. Those who see themselves as having control are likely to see themselves as more personally responsible. Put another way, those who see themselves as having more control have more (self-esteem) to lose by behaving unethically. As a result, those who see themselves as having greater control may anticipate that they will feel particularly bad about themselves if they behave unethically, making them less likely to engage in misconduct. The knowledge that they will have only themselves to blame for behaving un-ethically may make them less likely to do it. Furthermore, knowing that they can take credit for behaving ethically may make them more likely to do the right thing.

*Assessing the Importance of Morality
to Your Own Sense of Identity*

When a situation focuses people's attention on them-selves it makes their personal standards of morality sa-lient, which leads them to behave ethically. The salience of moral standards doesn't simply vary by situation; it also varies by people. Whereas morality is important to the identity of most people, there is variability along this di-mension, which is known as moral identity. Karl Aquino developed a valid measure of moral identity, which has been shown to predict the honesty and ethicality with which people behave. For example, those scoring high in moral identity were more likely to donate to a food drive, to make charitable contributions to a group outside their inner circle, and to play fairly in a sporting event. Not only does moral identity influence people's ethicality, it also in-fluences how much they are affected by the fairness with which others treat them. For instance, employees' ten-dency to reciprocate to customers the respect with which customers treated them was stronger among employees higher in moral identity.[24] (If you would like to assess your own moral identity, see appendix G.)

Self-Control Influences Ethicality

There is another way in which people's selves are related to their ethicality. To this point we have considered how people's *reflections about* their identity, esteem, and control affect their tendency to behave ethically. Ethicality is positively related to how much people (1) feel connected to their true selves (unless, perhaps, they see themselves as evil), (2) evaluate themselves favorably, and (3) see themselves as having control over their behavior and its ensuing outcomes. However, there is another important way that we need to talk about the self and its effect on ethicality. The self is not only the *object* of what people attend to; it also is the *subject* that drives behavior. More than a hundred years ago William James called the former the "me-self" and the latter the "I-self."[25]

Up until this point in the book we have been talking only about the "me-self." However, the "I-self" also may affect people's ethicality. The "I-self" exercises an executive function that leads people to think, feel, and do certain things and not others. In other words, the "I-self" enables us to exert self-control. As we will see, ethicality does not depend merely on how much people *see* themselves as having control; it also depends on how much they are *forced to engage* in self-control. Engaging in self-control is all about overriding our impulse to think, feel, and do something else.[26] For example, people trying to lose weight must resist the temptation to eat the delicious dessert in front of them. An organization trying to bring about an enduring competitive advantage needs to resist the temptation to go instead for a quick fix.

Being successful often requires people and organizations to exert self-control. Behaving ethically also often requires self-control, for instance, resisting the temptation to behave unethically. Ironically, however, being forced to exert self-control can come at a price. As Martin Hagger and his colleagues recently suggested, "Engaging in acts of self-control draws from a limited 'reservoir' of self-control which, when depleted, results in reduced capacity for further self-regulation. . . . Self-control is viewed as analogous to a muscle. Just as a muscle requires strength and energy to exert force over a period of time, acts that have high self-control demands also require strength and energy to perform. Similarly, as muscles become fatigued after a period of sustained exertion and have reduced capacity to exert further force, self-control can also become depleted when demands are made of self-control resources over a period of time. Baumeister and colleagues termed the state of diminished self-control 'strength' [as] ego depletion."[27]

What does exerting self-control have to do with people's tendencies to behave ethically? Even though behaving ethically may require self-control, the very act of exercising self-control—even in ways unrelated to ethicality—may bring about ego depletion and thereby reduce people's ethicality, at least for a while. Consider the following examples.

A. Kristin and Logan, a married couple, are midlevel managers in the same media company who have decided not to have children. In recent years they have grown increasingly angry about the company's attempt to address employees' needs for work-life balance. The problem is that whereas the company has done a lot for employees with children (e.g., flextime, telecommuting, and on-site childcare), it has done nothing for childless employees. Kristin is a marathon runner who would like to have greater flexibility for a few months to train for an upcoming race. Logan's aging parents are requiring more attention; he, too, would greatly value some of the flexible arrangements offered to employees with children. They also have been told that it is inappropriate or "unprofessional" to express anger about what they perceive to be unequal treatment of employees without children. Unfortunately, anger is exactly what both of them are feeling. Initially, they worked hard to bring about change in company policy so that childless employees would be given benefits commensurate with those given to employees with children. Over time, however, they find themselves increasingly demotivated to take on this challenge.

B. Kara is a longtime employee in a financial services organization that is undergoing massive changes brought on by new regulatory requirements as well as by new technology. The changes are so fundamental that they have forced Kara to discard her former ways of doing her job, which by this point had become practically habitual, and to learn entirely new ways of doing things.

C. Tim is in sales in a pharmaceutical organization whose boss's leadership style can best be described as micromanaging. Micromanagers require strict adherence to what they are trying to accomplish and to their methods of getting there. For example, even though Tim has his own good ideas on how best to connect with customers, his micromanaging boss will not let him put them into practice. As a salesperson himself years earlier, Tim's boss had developed successful ways to connect with customers. However, his methods were established in a different era, and while not irrelevant in today's environment, they are not the *only* path to success. In fact, Tim's own methods are equally if not more effective than his boss's.

In all of these examples employees must exert self-control in order to override their own natural tendencies. Kristin and Logan have to exert self-control over their emotions. They have been told that it is not okay for them to express the negative emotions that they are feeling. The organizational sociologist Arlie Hochschild has written eloquently about the concept of emotional labor, which requires employees to display emotions other than those they are experiencing, in the service of influencing other people's emotions. Sometimes emotional labor is caused by organizational norms. In many organizations, expressions of emotion in general and anger in particular are particularly frowned upon. Emotional labor also may be built into the job itself. For certain professionals, such as nurses, physicians, therapists, protective service workers, and health service workers, emotional labor pretty much goes with the turf.[28]

Kara has to exert self-control not so much over her emotions but over her behavior. She had become accustomed to doing things a certain way, but she now has to do things differently. In her case, it isn't so much organizational norms or the occupation but rather changes in the external environment that require her to exert self-control over her behavior.

Tim also has to exert self-control over his behavior, but in this case the root cause is different from what it was in the previous examples. In this case it's the process. How his boss manages requires Tim to exert self-control. Left to his own devices, Tim would rely upon his own ways of connecting with his customers. Unfortunately, his micro-managing boss, who insists on things being done his way, has forced Tim to act in a way that is not natural for him.

Regardless of the source (organizational norms, the oc-cupation, changes in the environment, the process), vari-ous features of the workplace require employees to exert self-control. Their resultant state of ego depletion leaves them with fewer resources in their self-control tanks, which can lead to all sorts of counterproductive behavior, such as reduced ethicality. Indeed, the situations in which Kristin and Logan, Kara, and Tim find themselves may af-fect how ethically they behave.

The latter idea fits with a broader view that when people behave unethically it may not be because they are bereft of moral fiber. Rather, good people can do bad things be-cause of the situation. Another desirable feature of the ego depletion explanation is that it locates the tendency to be-have unethically as part of a bigger story, which goes as follows: whenever people have to exert a lot of self-control their ego-depleted state may render them less effective at subsequent activities that also require self-control, at least for a while.

And, once again, the process matters. In chapter 4 (and earlier in this chapter) we considered how the process ac-companying certain events and decisions influenced the "me-self" (self-perceptions of esteem, identity, and con-trol), which in turn influenced employees' productivity, morale, and ethicality. Here I am making a related point: the process accompanying certain events and decisions also influences the "I-self," that is, how much employees are required to exert self-control. The more the process requires self-control to be exerted, the more likely employees are to be ego depleted, which will adversely affect their productivity, morale, and ethicality. For example, in situations like the one that Kristin and Logan were facing, namely, employees trying to bring about change, organizations vary in terms of how much latitude they give employees to express their emotions. Kristin and Logan were told that expressing anger was not acceptable, which somewhat ironically may have made them less motivated to bring about change in the very policy that was causing them to feel angry in the first place.

That last sentence is not merely idle speculation. Katy DeCelles and Scott Sonenshein recently found that angrier employees were less motivated to bring about change in their organizations. Outside the organization, however, angrier people have been shown to be more motivated to bring about change. Why the differing effects of anger on insiders and outsiders? Both groups feel angry, but insiders are more likely to receive the message that expressing anger is unacceptable. Hence, relative to outsiders, insiders have to exert greater self-control. Feeling more ego depleted, insiders may be less able to take on activities requiring further self-control, such as the considerable effort needed to be an agent of change.[29]

Suppose, however, that employees like Kristin and Logan were treated differently by their employers. What if they were told that healthy expressions of emotion about organizational policies are tolerated or, even better, welcomed? My hunch is that they would be less likely to use up self-control resources trying to suppress what they are feeling. Consequently, they would probably be more motivated to bring about constructive change and more generally, I would surmise, to behave more ethically.

Research has shown how exercising self-control in one activity makes people less likely to do so in a subsequent one, even when both are unrelated to ethicality. In the initial studies, Roy Baumeister and his colleagues required some participants to exert self-control by suppressing their feelings while watching an emotionally arousing video whereas others were allowed to openly express their feelings. Both groups were then asked to grip a handle as tightly as possible for as long as they could. Even though participants in both groups began the study feeling the same amount of physical strength, those who subsequently exerted self-control gripped the handle for a much shorter period of time than those who did not. In another study by Baumeister and his colleagues, participants in the self-control group ate radishes and resisted eating chocolates whereas those in another group were allowed to eat the chocolates and "resisted" eating the radishes. The results showed that members of the group that exerted self-control were subsequently much less motivated to work on a demanding cognitive task requiring self-control than were those from the other group.[30]

At a surface level, the second activity subsequent to the initial one requiring self-control is unrelated to ethicality. However, at a deeper psychological level the second activity overlaps greatly with behaving ethically, particularly when behaving ethically requires people to exert self-control, as it often does. Therefore, if exerting self-control subsequently makes people less likely to do so, it stands to reason that exerting self-control may reduce people's tendency to behave ethically.

Francesca Gino and her colleagues recently found this to be the case. In one study participants watched a video of a woman being interviewed, in which common words would periodically pop up at the bottom of the screen. Participants forced to exercise self-control were told to do something that would not come naturally: "Do not read or look at any of the words that may appear on the screen. If you find yourself looking at the words, immediately re-orient your attention toward the woman's face." In contrast, those in the group not required to exert self-control were told nothing about the words that appeared at the bottom of the screen. All participants then worked on a task in which they were told that they would be paid in proportion to how well they had performed. Gino and her colleagues measured how much participants lied by reporting that they had done better than they actually had. Those who had done the ego-depleting version of the exercise first were more likely to lie than were their counterparts who had not done the ego-depleting version of the task.

In a second study the ego-depleting task consisted of having participants do something else that does not come naturally: writing an essay in which they had to avoid using common letters (A and N). In contrast, those in the control condition were asked to write the same essay avoiding the use of uncommon letters (X and Z). Participants subsequently did another task, in which they had an opportunity to lie about their performance and thereby earn more money. Once again, those who did the ego-depleting essay were more likely to lie.[31]

At the outset of this chapter I mentioned that *when* decisions are made is an important element of the process. "When" can refer to a month or season. For example, although layoffs are typically experienced as bad news, the process may be experienced as more insensitive if the layoffs are carried out shortly before Christmas than if they are introduced after the first few months of the next year. "When" also can refer to the time of day. If people are called upon to make certain decisions that tempt them to behave unethically, the time of day in which such decisions are made may influence their behavior. Maryam Kouchaki and Isaac Smith have suggested that "the mere experience of everyday living can reduce one's self-control as the day progresses. . . . Gradual fatigue associated with unremarkable daily activities (e.g., making decisions, and regulating behavior)" uses up people's self-regulatory resources and therefore makes them more likely to behave unethically.

Kouchaki and Smith tested this idea in a very straightforward way. Two groups of people took part in a study in which they could earn money by lying. The only difference between the two groups was the time of day in which the study was conducted. Half of the participants were randomly assigned to take part in the morning and the other half did so in the afternoon. The results showed that the afternoon group was significantly more likely to lie than was the morning group, a result the authors called the "morning morality effect." Moreover, the morning morality effect occurred because those who did the study in the afternoon had lower moral awareness than did their counterparts in the morning. For example, in a word completion task the afternoon group was more likely to see the word "_ _ RAL" as "VIRAL" whereas the morning group was more likely to see it as "MORAL."[32]

If managers want their employees to be at their best when making decisions, they should pay attention to the nuances that may influence their ethicality. A literal application of the morning morality effect is that whenever possible, decisions with an ethical dimension should be made in the morning rather than in the afternoon. Furthermore, knowing the reason for the morning morality effect leads to other practical insights. For instance, if the morning morality effect is a result of people having fewer self-regulatory resources later in the day than earlier, then other factors that influence people's self-regulatory resources also should be taken into account as managers consider when it would be best to make ethically laden decisions. When people have had experiences that required them to exert self-control they may be predisposed to behave less ethically. For instance, just after employees have had an encounter with their micromanaging boss or shortly after they have completed a rigorous training program in which they had to discard old work habits and adopt new ones would not be ideal times to have them make an ethically laden decision, no matter what the time of day.

Kouchaki and Smith found that exercising self-control reduced ethicality because it made people less morally aware. If this is true, then having a mechanism in place to heighten moral awareness could be a great antidote. To offset groupthink (in which all members of a group are looking at a complex problem too similarly), group dynamics scholars such as Irving Janis have suggested that the group should assign someone to play the role of "devil's advocate." This person's responsibility is to point out problems associated with the group's predominant way of thinking, in the hopes of stimulating discussion about other ways to deal with the problem.[33] Since engaging in self-control has the potential to make people less morally aware, what might be needed is an "angel's advocate," someone who is responsible for reminding people of the moral dimension of the decision at hand.

Other research has shown that the time of day may affect decisions, including but not limited to those with an ethical dimension. For example, relative to mornings, evenings are associated with a greater incidence of numerous breakdowns in behavior, such as impulsive crimes, violent attacks, addiction relapses, and inebriation. Furthermore, in a recent study appropriately titled "Extraneous Factors in Judicial Decisions," Shai Danziger and his colleagues showed that judges' parole decisions were affected by when they were heard. A typical day for judges consists of three decision periods: (1) the start of the day until midmorning snack, (2) post-midmorning snack until lunch, and (3) post-lunch until the end of the day. Prisoners applying for parole had a much greater likelihood of receiving a favorable ruling if their case was heard earlier rather than later in the order of cases within a given decision period.[34] Although multiple factors undoubtedly explain why people demonstrate behavioral breakdowns later in the day, and why judges are likely to be less lenient later rather than earlier in the decision period, in both instances one likely candidate is ego depletion borne of exerting self-control.

In short, when people have to exert self-control over behavior unrelated to ethicality, they are more likely, at least for a while, to behave unethically. Other studies have shown that having to exercise self-control also makes people less likely to behave in ethically correct ways such as helping others in need. Hanyi Xu and colleagues had one group of participants do the ego-depleting task of suppressing their feelings while watching an emotionally arousing movie whereas the other group watched the same movie with no such restriction. Then all of the participants were given several opportunities to help others (e.g., by donating to an anti-AIDS charity). The group that previously had to suppress their emotions behaved less charitably.[35]

Here is another way to think about the relationship between ego depletion and ethicality in the workplace. When the impetus for ego depletion is ethics related, for instance, resisting the temptation to behave unethically, employees subsequently may be less likely to exercise self-control effectively, in ways either related or unrelated to ethicality. Previously we discussed how exercising self-control in ways unrelated to ethicality can spill over to reduce people's subsequent ethicality. In fact, the spillover effect also can go in the other direction: when exercising self-control takes the form of resisting the temptation to behave unethically, it reduces people's self-control in other ways. Thus when employees are tempted to lie, cheat, or steal, they may pay a price even when they successfully resist. At least for a while, they may do less well on subsequent tasks that require them to exert self-control.

In one study, participants who resisted the temptation to cheat (by not over-reporting how well they had performed) did poorly on a subsequent test unrelated to ethics but that requires self-control: the Stroop test, named after its founder, the psychologist John Ridley Stroop. Here is how it works. People are shown a list of words of colors (e.g., "RED") that appear in colors that do not match the word (e.g., the word "RED" is in green type).

Participants must name the color of the type as quickly as possible (e.g., to say "green" when the word "RED" is printed in green).[36]

In seeking to explain why good people do bad things, organizational scholars have articulated the many ways in which the workplace influences people to behave unethically or not to behave ethically. Sometimes it's a matter of bosses putting pressure on employees to not do the right thing. Sometimes it's the reward system that leads employees astray. It can also be the work culture; if you look around and see your fellow employees behaving unethically, it's a lot easier to do so yourself. Furthermore, organizations can not only motivate people to do the wrong thing but also enable them, for instance, by making it difficult for employees to know where to turn if and when they see ethical wrongdoings. In short, once we appreciate how various forces at play in the workplace motivate and enable employees to behave unethically, it becomes easier to understand why good people behave badly. In many cases, it's the place, not necessarily the people.[37]

But there is another potentially dangerous force lurking here as well. Even when moral employees are able to muster up the self-control to not behave unethically, they may become ego depleted, which has two downsides. First, it can adversely affect how well they do on subsequent tasks requiring self-control unrelated to ethicality, as the study using the Stroop test showed. Second, it can lower people's subsequent ethicality, particularly when the subsequent activity requires people to exert self-control, for example, resisting the temptation to behave unethically.

In fact, related research on "moral self-licensing" has shown that behaving ethically may subsequently make people more likely to behave unethically: "moral self-licensing occurs because good deeds make people feel secure in their moral self-regard. For example, when people are confident that their past behavior demonstrates compassion, generosity, or a lack of prejudice, they are more likely to act in morally dubious ways without fear of feeling heartless, selfish, or bigoted." According to this view, prior ethicality "frees" people up to behave less ethically going forward because their earlier ethicality demonstrated that they are fine, upstanding citizens.[38]

The ego-depletion effect also reflects the tendency for ethical behavior to give rise to less ethical behavior but for a different reason than the one underlying moral self-licensing. In moral self-licensing, the self is the object. Having already proven themselves to be moral, people subsequently may behave less ethically without having to worry about the potential negative implications for how they think about themselves. In chapter 4 we discussed how engaging in self-affirmation enables people to tolerate and even accept information that might otherwise be experienced as self-threatening. In like fashion, behaving ethically affirms people's sense of their own morality, thereby making them more immune to the self-threat they might experience if they were to behave unethically at a later point in time.

In ego depletion, the self is the subject. Prior acts of ethicality may have required people to exert self-control, thereby leaving them with fewer self-control resources needed to behave ethically in subsequent situations. The net result in the case of both moral licensing and ego depletion is the same: their prior acts of ethicality make employees less likely to behave ethically. However, it is important to be clear about the difference in the underlying mechanism, not only for theoretical reasons but also for practical ones. After all, if one wanted to interrupt the tendency for acting ethically to reduce subsequent ethicality it is necessary to understand why it is happening in the first place. For example, if the tendency was based on the mechanism underlying moral self-licensing, then one intervention might take the form of getting people to consider that ethicality is not a one-shot deal but an identity to be affirmed on a regular basis. Alternatively, if the tendency was the result of the mechanism underlying ego depletion, then an intervention might take the form of reducing the extent to which the initial activity required self-control to be exerted. The intervention to counter the effect of ego depletion on ethicality also could be based on the ideas presented in the next section.

Is It Inevitable for Ego Depletion to Reduce Ethicality?

Thus far our discussion of the relationships between organizational life, self-control, and ethicality has been decidedly pessimistic. I have been suggesting that the workplace exposes employees to conditions that require them to exert self-control, which makes them ego depleted and, as a result, more likely to behave unethically. The stark reality of organizational life is that it forces people to do things that require them to exert self-control, such as learning a new technology, dealing with insulting customers, and resisting the temptation to engage in short-term fixes.

Fortunately, in considering the relationships between organizational life, self-control, and ethicality, we have reason to be optimistic as well. Exerting self-control does not always lead to ego depletion. It can, but it doesn't have to. Whenever exerting self-control makes people less ego depleted, it stands to reason that they will be less likely to behave unethically. In fact, a slew of recent studies have identified conditions that make people less likely to become ego depleted even after exercising self-control. Indeed, I will discuss two broad categories of conditions. One category refers to positivity. You have probably heard of the power of positive *thinking*. It turns out that the link between exercising self-control and ego depletion may be mitigated not only by positive thinking but also by positive *feeling* and by positive *doing*. The other category I will discuss pertains to additional sources of motivation that may be introduced as antidotes to the experience of ego depletion.

In none of the studies discussed in the text that follows did the researchers examine people's ethicality. However, the studies have implications for ethical behavior in the following sense: exercising self-control makes people ego depleted, which in turn decreases ethicality. If, as the following studies demonstrate, there are circumstances under which exercising self-control does not lead to ego depletion as much, then these are the very circumstances in which the exercise of self-control should not lead to a reduction in ethicality.

The Power of Positivity

The power of positive thinking is illustrated in a study by Joshua Clarkson and his colleagues, in which participants worked on a task requiring them to exert self-control. First, they were given a few pages from a statistics textbook and were asked to cross out every letter "e" that they saw. They were then given a second task in which they also had to cross out every letter "e" but this time there were some exceptions; for example, when another vowel came after the "e" in the same word (as in the word "read") or when another vowel was one letter removed from the "e" in either direction (as in the word "vowel"), they were instructed not to cross out the "e." Given that participants had habituated to the rather straightforward procedure on the first task, doing the second task in a different way required them to exert self-control.

Next, all participants did an activity designed to affect their beliefs about how depleted they were. All of them were told that the color tone of the paper they were working on influences people's level of mental abilities. Half of them were told that the color tone has negative effects on people's mental abilities (exhausting their ability to attend to information and to think carefully), whereas the other half were told just the opposite, that the color tone has a replenishing effect on their mental abilities.

How do you think the information people were given influenced their beliefs about their level of depletion? You might expect that those who were told the color would deplete their energy would believe that they were more depleted than those who were told that the color would replenish their energy. However, just the opposite happened. Why? Participants who were told that the color would deplete them now had a handy external reason to feel depleted: the color of the paper. As a result, they may have inferred that their "real" level of depletion, deep down inside, was considerably lower. Those told that the color would replenish them had no such excuse. In fact, they may have inferred that they were "actually" quite depleted because they felt the way they did *in spite of* the fact that they should have felt more replenished. Believing their "true" level of depletion to be lower, those who thought the color of the paper would deplete them did much better on a subsequent measure of self-control than did their counterparts who were led to believe that the paper color would replenish them.[39] Although it seems counterintuitive that those told that the color of the paper would deplete them had more positive beliefs about their actual level of depletion than those told that the color of the paper would replenish them, those with more positive beliefs about their level of depletion were subsequently more able to exert self-control: the power of positive thinking!

The power of positive feeling was demonstrated in a series of studies by Diane Tice and colleagues in which they examined the role of mood. In all of the studies half of the participants did something that required them to exercise self-control. For instance, some were told to write down the thoughts they were having but were instructed that the one thing they should not think about is a white bear. Did you ever try to suppress a thought? If so, I bet that one of the first thoughts that came to your mind is the very one you were trying to suppress. Suppressing unwanted thoughts requires self-control. In another study some participants formed a habit but were then required to break the habit, much like the group that crossed out every letter "e," only to be told that there were certain instances in which the "e" should not be crossed out. In yet another study some participants had to resist the temptation to eat tasty snack foods. The other half of the participants in all three studies were not required to exert self-control.

Regardless of whether their initial activity required them to exert self-control, all participants in all three studies then did a second task that required them to exert self-control. In between the two tasks, however, some of the participants were induced into a positive mood, for instance by watching stand-up comedy routines by Robin Williams or Eddie Murphy, whereas others were not. In the absence of the positive mood enhancer the typical ego-depletion effect emerged: those who took part in an initial exercise requiring self-control had less in the tank on the second task than did those who did not take part in an initial exercise requiring self-control. However, the ego-depletion effect disappeared among those who were led to experience a positive mood.[40]

Brandon Schmeichel and Kathleen Vohs illustrated the power of positive doing by showing that engaging in self-affirmation can counteract ego depletion. Once again, some participants were forced to exert self-control whereas others were not. In one study the task requiring self-control exertion consisted of participants writing a story about a recent trip they had taken without using the letters A or N. In a second study, the self-control task entailed watching a video in which words periodically appeared on the screen that they had to ignore. In both studies participants then did another task that required them to exert self-control, such as seeing how long they could keep their hand in cold water or how long they could persist at a challenging puzzle. As expected, those who were forced to exert self-control on the first task did not persist as long on the second task, relative to those not forced to exert self-control on the first task. However, this effect went away when, in between the two tasks, participants engaged in self-affirmation.[41] As was the case in several studies discussed in chapter 4, the self-affirmation activity consisted of ranking values in terms of their personal significance and then briefly writing about why their most highly ranked value was important to them.

Although none of these studies examined ethical behavior, they have significant implications for the question of when exerting self-control may be less likely to lead to subsequent lapses in ethicality. Positive thinking, feeling, or doing may be effective antidotes. For example, the morning morality effect, whereby people behave less ethically later in the day than in the morning, may be weakened or eliminated if employees are led to believe that they still have self-control resources in their tanks (positive thinking), if they are exposed to information that puts them in a good mood (positive feeling), or if they take part in an activity that reaffirms their sense of self (positive doing). Positive thinking may be engendered by pointing out role models who persevered in the face of ego-depleting obstacles and ultimately prevailed ("If they can do it, so can I"). Positive feeling may be elicited by giving employees some uplifting news about themselves or the organization. And, as we saw in chapter 4, positive doing via taking part in a self-affirming activity can be brought about in a number of ways, such as taking part in a corporate-sponsored volunteer activity.

The Power of Motivation, or Fighting Fire with Fire

At its core ego depletion reflects reduced striving. By exerting self-control, people have fewer psychological resources to take on subsequent activities requiring self-control. However, what if it were made clear to employees how important it is for them to try to continue to exert self-control? Would this help them get over the hump of ego depletion? For example, suppose that employees are being driven crazy by their micromanaging boss who insists on things being done his way. Or imagine that employees have to learn a new procedure that requires them to discard all their old methods of doing things. In both instances, their experience of ego depletion may render them less equipped to withstand the temptation to lie, steal, and cheat.

Suppose that in both of these examples employees are induced to focus on the importance of behaving ethically. For instance, the home page of the organization's website could highlight the many ways in which the corporation behaves socially responsibly, such as by supporting its employees' volunteer efforts, by taking the lead on environmental sustainability, and so on. Several studies have shown that even ego-depleted people are able to maintain higher levels of self-control when the importance of doing so is emphasized. Mark Muraven and Elisaveta Slessareva depleted some of their participants by requiring them to suppress certain thoughts, such as thinking about a white bear; those in the control condition did not have to suppress any of their thoughts. Then all participants worked on a task that they were led to believe was a measure of creativity. The task required participants to trace geometric figures with a highlighter without retracing the same line and without lifting the highlighter from the page. Unbeknownst to participants, the task was actually insoluble. The measure of self-control consisted of how long participants were willing to persist in the face of the frustrating experience of not being able to complete the task. Relative to those in the control condition, those asked to avoid thinking about a white bear did not persist as long on the "creativity" task, which is a typical ego-depletion effect.

However, when participants were led to believe that working on the creativity task was part of a study with a very important purpose ("to provide scientific evidence for the development of new therapies for patients with Alzheimer's disease"), those who previously were asked to avoid thinking about a white bear continued to work at the task much longer; they were more persistent than those who suppressed thoughts of a white bear but who were not told of the importance of the study, and they were just as persistent as their counterparts who were told of the importance of the study but did not have to suppress their thoughts beforehand.[42]

When people believe that they are doing something important it gives them an incentive to try hard. Of course, one way to incentivize people, especially in the workplace, is with money. Does offering people money or tangible rewards provide another way to motivate ego-depleted employees to behave ethically? Suppose that ego-depleted employees are offered a lot of money to do the right thing or are threatened with having to pay a lot of money if they do not. Let's look at both the pros and cons of this idea; ultimately, I will tell you where I stand on this matter.

THE PROS

There is evidence that paying people more money can counteract the effects of ego depletion. Muraven and Slessareva induced some participants to be ego depleted whereas others were not. They then took part in another activity that required self-control, which consisted of drinking a beverage that practically everyone would *not* want to drink: Kool-Aid spiked with vinegar. All participants were instructed to drink as much as possible. Some were paid more money whereas others were paid less. Particularly among the ego depleted, those who were paid more drank more.[43] Although drinking awful-tasting Kool-Aid is not a measure of ethicality, both drinking this Kool-Aid and behaving ethically require people to exert self-control. One indicator of how these two are similar is that people are less likely to do both if they have been put into an ego-depleted state. It is therefore entirely plausible that paying ego-depleted people more money would not only motivate them to drink more of the awful Kool-Aid but also increase their tendency to behave ethically.

Furthermore, using money could work for a reason over and above the incentive that it gives people. Money has not only material or substantive value but also symbolic value. Studies show that subtly inducing people to think about money can get them to experience self-sufficiency, strength, and confidence. Previously we talked about the power of positive thinking, in which optimistic beliefs counteracted the effects of ego depletion. One study showed that *the mere idea of money* can bring about positive thinking. Under the guise of studying "finger dexterity," Xinyue Zhou, Kathleen Vohs, and Roy Baumeister asked participants to count out eighty $100 bills in one condition or eighty pieces of paper in another. They then measured participants' psychological strength, in the form of how much distress they experienced in response to social pain and physical pain. Relative to those who simply counted pieces of paper, people who counted out money felt stronger; they were less distressed by the socially and physically painful events they endured.[44]

If simply thinking about money can confer strength, then it should buffer the effects of exerting self-control. Helen Boucher and Monthe Kofos tested this idea, while cleverly getting people to think about money in a different way. First, participants did something in which they had to either exert self-control (suppress thoughts of a white bear) or not exert self-control. Next, they completed a sentence descrambling task in which they were given thirty sets of five words and had to make a sentence using four of the words. For example, in the "Money" condition the words were "won green the lottery I," which could be made into "I won the lottery." In the "Neutral" condition the words were "metal I wrote letter the" which could be made into "I wrote the letter." The researchers then evaluated people's subsequent tendencies to exert self-control, as reflected in their performance on a difficult cognitive task. The results in the Neutral condition were typical: those who previously had to exert self-control did a lot worse than those who did not. However, the results in the Money condition were quite different: those who previously had to suppress thinking about a white bear did no worse than those who did not. In other words, among those who had to suppress thinking about a white bear, performance was much better if they simply thought about money than if they did not. Moreover, these results seem to be due to the fact that the mere idea of money elicited positive thinking. Those who thought about money saw the difficult cognitive task as less difficult, which reflects positive thinking.[45]

What does this suggest about whether organizations should pay employees to be ethical, especially when employees are experiencing ego depletion? On the one hand, paying people to be ethical seems like a good idea because money can deter ego-depleted employees from behaving unethically for several reasons. Money can *motivate* the ego depleted by serving as an incentive to do the right thing. Furthermore, money can *empower* the ego depleted by activating feelings of confidence and related forms of positive thinking, which has been shown to be an antidote for the tendency of ego depletion to reduce ethicality.

THE CONS

On the other hand, paying employees to be ethical is unlikely to be the silver bullet for at least three reasons. First, just because the mere thought of money *can* lead to positive thinking does not mean that it *will*. It is not too difficult to imagine how thinking about money may be disempowering rather than empowering. For example, for people pessimistic about their chances of closing the gap between how much money they have and how much they would like to have, the idea of money may call to mind what they do *not* have, which is hardly likely to elicit feelings of confidence and power. Maryam Kouchaki and her colleagues recently demonstrated that the idea of money can trigger thoughts about dimensions far more nefarious than empowerment or disempowerment. In a series of studies participants were asked to rearrange words into sentences. In the "Money" group the sentences made reference to money (e.g., "She spends money liberally") whereas in the "No Money" group they did not (e.g., "She walked on grass"). Those in the Money group were more likely to view a decision they had to make through the lens of a business frame, which in turn led them to behave more unethically.[46]

Second, paying employees to promote ethical behavior or to deter unethical behavior can get expensive very quickly. There are certainly more cost-effective ways for employers to signal the importance of ethicality. For instance, when employees can clearly see the intrinsic benefits of doing the right thing ("the fruits of their labor"), they are more likely to assign importance to doing the right thing.

Suppose people are asked to donate time or money to a charitable cause when they are in an ego-depleted state; for instance, imagine that the request is made later rather than earlier in the day. Adam Grant has shown that personal testimonials from beneficiaries of charitable causes are highly motivating; this may be especially so when people are ego depleted and therefore in need of energy and inspiration.[47]

Third, the use of money can lead to a dangerous shift in people's beliefs about why they are acting ethically or not acting unethically. Most of us know the difference between what's ethical and what's unethical, and the vast majority of us are intrinsically motivated to do the former rather than the latter. What would happen, however, if people were financially (that is, extrinsically) motivated to do an activity for which they already were intrinsically motivated? At first blush, the simplest answer to this question is that people would be especially likely to engage in the behavior; after all, now they have two reasons, an intrinsic one and an extrinsic one.

However, the results of well over a hundred studies reviewed by Ed Deci and his colleagues have shown that the simplest answer is not always the most accurate. It turns out that adding an extrinsic motivator such as money to encourage people to do something they are already intrinsically motivated to do does not make them extra likely to engage in that behavior.[48] Instead, adding an extrinsic motivator may cause people to change their beliefs about why they are engaging in the behavior. According to the "over-justification effect," people no longer believe "I am doing this because the activity itself serves as its own source of reward" but rather "I am doing this for the money." Conse-

quently, an activity that previously was intrinsically motivated comes to be seen as extrinsically motivated.

A particularly compelling example of the overjustification effect was recently demonstrated by Amy Wrzesniewski and Barry Schwartz, who examined the motives of
more than eleven thousand cadets for entering the United
States Military Academy. All cadets rated the importance
of both intrinsic motives to join (e.g., their desire to be
trained as a leader in the army) and extrinsic reasons (e.g.,
to be able to get a better job or to make more money). The
researchers were particularly interested in how the cadets'
initial motives influenced their commitment and productivity, as reflected in their likelihood of graduation, in
their likelihood of becoming commissioned officers after
graduation, and in how well they performed as commissioned officers. Let's compare those who rated themselves
high in both intrinsic and extrinsic motives to those who
rated themselves high in intrinsic motives and low in extrinsic motives. Interestingly enough, the ones who were
intrinsically motivated but not extrinsically motivated to
join the army did significantly better on all measures relative to those who were intrinsically *and* extrinsically motivated to join.[49]

Thus while in some ways it makes sense to pay employees to behave ethically (especially when they are ego
depleted), there are even stronger reasons to believe that
this is not the right way to go. Just because money can
counteract ego depletion does not mean that it will, depending on the thoughts that it calls to mind. In addition,
paying employees to be ethical can be quite expensive and
therefore is unlikely to be economically sustainable. Finally, given the overjustification effect, the use of money

actually may be *counterproductive* for the sizable number of ego-depleted employees who are already intrinsically motivated to do the right thing.

More on Counteracting Ego Depletion:
Doing More by Doing Less

Motivation provides one strategy for managers to weaken the link between employees' ego depletion and their tendency to behave unethically. When managers convey how important it is to behave ethically, employees don't allow their ego depletion to rule them. This reasoning seems to suggest that managers have to "do something" if they want to get employees to fight through their ego depletion. Given the nature of self-control exertion, however, sometimes it may be better for managers to do less rather than more. Exerting self-control is like using a muscle: the more it is done, the more fatigue sets in. Much like muscle strength, however, our capability to exert self-control has a natural tendency to be restored, provided that we allow that natural restorative process to unfold. Just as taking a break from strenuous physical activity allows us to "get our strength back," the same can be said about exertion of self-control. Therefore, sometimes the best thing managers can do when dealing with ego-depleted employees is to create a space for their self-control resources to be replenished. As suggested by the following example, ensuring that employees are not incessantly overburdened with activities is one way to go.

A number of years ago I assumed the position of faculty director of a leadership development program at Columbia Business School. At the time that I took over, the program started at 8:30 in the morning and ended at 10:30 at night for three straight days. The only down times were for meals and short coffee breaks midway through the morning and afternoon sessions. Although participants' level of engagement was generally quite high across the three days, one of my first decisions as faculty director was to end at 5:00 PM on the second of the three days. I was conflicted about this decision. On the one hand, I was concerned that the learning experience might suffer, given that participants would now have less formal contact time with the faculty in the program. On the other hand, the program takes participants out of their comfort zones in a variety of ways. For instance, the program is conducted in English, which was not the first language for many of the participants. I figured that giving the participants some time off would reduce the amount of time that they were in the mode of using up self-control resources while simultaneously allowing the self-restoration process to unfold. In fact, the decision to end earlier on the second day has enhanced the overall experience for participants. They may not be working harder, but they certainly are working smarter. With their batteries recharged, they show up raring to go on the morning of the third day.

How does the idea of doing more by doing less relate to our discussion of the effect of ego depletion on ethicality? A recent study examining the effect of amount of sleep on how ethically people behave may help make the connection. Chris Barnes and his colleagues asked employees to report how much they had slept over the previous three months as well as how ego depleted they had felt during that same time period. Their bosses independently rated the frequency with which employees engaged in ethical behavior during the same time period, such as by not taking credit for someone else's work. The more employees slept the less ego depleted they felt, and the less ego depleted they felt the more their bosses rated them as behaving ethically.[50] Particularly when time is not of the essence, rather than doing something to motivate employees to fight through their ego-depleted state, the best process may be one in which managers do nothing more than make space for employees to recover and rest, and thereby nurture their natural tendencies to restore their self-control capabilities.

A related point can be made about the process of managing change, the topic we considered in chapter 3. The fast-paced environments in which most companies operate often leave managers and employees breathless. Just when employees are finished with one change, their bosses tell them that it's on to the next one. Asking employees to change, by its very nature, requires them to exert self-control. They have to override their natural impulse to behave one way, often built up over years, and do things differently. Little wonder that never-ending change often brings about employee burnout: they have to deal with change even when they barely have time to recover from earlier changes. Although it is certainly true that the only constant in environments is change, it is also true that at different points in time there is variability in how much the environment mandates change. When the environment requires less change, managers may be well served to deliberately *not* introduce new initiatives. By doing less (not introducing new initiatives), they are doing more: allowing for the restoration of employees' self-control capabilities. In fact, even when the environment mandates change it is important to take into account the timing with which new initiatives are rolled out. One important timing consideration is whether employees are at a moment in which they have enough self-control reserves to take on what is likely to be an arduous activity.[51]

Chapter Summary

Drawing on process dimensions considered in previous chapters, this chapter began by discussing how the ways things are handled influence employees' tendencies to behave ethically. First, those on the receiving end of high process fairness behave more ethically. Not only do they steal less but they also show their ethicality by behaving with greater process fairness toward others. People's tendency to return or pass along the process fairness with which they have been treated is motivated by reciprocity and enabled by learning. Second, the chapter discussed how workplace processes affecting employees' global self-integrity affect their ethicality. The more that the process causes people to see themselves as having esteem, identity, or control, the more ethically they behave.

We also considered how a different way of conceptualizing the self, that is, as subject (I-self) rather than as object (me-self), affects employees' ethicality. In its role as executor, the I-self may burn up resources that leave people feeling ego depleted and, as a result, less capable of exerting self-control, at least in the short run. Drawing on this basic principle from the ego-depletion literature, we discussed how (1) exerting self-control in activities unrelated to ethicality spills over to reduce people's likelihood of behaving ethically, and (2) exerting self-control in activities related to ethicality spills over to reduce people's ability to exert self-control in activities unrelated to ethicality. In addition, behaving ethically may lower people's tendency to do so subsequently, an effect that may be explained based upon the self as object (moral licensing) as well as the self as subject (ego depletion).

On a more optimistic note, I suggested that organizational factors that require employees to exert self-control need not summarily lead to ego depletion and corresponding breaches in ethicality. When an activity requiring self-control exertion is accompanied by positive thinking, feeling, or doing, employees are able to exert self-control on a subsequent activity. Other mitigating influences on ego depletion are sources of intrinsic *or* extrinsic motivation, not intrinsic *and* extrinsic motivation. Research on the overjustification effect has shown that the addition of an extrinsic incentive to encourage people to do something that they were already intrinsically motivated to do may actually backfire. A smarter way to proceed is to offer little extrinsic reward for people to engage in some activity when they are already intrinsically motivated to do so. Finally, given the tendency for self-control capabilities to restore themselves when they are not used up, sometimes managers' best way to address ego depletion is to create conditions for rest and recovery.

6 → A High-Quality Process: Easier Said Than Done

By this point I hope that you are pretty well convinced that the process matters. When the process is fair (chapter 2), when the process accompanying change adheres to the principles set forth in chapter 3, when the process allows employees to see themselves as having esteem, identity, and control (chapter 4), and when the process is not ego depleting (chapter 5), good things happen, such as high employee productivity, positive morale, and ethical behavior. All of this raises an important question: If the process matters, what gets in the way of doing it right? And, given the obstacles, what can be done to deal with them?

What makes the question about obstacles a puzzling one is that doing the process well sometimes may not even be very costly, as Winston Churchill recognized. The day after the attack on Pearl Harbor Churchill wrote a declaration of war letter to the emperor of Japan, ending it as follows: "I have the honour to be, with high consideration, Sir, Your obedient servant, Winston S. Churchill." Upon being castigated by his countrymen for writing such a respectful letter while declaring war, Churchill responded,

"When you have to kill a man, it costs nothing to be polite." Of course, doing the process in a high-quality way usually is not without expense. In fact, quite the contrary: in this chapter I will discuss some of the costs of doing the process well and what can be done to address them.

Organizing the Barriers

A high-quality process equips and engages those on the receiving end to do their jobs well, happily, and ethically. Being equipped speaks to ability whereas being engaged refers to motivation, the two key determinants of all human behavior. It therefore stands to reason that the two obstacles to managers' delivering a high-quality process are a lack of resources and a lack of desire. Lacking resources, they are not *able* to do the process in a high-quality way. Lacking desire, they are not *motivated* to do things in the right way. Lack of resources and lack of desire are manifested in a variety of forms and for a variety of reasons.

Lack of Resources

One important resource is knowledge. Sometimes managers simply may not know how, when, or why the process matters. For example, they may mistakenly believe that those on the receiving end of "tough decisions" are reacting badly because of the unfavorable outcome when the real cause is *the combination of* an unfavorable outcome and an unfair process. Take the case of Kaci Hickox, the nurse from Maine who returned to the United States from West Africa in October 2014 after treating Ebola patients. Ms. Hickox created quite a stir when she wrote to the *Dallas Morning News*, complaining about how she was treated when she was told she was under quarantine. Among other things, she was accused of being a whiner and self-centered. In my view, this was because of a misperception of what she was complaining about. Many who spoke out against her believed she was complaining about the outcome: being quarantined. After all, they reasoned, Ms. Hickox should have recognized that she was a public health hazard and that the decision to quarantine, while unfavorable to her, was legitimate. However, Ms. Hickox was not simply complaining about being quarantined. Rather, she *also* felt that she had been mistreated by the authorities in the process. According to the October 25, 2014, issue of the *New York Times*, Ms. Hickox believed that the process accompanying the quarantine was unfair in a variety of ways. She felt that (1) the decision was not made on the basis of accurate information, (2) she was not given a clear and adequate explanation of why the decision was made, and (3) she was not treated with dignity and respect.

Regarding accuracy, there was some question about the extent to which she showed signs of being ill. An initial scan of her forehead suggested that she had a temperature of 101. When retested a little later, she had a temperature of 98, at which point a doctor told her, "There's no way you have a fever. Your face is just flushed." She also described being kept "in isolation for about seven hours . . . left alone for long stretches and given only a granola bar when she said she was hungry . . . and being held with no explanation." Regarding dignity and respect, Ms. Hickox told her mother that she felt that a dog would have been treated better than she was.[1] I bet that she would have reacted to the same decision to be quarantined quite differently if it had been accompanied by a fairer process, that is, based on accurate information, with clear explanations, and in ways that preserved her dignity and respect. She may not have been happy, but she would have been *a lot* less angry.

It's somewhat understandable that managers may mis-perceive the way in which those on the receiving end of tough decisions are upset about an unfavorable outcome; in reality, they may be bothered by the combination of the bad outcome *and* the poor process. After all, if those on the receiving end actually are upset about the outcome and the process, then those carrying out the process may feel criticized. In any event, when managers do not recognize that recipients are upset because of the outcome *and* the process and not just because of the outcome, they are likely to continue doing the process in the same regrettable ways.

Managers' misguided beliefs about the process also can come from a benign rather than self-protective place. Often the idea that the process matters is pretty self-evident, even "common sense." But not always: throughout the book we have seen instances in which small differences in how things are handled had disproportionately large effects. For example, who could have imagined that giving nursing home residents control over caring for a plant or selecting the night on which a movie would be shown would positively influence their physical and emotional well-being?[22] Who would have thought that taking an extra hour when onboarding employees to encourage them to identify their signature strengths and how to enact them would lead to higher customer satisfaction six months later?[23] Who could have predicted that giving African American middle school children an opportunity to do short self-affirmation exercises at the beginning of the school year would have positive effects on their academic achievement months and even years later?[4] Who could have known that the time of day influences the ethicality with which decisions are made?[5] In short, sometimes it's a knowledge gap that interferes with a high-quality process.

Even knowing about the importance of the process does not ensure that it will be handled well. Managers also must have the skills needed to carry out the process, such as the ability to stay calm under trying circumstances. Andy Molinsky and Joshua Margolis have shown that when managers have to dole out unfavorable outcomes ("necessary evils"), the way they go about it often leaves a lot to be desired.[6] Note the unfortunate irony: as mentioned in chapter 2, when outcomes are unfavorable the quality of the process has an especially big effect on employees' productivity and morale.[7] And yet it is precisely when outcomes are unfavorable that managers often come up short in how they implement the decision, in part because they don't have the intrapersonal and interpersonal skills needed to deal with difficult circumstances.

Consider, as Molinsky and Margolis did in one of their studies, the difficult task that managers face when they have to lay off employees. It is an emotionally loaded time for the people losing their jobs, who understandably feel angry, worried, and sad. It's also emotionally trying for the managers who have to deliver the bad news. As one manager put it,

> Internally, there is a nervous stomach, you feel on edge. Sometimes you get physically nauseous or a headache. Very often you have bad dreams that are not necessarily related to the downsizing itself, but from that stress. There is a degree of nervousness that almost makes you have to step back and say, "I have to be calm, I can't show that I am nervous about delivering this message."

Another manager described it this way:

> If I am about to cry because this is upsetting me as much as it is upsetting the other individual, I am definitely going to try not to cry. But the emotion that I feel is genuine in terms of the unhappiness or the sorrow that I am feeling that I have to deliver this message to someone.[8]

Managers may also feel angry about the layoffs themselves if, for example, they don't see the need for them in the first place, their good friends are being let go, or, in the course of delivering the news, they are blamed or insulted by the people losing their jobs. In addition, they may feel guilty, either because they see themselves as responsible for the layoffs or because they think it is not right for them to have their jobs when their coworkers do not ("survivor guilt"). At times like these managers need to have the capacity to regulate negative emotions in order to do the process well, which entails delivering the news in a forthright manner while also preserving the dignity and respect of those on the receiving end. Managers have to be honest without coming on too softly or too strongly. And yet instances of coming on too softly or too strongly abound. For example, if the recipients of the bad news show signs of feeling sad or worried, managers may be tempted to backtrack in a well-intentioned but shortsighted attempt to make the recipients feel better. If the recipients lash out and blame the managers, the latter may feel the urge to respond with anger themselves. In different ways, then, delivering the news too softly or too strongly is not respectful to the recipients.

Given the many painful negative emotions that managers and recipients are feeling when the former have to communicate bad news to the latter, it is no wonder that the delivery process often goes awry.[9] But it's not simply that managers are feeling a lot of negative emotion. Adding to the psychological burden is their sense that the emotions are inadmissible, that they must be suppressed. Recall the above quotes: one manager said, "I have to be calm, I can't show that I am nervous about delivering this message." Another said, "If I am about to cry because this is upsetting me as much as it is upsetting the other individual, I am definitely going to try not to cry." Having to deal with the inadmissibility of emotions when delivering bad news may contribute to managers' ego depletion; after all, it takes self-control to hide strongly felt emotions.

Whereas the previous chapter illustrated how ego depletion can predispose decision makers to behave less ethically, recent research shows that ego depletion also detracts from the quality with which bad news is communicated. Dave Whiteside and Laurie Barclay asked participants to play the role of managers delivering bad news to one of their employees (Jim) either about his impending layoff or about a negative performance review. Prior to the delivery, some of the participants were induced to be more ego depleted than others. For instance, in one study everyone watched a video of a woman being interviewed about a job without audio. Allegedly, as participants were told, this was because the researchers wanted to evaluate how people make judgments based on body language. Every so often, common words were shown at the bottom of the screen. To induce ego depletion, some participants were explicitly instructed to betray their natural instincts: they were told that whenever words appeared at the bottom they should ignore them and redirect their attention back to the person being interviewed. Another group of participants were not given specific instructions about what they should do when they saw the words appearing; this group was less ego depleted. Participants then recorded the message they would send to the people on the receiving end of the bad news. Participants who watched the video that didn't require them to exert self-control were respectful in their delivery. For example, in communicating to Jim that he was being laid off, one of them said:

> Our organization's poor performance has forced us to make some really tough decisions. In order to make the process as fair as possible, we used a number of criteria to determine which staff members are to be laid off: department performance, employee seniority, and employee performance. You are one of our most recent hires, and while your performance has improved, it is still below average for this department. So, we are laying you off effective July 1. I can't tell you how sorry I am to have to tell you this. We really do appreciate your contribution to the organization, and we will be providing you with job search assistance as well as two months of severance pay to hopefully make this transition a little easier on you and your family. Again, I'm really sorry, Jim. Please let me know if there is anything else I can do.

Contrast this approach with the more disrespectful style of message written by those who previously had to exert self-control while watching the video. For instance, one of them curtly wrote:

> Jim, since sales have declined significantly, the company has made a decision to cut costs, which includes laying off a certain percentage of the staff. Unfortunately, in

this department you are one of the people to be laid off effective July 1. You will have access to job search assistance and a severance package of two months' pay. I'm sorry to give you this news and I wish you well.

Note that the substance of the two messages was pretty much the same. In both instances the date that the layoff became effective was identical, as was the assistance given to Jim in the form of finding a job elsewhere and the amount of severance pay. However, by being more informative in content and sympathetic in tone, the first message preserved Jim's dignity to a much greater extent than did the second.[10]

Another study that shows how ego depletion fosters disrespectful behavior was done at the airport, only this time the people behaving badly were customers rather than managers. If you have flown recently, you probably have noticed no shortage of emotionally draining conditions such as slow-moving security lines, oversold seats, crowded waiting areas, flight delays, and so on. It's like one big exercise in self-control, and most of us are up to the challenge. But even when we are up to it, we may pay a price in the form of ego depletion. Katy DeCelles and her colleagues examined the behavior of airline passengers in the gate area and found that those exposed to more draining conditions such as those described above showed a greater tendency to behave disrespectfully toward the airline personnel. For example, they were more apt to sigh loudly, pound their fists on the counter, roll their eyes, or curse at gate agents for not being able to change their seat or get them an upgrade. In one instance, a passenger who had been drinking a very large bottle of water threw it near the gate agent when he was told that the airline wouldn't hold the plane because he'd forgotten his cell phone in the lounge and wanted to go back for it. On another occasion a young couple who had missed their overseas flight was so irate that the gate agent needed to call airport police. There also were stories of passengers assaulting agents by pulling on their lanyards, which now have an emergency release for this very reason.

Of course, one interpretation of these findings is that some people are simply more likely to fly off the handle than others. How do we know that ego depletion played a role in these instances of "air rage"? In a follow-up study, participants were asked to imagine that they had an annoying experience at the airport, such as being the victim of an oversold flight. Beforehand, one group had been induced into a state of ego depletion by having to write an essay about their daily life without using the letters A and N, whereas another group wrote the same essay under much less draining conditions; they merely had to avoid using the letters X and Y. Then everyone indicated how angry they would feel as well as how likely they would be to behave rudely toward the gate agents, such as rolling their eyes or sighing when talking to them, and by blaming them for problems that were clearly beyond the agents' control. Not surprisingly, those who felt angrier about being the victim of an oversold flight said they would be more likely to behave rudely. However, this was particularly true for those who wrote the ego-depleting version of the essay. In other words, it wasn't only anger that led to disrespectful behavior; people were inclined to behave disrespectfully when they were angry *and* when they had been exhausted of their ability to regulate their anger.[11]

Lack of Desire

Knowing that the process matters and having the necessary skills do not ensure that the process will be carried out well. Another essential component is desire or motivation. For a variety of reasons, managers may not want to engage in behavior that comprises a high-quality process. For one thing, such behaviors may have additional consequences that are not particularly welcome; let's call this the problem of "unwanted side effects." Furthermore, the realities of organizational life activate other motives that are at cross-purposes with the desirability of a high-quality process; let's call this the dilemma of "competing interests."

UNWANTED SIDE EFFECTS

High process fairness has many benefits, but it also has its costs. Consider two of the main pillars of a fair process: participation and explanation. Managers may be reluctant to involve others or to explain why they make certain decisions for fear of looking powerless or weak. When managers maintain a zero-sum view of power, involving others in decisions or explaining decisions might feel uncomfortable. The more they allow their employees to participate in decision making, the less power they may see as being left over for them. Explanations impart knowledge, and in so doing may empower those on the receiving end. Here again, managers with a zero-sum view of power may not want to give explanations for their decisions. For example, legal counsel typically advises downsizing organizations to provide little explanation and information about layoffs, on the grounds that anything they say can and will be used against them in court by those filing a suit for wrongful termination. Ironically, withholding information may in fact generate more anger and legal action against downsizing organizations than would be the case if they were to be more revealing and less defensive.

That said, managers are not entirely wrong to believe that they will be seen as less powerful if they are participatory or explanatory. Naomi Rothman, Batia Wiesenfeld, and their colleagues recently conducted a study in which participants made judgments about a supervisor at an investment bank, John, who was deciding how to allocate bonuses. Half of the time John was described as involving others in decisions: "He has been actively soliciting input from his subordinates about their own and others' contributions over the last year, rather than making the decision independently." The other half of the time John was nonparticipatory: "He is making the decisions entirely independently rather than soliciting input from his subordinates about their own and others' contributions over the last year." John was rated as significantly more powerful when he was not participatory; for instance, he was seen as having greater control over people and resources.[12]

In a second study by Rothman, Wiesenfeld, and their colleagues, participants were asked to make judgments about decision makers who gave varying degrees of explanation. First, participants watched an encounter between two people who had taken part in a previous study in which one of them made a decision about how much to reward the other. The person on the receiving end, who was given what he thought was a low reward, said, "I have a question. How did I end up with this amount?" The person who made the decision responded in one of two ways. Half of the time he provided an explanation in a positive tone: "I'm so sorry. Let me see if I can explain. You didn't actually get less than average. There just wasn't that much to go around. I'm really sorry! I wish I had more time to explain but I am running late for another study." The other half of the time the decision maker did not provide an explanation and also adopted a defensive stance, saying, "What's the big deal? I'm not going to explain myself to you." After watching the encounter, participants rated how much they saw the decision maker as powerful. The decision maker was seen as more powerful when he did not give an explanation than when he did.[13]

One implication of these findings is that managers will shy away from being participatory and explanatory in order to be seen as powerful. Even though participatory and explanatory managers were rated as less powerful than their nonparticipatory and nonexplanatory counterparts, I believe we need to rethink the idea that managers' actual power declines when they are participatory and explanatory for two reasons. First, research has convincingly shown that participation and explanation foster employees' commitment to their bosses and their bosses' decisions.[14] If managers gain commitment from their employees by being participatory and explanatory, then managers' power base, if anything, goes up rather than down.

Second, even if managers are concerned about how they will be viewed by being participatory and explanatory, they run another risk to their reputation by *not* being participatory and explanatory. Rothman, Wiesenfeld, and their colleagues asked participants to judge not only the managers' power but also their status. Power and status are related, but they are not the same thing. Power refers to control over valued resources. Status refers to how much people are respected or have prestige in the eyes of others.

Although participatory and explanatory managers were rated as lower in power, they were judged as higher in status.[15] Hence managers who do not want to involve others or to provide explanation out of a fear of appearing weak are at best misguided and at worst flat-out wrong. They are misguided in that the commitment they gain from their employees by being participatory and explanatory puts them in a position to be more powerful. They are flat-out wrong in that the higher status they attain makes them anything but weak.

COMPETING INTERESTS

The realities of organizational life activate other desires for managers that may interfere with their tendency to carry out a high-quality process. One such competing interest is reflected in the following situation that I recently witnessed firsthand.

Jay, a vice president at a midsized bank, was approached by one of his direct reports, Susan, with a suggested change designed to improve how the company presented financial reports to its clients. Viewing Susan's recommendation strictly as a business decision, Jay was not opposed to it. However, Jay knew that going in the new direction would create hardship for David, the person in charge of the existing report process. Jay suggested to Susan that the two of them meet with David to discuss the new way of doing things. Susan readily agreed to meet with Jay and David, but she strongly believed that one topic of conversation should not be broached: the discomfort that the change was going to cause for David. In her words, this was a "business decision," therefore, it would be "unprofessional" to talk about the emotional turmoil it might cause in the people affected by it.

Organizations are "in business." Given their business imperative, organizations have economic goals that lead to an emphasis on motives such as rationality, efficiency, and the bottom line. Recent research by Andy Molinsky, Adam Grant, and Joshua Margolis has shown that when an economic way of thinking (also known as an economic schema) holds sway, decision makers are less likely to treat the affected parties with dignity and respect. In other words, compassionate interpersonal treatment may be less emphasized when managers view the world through the lens of economics. Participants in one study had to deliver the news that because of financial hardships, their school was reducing the scholarships that had already been awarded to students who were writing honors theses. Before delivering the bad news to the affected parties, all participants completed a storytelling exercise. Half of them were induced into an economic mind-set by virtue of their story having to include the words "economically rational, logical, fiscally responsible, efficient, profitable, self-interested, cost-benefit analysis, businesslike, and professional." The other half was put into less of an economic mind-set; their story had to include words such as "book, car, chair, computer, desk, pen, street, table, and trashcan."

Those put into an economic mind-set communicated the bad news with relatively little compassion. For example, one of them simply said, "I regret to inform you that we will have to cut $3,000 from your scholarship. With the economy as it is we have had less money to supply our students." In contrast, those who were not thinking in economic terms were far more compassionate. As one of them wrote, "I would like to speak to you regarding your scholarship. Unfortunately, the funding has been cut and the scholarship has been reduced. I know this is upsetting and probably means you have some decisions to make, but feel free to ask questions and the department will do its best to help you find other ways to get funding. I am very sorry that this had to happen but the financial markets are such that we simply cannot afford to continue providing this level of assistance. Again, I am sorry and feel free to come in at any time with questions or for help."[16]

By asking participants some additional questions, the researchers also identified two reasons why those with an economic mind-set were less compassionate. One reason pertained to participants' experience of emotion whereas the other reflected their expression of it. First, those in an economic mind-set felt less empathy for the affected parties than did those not in an economic mind-set. Second, much like Susan in the story above, they also were more likely to think it unprofessional to share their true feelings, relative to those who had been put into less of an economic mind-set.[17] Economic motives pervade the workplace. Unfortunately, they can bring to the fore other desires, such as not wanting to appear unprofessional, that can crowd out compassion, an important element of a high-quality process.

But it's not simply economic desires that compete with managers' tendencies to deliver a high-quality process. Psychological motives can get in the way as well. Although a high-quality process is multifaceted, a central tenet of this process is that managers must be other-directed rather than self-directed. When they are other-directed, they give priority to what their employees need to function effectively. Behaviorally, an other-directed orientation translates into managers doing things that decrease the psychological distance between themselves and their employees. It means making themselves available, hearing others out, and providing not only compassion but also direction. However, the nature of organizational life can make managers more self-directed, which can detract from the quality of the process.[18]

Let me provide an example. A number of years ago I was asked to speak to a group of managers after their employer, an organization in the telecommunications industry, introduced the first layoffs in the company's history. This was a very significant moment for the organization, which until that time had been known for its paternalistic corporate culture. The layoffs came as quite a shock. The surviving managers I spoke to were under a great deal of emotional duress. They felt angry about the company's departure from its typical paternalism, felt guilty that they had not done more to prevent the layoffs, and were worried about when the next shoe was going to drop. If there ever was a time for them to be available to their people, this was it. Unfortunately, just the opposite occurred. The emotional distress brought on by the layoffs put them into a self-protective mode. The change in corporate culture signified by the layoffs was something that deeply affected the managers as well as their direct reports. Put differently, they were not merely agents of change but, like their employees, recipients of the change. Thus managers' motivation to protect themselves outweighed their desire to take care of their direct reports, detracting from how well they handled the implementation of the layoffs.

And, there's another important part to this story. That was a tough audience to be around that day. Quite literally, I felt their pain—emotions are contagious. Studies have shown that it's depressing to be around depressed people and anxiety provoking to be around anxious people.[19] True to form, I found it challenging to be surrounded by people feeling the turmoil that this group was experiencing. It soon became apparent that they wanted to withdraw from their employees. Given emotional contagion, I must confess that a small part of me felt like withdrawing from them. But only a small part; an even bigger part of me felt empathic about what they were going through, which helped me be emotionally present. We spent much of the day focusing on how they could constructively help one another and their direct reports adapt to their new organizational landscape in the aftermath of the layoffs.

In sum, an important element of a high-quality change process is to be other-directed. Particularly when tough decisions have to be made and negative emotions are running high, managers understandably feel the urge to go into a self-protective mode. The negative emotions that make managers feel like withdrawing could be their own, such as anger, anxiety, and guilt, or they could be those of their employees, which they do not want to "catch." If they give in to the urge to withdraw they are unlikely to reach out to others, in which case the quality of the process will be compromised.

So much to do, so little time. Another reality of organizational life is that time generally is a precious commodity, especially in periods of change. In chapter 3 we talked about the many elements that go into a well-managed change process, as reflected in the framework

$$\text{Change} = (D \times V \times P) > C,$$

in which D refers to surfacing dissatisfaction with the current state, V refers to providing a vision of the future state, P refers to the process of moving from the current state to the future state, and C refers to reducing the costs of change. I have presented the "DVP" framework to executives from all over the world. The overwhelming majority completely agree with it. They know that if they want their employees to be engaged rather than resistant they need to implement change in the right ways. I then ask them a simple question: Why is the framework easier to talk about than to actually carry out? There are lots of answers to this question, but the one I hear perhaps most of all is, "We don't have the time." After all, they rightfully say, the framework requires a lot of things to be done. It is also a model in which *all* of the elements need to be done; the chain is only as strong as its weakest link. So they are quite correct to *feel* like they don't have enough time.

I wish I could wave a magic wand to make more time available for those trying to bring about change. Alas, that is not possible, but I do have some ideas to make the time crunch accompanying organizational change more manageable. First, although lots of elements go into a well-handled change process, it is not as if each manager needs to spend a lot of time with all of the elements. My advice for the team of change managers is to organize themselves around the framework and then to "divide and conquer" the various elements. Second and perhaps even more important, managers responsible for bringing about change need to reconsider how they think about time. It may seem tempting for them to say, "We don't have the time to do this DVP stuff now; maybe we will get to it later. Right now, we just have to get this change done, no matter how we do it."

This way of thinking is wrong on two fronts. First, if the change process is not handled well in the present, it is unlikely that there will be more time in the future. Second, if change implementers don't handle the change process well early on, they are likely to create an even bigger mess for themselves later. At the later point they will have to address the compound problem of (1) the change not taking hold and therefore not bringing about the benefits it was supposed to bring, and (2) having to explain and correct for the flawed way they went about it in the first place. Furthermore, are the implementers of change who flubbed the process earlier on going to have the time to do things in the right way later? Unlikely. To those who believe that they don't have the time to do the change process well in the first place, I say the reality is not simply "pay now or pay later"; it is "pay now, or pay (even more) later." When it comes to handling a change process well, the ounce of prevention truly is worth the pound of cure.

Toward Overcoming the Barriers

By talking about the barriers to the delivery of a high-quality process, we can better understand how it is easier to talk about delivering a high-quality process than it is to actually deliver one. As we have seen, the barriers come in a variety of forms. Sometimes it is simply not clear that the process matters or just how much it matters. Sometimes it is a skills gap; those who plan and implement decisions may not have the requisite interpersonal savvy or self-management capabilities. And sometimes it's a matter of a lack of will rather than a lack of skill. Having identified the barriers, though, we can better discuss what can be done to overcome them and thereby boost the odds that the process will be carried out in an effective way. Working through the barriers is a joint responsibility: there are things that individual managers can do and there are things that organizations can do.

What Individuals Can Do

Most managers, most of the time, know that the process matters, at least as a guiding principle. While most managers generally know that the process matters, they may have difficulty recognizing this in specific situations, especially when they have to decide how they want to handle things. Why? One of the major challenges managers face is that doing the process well requires them to regulate their negative emotions. Negative emotions are felt in part because the nature of managerial work often requires making difficult decisions that will not be received well. Managers may feel angry, anxious, or guilty about making these decisions in their own right, and they also may find themselves the target of negative emotions from an unappreciative audience. This is particularly so when managers have to tell people that they are losing their jobs. Even in less emotionally fraught instances, however, such as organizational change in which no employees are losing their jobs, the change may nonetheless represent to employees losing aspects of their job that they would prefer to keep. Making matters even more challenging for managers as implementers of change is that they often feel pressure to not let their negative emotions show, which requires a significant amount of self-control.

In short, that's a lot of emotional pressure. If it is not addressed effectively the chances of doing the process in a high-quality way are greatly reduced. For instance, managers will be less likely to communicate in a forthright and yet respectful way about the nature of the change. At a time when they need to be available to their employees they may withdraw in the service of self-protection.[20] Or they may worry about some of the unfavorable side effects of handling the process well, such as appearing weak if they involve others in decisions or explain to them why certain decisions were made.[21]

Yet studies show that it is not inevitable that people will be derailed by emotionally trying working conditions. Some people are able to regulate their negative emotions and as a consequence behave constructively. One recent study examined how employees' ability to regulate negative emotions enabled them to deal with a difficult work environment, in which they perceived their employers' decision-making processes as unfair. As previously discussed, employees subjected to unfair processes usually react badly. They may retaliate, for example, by stealing from their employers. Or they may withdraw, such as by not performing well at their jobs. What happens, however, if retaliation or withdrawal is not possible or is not in employees' best interests? Is there anything they can do to make the best of a difficult situation?

This is the question Marius Van Dijke, Niels Van Quaquebeke, and I set out to answer in a multi-industry study of employees from the Netherlands. Participants rated the fairness of the procedures used to arrive at outcomes they care about, such as salary and promotion opportunities. For example, they were asked questions such as "How much have you been able to express your views and feelings during those procedures?" and "How much have these procedures been applied consistently?" Independently, one of their coworkers evaluated their job performance, for instance, how willing they were to do more than required ("How much does this employee go above and beyond the call of duty when serving customers?").

Not surprisingly, many employees who perceived their organization's procedures as unfair did not perform well.

However, this was not always the case. It all depended on how much those on the receiving end of the unfairness regulated their negative emotions. Those who regulated negative emotions effectively performed well even in the face of being treated unfairly.[22] One way to regulate negative emotion is by appraising potentially emotionally arousing situations in ways that make them less loaded. For example, when employees are receiving a performance appraisal from their boss, rather than worrying about the impression they are making they should try to view the conversation as an opportunity to receive feedback to help them achieve the potential that their employer sees in them. The results showed that emotional reappraisal served as a buffer by getting employees on the receiving end of low procedural fairness to not see it as a sign of personal disrespect. For instance, employees may have reasoned, "Yes, my boss was unfair, but s/he is stressed," or "This procedure is not really all that unfair because my boss behaves this way toward everyone."

The scale used to measure "emotional reappraisal" in the above-mentioned study was developed by the Stanford University psychologist James Gross (see appendix H). You can see that it talks in generalities, for example, "When I want to feel less negative emotion, I change the way I'm thinking about the situation" or "When I'm faced with a stressful situation, I make myself think about it in a way that helps me stay calm."[23] Andy Molinsky and Joshua Margolis offer specific examples of what it looks like to do these things in their study of managers facing the unenviable task of telling employees that they are being laid off. Some of the effective methods managers used, as summarized in table 6.1 with illustrative examples, were justifying one's actions, quarantining emotion, releasing emotion, and diverting attention.[24]

Table 6.1. Managers' Emotional Regulation Strategies When Delivering Bad News

Strategy	Definition	Illustration
Justifying one's actions	Providing oneself with a convincing justification for one's actions in order to reduce guilt and personal distress.	"I look at the job market. It's hot right now. A lot of people at Apparel Inc. are young and have a lot to offer. Even the outplacement people told us ahead of time that Apparel Inc. people are employable. They almost made us feel better about it of what we were doing."
Quarantining emotion	Distancing oneself from one's emotions in order to deliver the difficult message.	"I find it's personally easier to put the emotions on the back burner. I'll deal with them prior to or after the fact, but during the meeting, I'm there to do a job and I just focus on my performance and get the job done."
Releasing emotion	Exhaling, or releasing, negative emotion to prepare for, or help recover from, a difficult conversation.	"Misery loves company; if you feel that other people are experiencing the same types of pain you are feeling, just to talk about it and talk about how the process makes you feel brings on a deep sigh of relief."
Diverting attention	Focusing on something other than one's own distress or that of the affected employee in order to facilitate delivery of the negative message.	"If I didn't have a checklist per se or even a mental checklist I think I definitely would have gotten off track, because you're anxious and the person's anxious and you might start to get to a point and they might cut you off with something else, then you just forget what your point is."

Source: A. L. Molinsky and J. D. Margolis (2006), "The Emotional Tightrope of Downsizing: Hidden Challenges for Leaders and Their Organizations," *Organizational Dynamics* 35: 154. Reproduced with permission from Elsevier.

Although somewhat different, all four methods require balancing acts on the part of managers. For example, justifying is a way for managers to get their guilt under control, but if they go too far they may come across as blaming the victim. Quarantining emotion or diverting attention helps managers focus on the task of delivering the news but runs the risk of making them seem callous and unconcerned. Releasing emotions is a fine idea as long as it is truly done before or after and not during the actual delivery of the bad news. While regulating negative emotion is challenging, it also is doable. The more managers can regulate negative emotion that inevitably accompanies the process of delivering bad news to people, the more likely those on the receiving end will react constructively rather than destructively.

What Organizations Can Do

Some managers are able to take it upon themselves to deal with the obstacles to delivering a high-quality process, but that is only part of the equation. The other part is what organizations can do to help managers deal with the obstacles. Some provide training. Studies have shown that teaching people how to be fair in planning and implementing decisions has positive effects on both the managers and their direct reports. In one study, managers who went through training changed their behavior to be fairer; for example, they were more likely to include others in decision making, to provide explanations for their decisions, and to treat people with dignity and respect.[25] Of course, an important question is whether participating in such a training program brings about lasting change. In this same study, participants who underwent process fairness training became more confident in their ability to behave fairly, which boded well for them to continue to behave fairly long after the training ended.

Equally important, the training program had demonstrable effects on the direct reports of managers who had gone through it. For instance, direct reports were more likely to do more than their jobs formally required them to do, which studies have shown is a clear indicator that their bosses were in fact treating them more fairly.[26] In another study the fairness training allowed direct reports to feel less personal strain in the face of a rather stressful event: being forced to take a pay cut. In this study, as part of a cost-cutting initiative, the employer (a hospital) changed the way in which employees (nurses) were compensated. Rather than being paid on an hourly basis, which allowed the nurses to be paid for overtime, they were now given a salary for working the same number of hours. This change in compensation structure reduced the nurses' pay by about 10 percent. Prior to the pay cut, some of the nurses' supervisors took part in a process fairness training program whereas others did not. The nurses of supervisors who had been trained experienced significantly less insomnia relative to the nurses whose supervisors had not done the training. To put it another way, the nurses whose supervisors had not been trained lost not only money but also sleep.[27]

Two other things about the process fairness training program should be noted, both of which are consistent with important themes of this book. First, the content of the training program was well within participants' intellectual grasp. They were trained in behaviors that were pretty straightforward but often get overlooked in the upheaval associated with change. These included treating others with dignity and respect, showing emotional support, making themselves accessible to their employees, and providing clear and reasonable explanations for why the pay cuts were being introduced. Second, the costs of the training program, while not trivial in terms of time and money, were not very high either. The total amount of training consisted of eight hours, carried out on two consecutive days in four-hour sessions. Once again, we see evidence of how processes that are not all that complicated and not all that costly can pay big dividends.

Whether done in the context of a training program or elsewhere, it is key for organizations to help managers regulate the negative emotions they experience in the process of making and carrying out decisions. Three ways in which organizations can play a constructive role are as follows: (1) by leading managers to expect that negative emotions are likely to be experienced; (2) by making discussion of negative emotions and the challenges in regulating them a legitimate topic of conversation; and (3) by helping managers reappraise the meaning of the events that gave rise to the negative emotional experiences.

SOMETHING TO BE EXPECTED

Because delivering a high-quality process is easier said than done, organizations should communicate to managers that they should expect to encounter obstacles. Being able to anticipate the painful emotions that managers may face is an important first step in dealing with them. When we expect difficult situations they are much less distressing than when those same situations catch us by surprise. This is the reason why, for instance, surgical patients are told in advance what to expect after their procedures.

The same rationale applies to why it is helpful for employers to tell prospective employees about what they can expect on the job. All too often, employers do not tell it like it is. In their effort to make themselves desirable to would-be employees, they tend to put their best foot forward. Although doing so may attract people to the firm, it may undercut the firm's ability to retain them. When the reality of the job is different from what people were led to expect, disillusionment and, with that, an early exit are more likely to occur. One way to reduce the problem of early turnover is by providing potential employees with a Realistic Job Preview, in which they learn about not only the upsides but also the downsides of the job.[28] Letting people know the reality of what they are getting into helps them be resilient in the face of the downsides they will inevitably encounter.

The same dynamics apply when managers are told in advance about the obstacles to delivering a high-quality process. If managers are given a "Realistic Process Preview" about the difficulties they may experience when trying to be fair or when trying to follow change management principles (as set forth in chapter 3), they may be resilient in the face of such difficulties. A key component of a Realistic Process Preview is to forewarn people of how emotionally challenging the process may be. If the same obstacles catch managers by surprise they are likely to go into a self-protective shell. For example, in the downsizing organization studied by Molinsky and Margolis, an HR executive went into a meeting in which the news of a layoff had to be delivered to an employee. The HR representative was accompanied by a burly and experienced business unit head who believed that he could handle being the bearer of bad news. "I got this," he confidently said to the HR manager. However, once the meeting started the business unit head was paralyzed by painful emotions, both his own and those of the person being laid off, forcing the HR executive to take over.[29] Just as people given the Realistic Job Preview remain present in the sense that they are less likely to exit the company earlier than they would have otherwise, those given the Realistic Process Preview may remain present in the sense of not withdrawing into themselves. They can focus on what others need and, as a consequence, handle processes well.

SOMETHING TO BE DISCUSSED

Experiencing negative emotion is a potential obstacle to handling the process well. Further contributing to the burden is when people believe that the negative emotion they are experiencing is not open for discussion. It's the proverbial elephant in the room. Not only is it felt, but it is draining, in part because people believe that they have to act as if they are not experiencing the negative emotion. After all, they don't want to be seen as "unprofessional." What if it were acceptable, however, to talk about the elephant in the room? It wouldn't make the negative emotion go away, but it would make the experience of it more manageable and, in so doing, better position people to deliver a high-quality process.

A number of years ago I saw these dynamics unfold firsthand. The CEO of a company I was working with had to make the tough decision to close a plant. The product made at the plant had been the core of the company's identity for many years, but this was no longer the case because of the product's declining profitability. The CEO did a great job making the business case for why it made sense to close the plant. But he didn't stop there. In the most authentic of ways, he told the team about the emotional anguish he had experienced in making this decision and how he was very conflicted about it, but he also told them how, at the end of the day, he was confident that this was the right decision for the long-term interests of the company. In doing so, he legitimized both the experience and the expression of painful emotions, which was greatly appreciated by the middle managers below him, who were dealing with related difficulties since they had the responsibility of actually implementing the plant closing. In chapter 3 we discussed how part of a well-managed change process consists of senior executives role modeling the new behaviors called for by the change. This executive didn't simply role model the new behaviors; he made it permissible to acknowledge the emotional nature of the decision and the conflict he experienced but also communicated that the organization nonetheless had to make decisions that were in its best long-term interests.

The team below him still had to do the tough job of implementing the plant closing. But because the CEO took the time to express the difficulty of what they were all experiencing, they were able to get through it in ways that preserved the dignity and respect of everyone who was affected. Inspired by the CEO's openness, the team even took it upon themselves to debrief with one another about the emotional turmoil they were going through, which also made their experience a lot more bearable. In a sense, the CEO implied that it would have been unprofessional for his team *not* to allow the discussion of negative emotion to be a legitimate topic of conversation.

SOMETHING TO REAPPRAISE

Our discussion of what individuals can do showed that those who reappraised negative events remained engaged with organizational priorities. (See appendix H for general descriptions of reappraisals and table 6.1 for specific examples of the form they may take.) Although individuals may take it upon themselves to reappraise, for each of the examples described in table 6.1 there are things organizations can also do to make them happen. For instance, for the strategy known as justifying, managers are better equipped to do so if their bosses give them a clear, credible explanation for why a particular course of action is being taken.

The strategy of diverting attention is also amenable to organizational influence. A particularly deft example was shown by administrators of Wesleyan University during the graduation ceremony in 2009, the year that our son graduated. Several weeks earlier, a student was tragically killed in a shooting incident in the campus bookstore. It cast a pall over the entire university community in the weeks leading up to the graduation. At the graduation ceremony the university paid homage to the slain student and her family in a very moving way. While this was a significant part of the graduation ceremony, it did not dominate the proceedings. This was because after due respects were paid, the president of the university, Michael Roth, artfully refocused everyone's attention on the regularly scheduled order of the day: the graduation ceremony for the class of 2009.

Molinsky and Margolis's analysis of attention-diverting strategies suggests that there are several ways in which organizations can implement them. For instance, when organizations provide clear and socially sensitive guidelines on how to deliver tough decisions, managers may be able to focus more on the delivery process than on the emotionally painful substance of the decision itself. Molinsky and Margolis also suggested that some managers in their study coped by deliberately focusing their attention away from what they had to do and toward other positive aspects of their lives. As one of them put it, "I try to think about other things, such as my family, you know, the games that my kids are going to or playing that evening."[30]

In like fashion, there are things organizations can do to influence managers' focus of attention. Moreover, specific forms of redirected attention may especially help managers get through tough times. Attention focused on reaffirming people's sense of self is likely to be particularly constructive. In the previously mentioned study I did with Marius Van Dijke and Niels Van Quaquebeke, we found that reappraisal buffered the negative effect of being on the receiving end of low procedural fairness by keeping people from feeling bad about themselves. For example, those who reappraised more in response to low procedural fairness agreed more with statements such as "I believe I have a good reputation in this organization" and "Most members of the organization respect me.[31] If diverted attention is most useful if it goes toward something self-affirming, then the ideas summarized in figure 4.1 may provide some useful leads on the kinds of things that organizations can do.

And Finally, Develop Engaging and Enabling Structures

My closing suggestions of what organizations can do harken back to where we started. The opening scenario in chapter 1 cautioned organizations not to emphasize outcomes only, in which they essentially tell their people, "I don't care how you get there, just get there." Of course outcomes matter, but they also have to be arrived at in the right way. It is not outcome *or* process, it is outcome *and* process. Most organizations do a decent job of emphasizing the importance of outcomes, although even here more work needs to be done. There is growing recognition that indicators of how well an organization is performing may take a variety of forms, as reflected in the fact that there is more talk today about "stakeholders" rather than simply "shareholders." Still, most organizations need to do a much better job of adding process considerations to the mix of important criteria.

In chapter 3 I talked about the need for organizations to put engaging and enabling structures in place when trying to bring about change. Such structures consist of formal organizational arrangements that engage people with the change (make them want to go there) and equip them to change (make them able to go there). Engaging and enabling structures also may help managers deal with the obstacles they face in delivering a high-quality process. Some obstacles are motivational, in which managers do not want to do what a high-quality process entails. One way to counteract motivational obstacles is by incentivizing managers to care not only about the outcomes but also about the process.

An excellent example is the diversity and inclusion initiative at PepsiCo. The CEO who started it, Steve Reinemund, was concerned about how the company was managing its diverse employees, namely people of color, ethnic minority group members, and women. When Reinemund took the helm in 2000, the company's record in attracting, retaining, and promoting diverse employees was woeful. He spearheaded a bold change in how managers were formally evaluated and rewarded. In addition to the usual "business" criteria (bottom-line profitability), Reinemund introduced "people" dimensions, with one such dimension being how well managers performed with respect to diversity and inclusion.

The people dimensions included bottom-line outcomes. Moreover, the evaluation process started at the top. Reinemund and his senior management team were compensated with respect not only to financial results but also to how well they did in attracting, retaining, and promoting diverse employees. In fact, in one year the company did very well financially but poorly with respect to the diversity dimensions. Exemplifying the need for change agents to walk the talk (and against the strong advice from PepsiCo's board of directors), Reinemund willingly accepted a much lower level of compensation than would have been the case prior to the diversity and inclusion initiative, when only traditional financial criteria were used.[32]

In rolling out the diversity and inclusion initiative to the rest of the organization, PepsiCo did not simply focus on the outcome criteria of attracting, retaining, and promoting diverse employees. The company also identified the behaviors that managers needed to exhibit while trying to reach these goals. In this way PepsiCo communicated to managers that their evaluation also depended on the process. It was important for them to arrive at their targets, but it was also important for them to arrive at their targets in the right way. Allan Church, an organizational psychologist at PepsiCo, led the design and institutionalization of an employee survey and manager feedback program to support the diversity and inclusion initiative. For instance, the compensation of senior leaders depended on how well they were evaluated on behaviors such as

"Demonstrates sensitivity and awareness of cross-cultural implications when conducting business or executing initiatives." For the next level of management, compensation depended on how much they "fostered a positive and inclusive work environment where all people feel respected and valued for their contributions." And the rewards given to all employees were based on behaviors such as "Demonstrates sensitivity to differences when dealing with people from different cultural backgrounds or other differences."[33]

In the spirit of truth in advertising, I should emphasize that it takes work to develop an appraisal system in which decisions and decision makers are evaluated on the basis of process and outcome. For instance, it is necessary to identify the behaviors that comprise a high-quality process, to assess the behaviors accurately, and to provide feedback in ways that people are willing and able to take in. All of these take time and effort, which may explain why many companies simply use outcome criteria. However, those who do not also take the process into account in evaluating decisions and decision makers do so at their own peril. Bad processes usually lead to bad outcomes; it's just a matter of when that will happen. Those who "don't have the time" to appraise decisions and decision makers based on the process will be even less likely to have the time later to deal with the difficult situation they created by not going about things the right way in the first place. Once again, pay now or pay (even more) later.

Appraisal and evaluation systems are not the only enabling structures that can help managers overcome obstacles to a high-quality process. Some organizations use After Action Reviews (AARs), in which decision makers take a hardnosed look at how to improve both the outcomes and the process. Naturally, the value of an AAR depends on how it is done. The work of Marilyn Darling, Charles Parry, and Joseph Moore illustrates a particularly constructive way to do an AAR. One of their many note-worthy observations is that the word "after" in an AAR is a bit misleading. A key aspect of a successful AAR is the "Before Action Review," in which decision makers iden-tify what they intend to accomplish and how that will be measured, the challenges they expect to encounter, what has been learned from similar projects in the past, and what they believe will enable them to succeed this time. Answering these questions beforehand sets the stage for a more useful AAR later.[34] Training programs such as the one on process fairness are yet another enabling structure that may help managers overcome obstacles.[35]

Engaging and enabling structures make process con-siderations more impactful at two levels, the concrete and the symbolic. Concretely, they can motivate people to care about the how, as in the case of the appraisal system accom-panying the diversity and inclusion program at PepsiCo, and they can equip people to be better at the how, as in the case of AARs or training programs. Equally important is the symbolic value of engaging and enabling structures. The very fact that an organization makes great efforts to put them in place sends a loud and clear message: the pro-cess matters.

Chapter Summary

Given how much the process matters, we need to under-stand why managers often fail to go about doing things in the right way. Accordingly, this chapter shined the spot-light on the barriers to managers' delivery of a high-quality process. I considered three types of obstacles: knowledge based, skills based, and desire based. Sometimes managers do not know that (or how much) the process matters. Even when they do know, they still may fail to deliver a high-quality process, either because of a lack of skill or because of a lack of will. Having delineated the obstacles, we can talk more sensibly about what can be done, by individual managers and their employers alike, to overcome them.

Handling the process well requires being able to deal with emotionally trying circumstances. For example, anxiety, anger, and guilt, which go with the turf of planning and implementing decisions, need to be regulated. These and other negative emotions can make managers self-focused, whereas handling the process well requires their attention to be other-directed. Managers who engage in the emotion regulation strategy of reappraisal are less self-preoccupied and more other-directed. Table 6.1 provides specific examples of what reappraisal looks like in the context of the managerially painful activity of telling people that they are being laid off.

Just as individuals can take it upon themselves to regulate negative emotions, organizations can create conditions that make it more likely for individuals to do so. For instance, organizations should help managers expect negative emotions, talk openly about them, and reappraise them. All of these actions will help managers be resilient in the face of emotionally difficult situations, thereby paving the way for them to deliver a high-quality process. Furthermore, formal organizational arrangements such as appraisal and reward systems, AARs, and training programs can encourage managers to handle processes well by engaging and equipping them and also by symbolically conveying the message that the process matters.

Appendix A

The Change Implementation Survey

The following questionnaire is designed to help managers diagnose their strengths and weaknesses as agents of organizational change. Please do not use this instrument without the permission of Joel Brockner.

Your Name: _____

Instructions: Leaders often have to play a significant role in planning and implementing change within organizations. Change can be organization wide, such as growth, restructuring, reengineering, introduction of new technology, mergers/acquisitions, or relocations. Change also could be smaller in scope, such as those that take place within a team or function. Sometimes change can even be on a smaller scale, such as trying to change the behavior of someone who works for you or with whom you work. The following questions pertain to behavioral tendencies when one is trying to effect change, no matter how large or small. Please indicate the frequency with which you believe you exhibit each of the following behaviors. Use the following scale:

1	2	3	4	5
Does not apply to me at all		Applies to me somewhat		Applies to me a great deal

____ 1. I clearly describe to people <u>why</u> the situation as it exists prior to the change is not acceptable.

____ 2. I help people have access to information (such as competitive conditions and firm performance) that allows people to see for themselves when and why change is necessary.

____ 3. I introduce change in anticipation of problems, not only in response to problems that have already surfaced.

____ 4. I create a sense of urgency for change even when recent performance has been favorable.

____ 5. I communicate to people that they should expect the organization to undergo change on a regular basis.

Note: The word "vision" in questions 6 through 9 refers to a mental image of the desired future state of the organization.

____ 6. I remind people of our common vision, throughout the change effort.

____ 7. I communicate a vision that people can easily understand.

____ 8. I communicate a vision that people feel enthusiastic about.

____ 9. I make people want to "buy-in" (be committed) to the vision.

____ 10. When telling people about the need to change our current practices, I show respect toward those practices that have served us well in the past.

____ 11. When describing the nature of the change, I also describe the things that will not be changing.

____ 12. When introducing change, I "walk the talk"; that is, I serve as a role model for the new behaviors that are needed.

____ 13. In the change process, I make efforts to ensure that people will be working on at least some tasks at which they are likely to succeed.

____ 14. I positively publicize the activities of people that are supportive of the change effort.

____ 15. I find out the opinions of key parties about the change, that is, whether the parties are likely to favor it or oppose it.

____ 16. I develop an action plan on how to bring out the support of those who are likely to favor the change.

____ 17. I develop an action plan on how to deal with those who are likely to oppose the change.

____ 18. I devote extra attention to "opinion leaders" to gain their support of the change effort.

Note: The word "plan" in questions 19 and 20 refers to a description of the concrete steps that need to be taken to actually implement the change.

____ 19. In crafting the plan, I seek input from numerous others on how to best implement the plan.

____ 20. I distribute the plan to the right personnel to gain support for it.

Note: The words "enabling structures" in questions 21 and 22 refer to formal organization arrangements designed to support a new way of operating. They include, but are not limited to, hiring practices, training programs, career paths, measurement and reward systems, organizational structures, task teams, etc.

___ 21. I take an active role in the <u>creation</u> of enabling structures, rather than leaving that job to others.

___ 22. I communicate how changes in the enabling structures symbolize the direction of the intended change.

___ 23. I communicate important information about the change effort in multiple different ways.

___ 24. After communicating information to people, I assess how they have interpreted the information.

___ 25. I give people the opportunity to initiate communications about the change effort (e.g., through an open-door policy, management by walking around, question-and-answer sessions at meetings, etc.)

___ 26. I provide ample advance notification of important changes that will affect people.

___ 27. When managing change, I make extra efforts to treat people with dignity and respect

___ 28. I give people considerable input into how the change should be implemented.

___ 29. I seek feedback about the consequences of the change effort while the change is in process.

___ 30. I make adjustments in response to the feedback received about the change effort.

___ 31. I show people sensitivity to the possibility that the change may be difficult for them.

___ 32. I make opportunities for people to learn or be trained in new skills required by the change effort.

___ 33. I openly allow people to talk about their reactions to the change.

___ 34. During a change effort, I provide opportunities for people to do things that put them "in control."

Appendix B

Scoring Guide for the Change Implementation Survey

Action Step	Survey Items		Personal Average
Analyze Need for Change (D)	#1–2	(Sum of Items 1–2)/2 =	_____
Create a Sense of Urgency (D)	#3–5	(Sum of Items 3–5)/3 =	_____
Vision (V)	#6–9	(Sum of Items 6–9)/4 =	_____
Separate from the Past (P)	#10–11	(Sum of Items 10–11)/2 =	_____
Develop a Strong Leader Role (P)	#12–14	(Sum of Items 12–14)/3 =	_____
Line Up Political Sponsorship (P)	#15–18	(Sum of Items 15–18)/4 =	_____
Craft an Implementation Plan (P)	#19–20	(Sum of Items 19–20)/2 =	_____
Develop Enabling Structures (P)	#21–22	(Sum of Items 21–22)/2 =	_____
Communicate, Involve, Be Honest (P)	#23–28	(Sum of Items 23–28)/6 =	_____
Monitor and Refine (P)	#29–30	(Sum of Items 29–30)/2 =	_____
Reduce the Costs of Change (C)	#31–34	(Sum of Items 31–34)/4 =	_____

Change = (D × V × P) > C

D   refers to surfacing dissatisfaction with the current state
V   refers to providing a vision of the future state
P   refers to the process of moving from the current state to the future state
C   refers to reducing the costs of change

The letters in parentheses refer to the category to which the action step belongs.

Appendix C

Measure of Regulatory Focus

Source: P. Lockwood, C. H. Jordan, and Z. Kunda (2002), "Motivation by Positive or Negative Role Models: Regulatory Focus Determines Who Will Best Inspire Us," *Journal of Personality and Social Psychology* 83: 854–64. Copyright © 2002 by the American Psychological Association. Reproduced with permission.

Please indicate how much you believe each of the following statements applies to you.

1	2	3	4	5
Does not apply to me <u>at all</u>		Applies to me <u>somewhat</u>		Applies to me <u>a great deal</u>

____ 1. In general, I am focused on preventing negative events in my life.

____ 2. I am anxious that I will fall short of my responsibilities and obligations.

____ 3. I often think about the person I am afraid I might become in the future.

____ 4. I often worry that I will fail to accomplish my academic goals.

____ 5. I often imagine myself experiencing bad things that I fear might happen to me.

___ 6. I frequently think about how I can prevent failures in my life.

___ 7. I am more oriented toward preventing losses than I am toward achieving gains.

___ 8. My major goal in school right now is to avoid becoming an academic failure.

___ 9. I see myself as someone who is primarily striving to become the self I "ought" to be—to fulfill my duties, responsibilities, and obligations.

___ 10. I frequently imagine how I will achieve my hopes and aspirations.

___ 11. I often think about the person I would ideally like to be in the future.

___ 12. I typically focus on the success I hope to achieve in the future.

___ 13. I often think about how I will achieve academic success.

___ 14. My major goal in school right now is to achieve my academic ambitions.

___ 15. I see myself as someone who is primarily striving to reach my "ideal self"—to fulfill my hopes, wishes, and aspirations.

___ 16. In general, I am focused on achieving positive outcomes in my life.

___ 17. I often imagine myself experiencing good things that I hope will happen to me.

___ 18. Overall, I am more oriented toward achieving success than preventing failure.

Items 1–9 measure prevention focus. The more you endorse those items, the stronger your prevention focus.

Items 10–18 measure promotion focus. The more you endorse those items, the stronger your promotion focus.

Measure of Work Regulatory Focus

Source: M. J. Neubert, K. M. Kacmar, D. S. Carlson, L. B. Chonko, and J. A. Roberts (2008), "Regulatory Focus as a Mediator of the Influence of Initiating Structure and Servant Leadership on Employee Behavior," *Journal of Applied Psychology* 93: 1220–33. Copyright © 2008 by the American Psychological Association. Reproduced with permission.

Please indicate how much you believe each of the following statements applies to you.

1	2	3	4	5
Does not apply to me at all		Applies to me somewhat		Applies to me a great deal

___ 1. I concentrate on completing my work and tasks correctly to increase my job security.

___ 2. At work I focus my attention on completing my assigned responsibilities.

___ 3. Fulfilling my work duties is very important to me.

___ 4. At work, I strive to live up to the responsibilities and duties given to me by others.

___ 5. At work, I am often focused on accomplishing tasks that will support my need for security.

___ 6. I do everything I can to avoid loss at work.

___ 7. Job security is an important factor for me in any job search.

___ 8. I focus my attention on avoiding failure at work.

___ 9. I am very careful to avoid exposing myself to potential losses at work.

___ 10. I take chances at work to maximize my goals for advancement.

___ 11. I tend to take risks at work in order to achieve success.

___ 12. If I had an opportunity to participate on a high-risk, high-reward project I would definitely take it.

___ 13. If my job did not allow for advancement, I would likely find a new one.

___ 14. A chance to grow is an important factor for me when looking for a job.

___ 15. I focus on accomplishing job tasks that will further my advancement.

___ 16. I spend a great deal of time envisioning how to fulfill my aspirations.

___ 17. My work priorities are impacted by a clear picture of what I aspire to be.

___ 18. At work, I am motivated by my hopes and aspirations.

Items 1–9 measure prevention focus. The more you endorse those items, the stronger your prevention focus.

Items 10–18 measure promotion focus. The more you endorse those items, the stronger your promotion focus.

Measure of "Openers"

Source: L. C. Miller, J. H. Berg, and R. L. Archer (1983), "Openers: Individuals Who Elicit Intimate Self-Disclosure," *Journal of Personality and Social Psychology* 44: 1234–44. Copyright © 1983 by the American Psychological Association. Reproduced with permission.

Please indicate how much you believe each of the following statements applies to you.

1	2	3	4	5
Does not apply to me at all		Applies to me somewhat		Applies to me a great deal

____ 1. People frequently tell me about themselves.

____ 2. I've been told that I'm a good listener.

____ 3. I'm very accepting of others.

____ 4. People trust me with their secrets.

____ 5. I easily get people to "open up."

____ 6. People feel relaxed around me.

____ 7. I enjoy listening to people.

____ 8. I'm sympathetic to people's problems.

____ 9. I encourage people to tell me how they are feeling.

____ 10. I can keep people talking about themselves.

Allport-Vernon-Lindzey Values

Source: G. W. Allport, P. E. Vernon, and G. Lindzey (1970), *Study of Values, Revised 3rd Edition* (Chicago: Riverside Publishing). Courtesy of Robert Allport. Reproduced with permission.

1. **Theoretical.** The theoretical person is primarily interested in the discovery of truth, in the systematic ordering of knowledge. The individual's interests are empirical, critical, and rational.

2. **Economic.** The economic person is primarily oriented toward what is useful. This individual is interested in practical affairs of the business world, in the use of economic resources, and in the accumulation of tangible wealth. This person is thoroughly "practical" and fits well the stereotype of the American business person.

3. **Aesthetic.** The aesthetic person's chief interest is the artistic aspects of life, although the person need not be a creative artist. Form and harmony are valued; the individual views experience in terms of grace, symmetry, or harmony.

4. **Social.** The essential value for the social person is love of people—the altruistic or philanthropic aspect of love. This individual values people as ends, and tends to be kind, sympathetic, unselfish.

5. **Political.** The political person is characteristically oriented toward power, not necessarily in politics, but in

whatever area he or she functions. Most leaders have a high power orientation.

6. **Religious.** The religious person is one whose mental structure is permanently directed to the creation of the highest and absolutely satisfying value experience. The dominant value is unity. The person seeks to relate to the universe in a meaningful way and has a mystical orientation.

Appendix G
Measure of Moral Identity

Source: K. Aquino and A. Reed II (2002), "The Self-Importance of Moral Identity," *Journal of Personality and Social Psychology* 83: 1423–40. Copyright © 2002 by the American Psychological Association. Reproduced with permission.

Moral identity measures how much moral traits are central to how we define ourselves. Some people consider morality to be more central to their identity than others.

Instructions: Here are some characteristics that might describe a person:

> *Caring, Compassionate, Fair, Friendly, Generous, Helpful, Hardworking, Honest, Kind*

The person with these characteristics could be you or it could be someone else. For a moment, visualize in your mind the kind of person who has these characteristics. Imagine how that person would think, feel, and act. When you have a clear image of what this person would be like, answer the following questions.

Answer anywhere from 1 to 7, in which 1 means "Strongly Disagree" and 7 means "Strongly Agree."

1. It would make me feel good to be a person who has these characteristics.

2. Being someone who has these characteristics is an important part of who I am.

3. I would be ashamed to be a person who had these characteristics.

4. Having these characteristics is not really important to me.

5. I strongly desire to have these characteristics.

Scoring Instructions: Subtract your answers to Questions #3 and #4 from the number "eight." Then add all five scores together. The higher the score, the more that morality is central to how you define yourself.

Appendix H

Measure of Emotional Reappraisal

Source: J. J. Gross and O. P. John (2003), "Individual Differences in Two Emotion Regulation Processes: Implications for Affect, Relationships, and Well-Being," *Journal of Personality and Social Psychology* 85: 348–62. Courtesy of James Gross. Reproduced with permission.

Instructions: Please indicate how much each of the following statements applies to you. Use the following rating scale:

Write 1 if you <u>strongly disagree</u> with the statement

Write 2 if you <u>moderately disagree</u> with the statement

Write 3 if you <u>neither agree nor disagree</u> with the statement

Write 4 if you <u>moderately agree</u> with the statement

Write 5 if you <u>strongly agree</u> with the statement

___ 1. I control my emotions by changing the way I think about the situation I'm in.

___ 2. When I want to feel less negative emotion, I change the way I'm thinking about the situation.

___ 3. When I want to feel more positive emotion, I change the way I'm thinking about the situation.

___ 4. When I want to feel more positive emotion (such as joy or amusement), I change what I'm thinking about.

___ 5. When I want to feel less negative emotion (such as sadness or anger), I change what I'm thinking about.

___ 6. When I'm faced with a stressful situation, I make myself think about it in a way that helps me stay calm.

Notes

Chapter 1 → Introduction

1. B. Carter, "Leno Blesses 'Tonight Show' Succession Plan," *New York Times*, April 3, 2013, C7.
2. J. Brockner and B. M. Wiesenfeld (1996), "An Integrative Framework for Explaining Reactions to Decisions: The Interactive Effects of Outcomes and Procedures," *Psychological Bulletin* 120: 189–208.
3. E. A. Locke (1968), "Toward a Theory of Task Motivation and Incentives," *Organizational Behavior and Human Performance* 3: 157–89.
4. E. Langer and J. Rodin (1976), "The Effects of Choice and Enhanced Personal Responsibility for the Aged: A Field Experiment in an Institutional Setting," *Journal of Personality and Social Psychology* 34: 191–98.
5. J. S. Adams (1965), "Inequity in Social Exchange," in *Advances in Experimental Social Psychology*, ed. L. Berkowitz (New York: Academic Press), 267–99.
6. J. Thibaut and L. Walker (1975), *Procedural Justice: A Psychological Analysis* (Hillsdale, NJ: Erlbaum); E. A. Lind and T. R. Tyler (1988), *The Social Psychology of Procedural Justice* (New York: Plenum Press).
7. E. Sherman (2014), "Ford Fires 100 Factory Workers by Robocall on Halloween," http://jobs.aol.com/articles/2014/11/04/fired-fires-factory-workers-robocall-halloween/?icid=maing-grid7|htmlws-main-bb|dl18|sec1_lnk2%26pLid%3D557327.
8. http://www.smh.com.au/technology/technology-news/oops-email-misfire-sacks-all-1300-staff-20120424-1xflp.html.
9. E. A. Lind, J. Greenberg, K. S. Scott, and T. D. Welchans (2000), "The Winding Road from Employee to Complainant: Situational and Psychological Determinants of Wrongful-Termination Claims," *Administrative Science Quarterly* 45: 557–90.

10. W. L. Levinson, D. L. Roter, J. P. Mullooly, V. T. Dull, and R. M. Frankel (1997), "Physician-Patient Communication: The Relationship with Malpractice Claims among Primary Care Physicians and Surgeons," *Journal of the American Medical Association* 277: 553–59.
11. E. Rosenthal, "Pre-Med's New Priorities: Heart and Soul and Social Science," *New York Times,* April 13, 2012.
12. J. R. Hackman (1987), "The Design of Work Teams," in *Handbook of Organizational Behavior,* ed. J. Lorsch (Englewood Cliffs, NJ: Prentice-Hall), 323.
13. M. Beer (1988), "Leading Change," Harvard Business School Background Note 488-037.
14. C. M. Steele (1988), "The Psychology of Self-Affirmation: Sustaining the Integrity of the Self," in *Advances in Experimental Social Psychology,* ed. L. Berkowitz (New York: Academic Press), 261–302.
15. D. M. Cable, F. Gino, and B. R. Staats (2013), "Breaking Them in or Eliciting Their Best? Reframing Socialization around Newcomers' Authentic Self-Expression," *Administrative Science Quarterly* 58: 1–36.

Chapter 2 → It's Only Fair

1. Adams, "Inequity in Social Exchange."
2. Thibaut and Walker, *Procedural Justice;* Lind and Tyler, *The Social Psychology of Procedural Justice;* R. Folger and J. Greenberg (1985), "Procedural Justice: An Interpretive Analysis of Personnel Systems," in *Research in Personnel and Human Resources Management,* ed. K. Rowland and G. Ferris (Greenwich, CT: JAI Press), 141–83.
3. G. S. Leventhal, J. Karuza, and W. R. Fry (1980), "Beyond Fairness: A Theory of Allocation Preferences," in *Justice and Social Interaction,* ed. G. Mikula (New York: Springer-Verlag), 167–218.
4. R. J. Bies (1987), "The Predicament of Injustice: The Management of Moral Outrage," in *Research in Organizational Behavior,* ed. L. L. Cummings and B. M. Staw (Greenwich, CT: JAI Press), 289–319.
5. Brockner and Wiesenfeld, "An Integrative Framework for Explaining Reactions to Decisions."
6. J. Brockner, M. Konovsky, R. Cooper-Schneider, R. Folger, C. Martin, and R. J. Bies (1994), "The Interactive Effects of Procedural Justice and Outcome Negativity on the Victims and Survivors of Job Loss," *Academy of Management Journal* 37: 397–409.
7. J. Brockner (2006), "Why It's So Hard to Be Fair," *Harvard Business Review* 84: 122–29.

8. J. Greenberg (1990a), "Looking Fair vs. Being Fair: Managing Impressions of Organizational Justice," in *Research in Organizational Behavior*, ed. B. M. Staw and L. L. Cummings (Greenwich, CT: JAI Press), 111–57.

9. Lind et al., "The Winding Road from Employee to Complainant"; Brockner et al., "The Interactive Effects of Procedural Justice and Outcome Negativity on the Victims and Survivors of Job Loss."

10. N. I. Eisenberger, M. D. Lieberman, and K. D. Williams (2003), "Does Rejection Hurt? An fMRI Study of Social Exclusion," *Science* 302: 290–92.

11. K. Van den Bos, J. Ham, E. A. Lind, M. Simonis, W. J. van Essen, and M. Rijpkema (2008), "Justice and the Human Alarm System: The Impact of Exclamation Points and Flashing Lights on the Justice Judgment Process," *Journal of Experimental Social Psychology* 44: 201–19.

12. R. C. Mayer, J. H. Davis, and F. D. Schoorman (1995), "An Integrative Model of Organizational Trust," *Academy of Management Review* 20: 709–34; D. M. Rousseau, S. B. Sitkin, R. S. Burt, and C. Camerer (1998), "Not So Different After All: A Cross-Discipline View of Trust," *Academy of Management Review* 23: 393–404.

13. J. Brockner, P. A. Siegel, J. Daly, T. R. Tyler, and C. Martin (1997), "When Trust Matters: The Moderating Effect of Outcome Favorability," *Administrative Science Quarterly* 42: 558–83.

14. E. C. Bianchi and J. Brockner (2012), "Dispositional Trust Predicts Employees' Perceptions of Procedural Fairness," *Organizational Behavior and Human Decision Processes* 118: 46–59.

15. P. Degocy (2000), "Contagious Justice: Exploring the Social Construction of Justice in Organizations," in *Research in Organizational Behavior*, ed. B. M. Staw and R. I. Sutton (Greenwich, CT: JAI Press), 51–102.

16. K. Van den Bos, J. Bruins, H. A. M. Wilke, and E. Dronkert (1999), "Sometimes Unfair Procedures Have Nice Aspects: On the Psychology of the Fair Process Effect," *Journal of Personality and Social Psychology* 77: 324–36.

17. J. Brockner (2002), "Making Sense of Procedural Fairness: How High Procedural Fairness Can Reduce or Heighten the Influence of Outcome Favorability," *Academy of Management Review* 27: 58–76; J. Brockner (2010), *A Contemporary Look at Organizational Justice: Multiplying Insult Times Injury* (New York: Routledge).

18. R. Janoff-Bulman (1979), "Characterological versus Behavioral Self-Blame: Inquiries into Depression and Rape," *Journal of Personality and Social Psychology* 37: 1798–1809.

19. C. S. Dweck (1999), *Self-Theories: Their Role in Motivation, Personality and Development* (Philadelphia: Psychology Press).

20. A. Grant, "Raising a Moral Child," *New York Times*, April 11, 2014.
21. T. Amabile and S. Kramer (2011), *The Progress Principle: Using Small Wins to Ignite Joy, Engagement, and Creativity at Work* (Boston: Harvard Business School Press).
22. Steele, "The Psychology of Self-Affirmation"; J. Brockner, D. Senior, and W. Welch (2014), "Corporate Volunteerism, the Experience of Self-Integrity, and Organizational Commitment: Evidence from the Field," *Social Justice Research* 27: 1–23.
23. R. Garonzik, J. Brockner, and P. A. Siegel (2000), "Identifying International Assignees at Risk for Premature Departure: The Interactive Effect of Outcome Favorability and Procedural Fairness," *Journal of Applied Psychology* 85: 13–20.
24. J. Greenberg (1994), "Using Socially Fair Treatment to Promote Acceptance of a Work Site Smoking Ban," *Journal of Applied Psychology* 79: 288–97.
25. J. Greenberg (1990b), "Employee Theft as a Reaction to Underpayment Inequity: The Hidden Cost of Pay Cuts," *Journal of Applied Psychology* 75: 561–68.

Chapter 3 → Making Change Happen: It's All (or at Least Largely) in the Process

1. J. O'Neill (2001), "Building Better Global Economic BRICs," Goldman Sachs Global Economic Paper: No. 66.
2. Beer, "Leading Change"; T. J. Jick (2002), "Managing Change," in *The Portable MBA in Management*, 2nd ed., ed. A. Cohen (New York: Wiley); J. P. Kotter (1996), *Leading Change* (Boston: Harvard Business School Press).
3. E. E. Morison (1966), *Men, Machines, and Modern Times* (Cambridge, MA: MIT Press).
4. Beer, "Leading Change."
5. Jick, "Managing Change."
6. E. Langer, A. Blank, and B. Chanowitz (1978), "The Mindlessness of Ostensibly Thoughtful Action: The Role of 'Placebic' Information in Interpersonal Interaction," *Journal of Personality and Social Psychology* 36: 635–42.
7. D. Kahneman and A. Tversky (1984), "Choices, Values, and Frames," *American Psychologist* 39: 341–50.
8. E. T. Higgins (1997), "Beyond Pleasure and Pain," *American Psychologist* 52: 1280–1300.

9. L. C. Idson, N. Liberman, and E. T. Higgins (2000), "Distinguishing Gains from Nonlosses and Losses from Nongains: A Regulatory Focus Perspective on Hedonic Intensity," *Journal of Experimental Social Psychology* 36: 252–74.

10. D. Van-Dijk and A. N. Kluger (2004), "Feedback Sign Effect on Motivation: Is It Moderated by Regulatory Focus?" *Applied Psychology: An International Review* 53: 113–35.

11. D. A. Stam, D. Van Knippenberg, and B. Wisse (2010), "The Role of Regulatory Fit in Visionary Leadership," *Journal of Organizational Behavior* 31: 499–518.

12. E. T. Higgins (1998), "Promotion and Prevention: Regulatory Focus as a Motivational Principle," in *Advances in Experimental Social Psychology*, ed. M. P. Zanna (New York: Academic Press), 1–46.

13. *New York Times*, October 12, 2000, http://www.nytimes.com/2000/10/12/business/2-americans-win-the-nobel-for-economics.html.

14. Jick, "Managing Change."

15. B. F. Skinner (1972), *Beyond Freedom and Dignity* (New York: Vintage Books).

16. S. Kerr (1975), "On the Folly of Rewarding A While Hoping for B," *Academy of Management Journal* 18: 769–783.

17. A. Bandura (1977), *Social Learning Theory* (Oxford: Prentice-Hall).

18. J. P. Kotter and J. L. Heskett (1992), *Corporate Culture and Performance* (New York: The Free Press).

19. P. Lockwood, C. H. Jordan, and Z. Kunda (2002), "Motivation by Positive or Negative Role Models: Regulatory Focus Determines Who Will Best Inspire Us," *Journal of Personality and Social Psychology* 83: 854–64.

20. R. W. White (1959), "Motivation Reconsidered: The Concept of Competence," *Psychological Review* 66: 297–333.

21. Amabile and Kramer, *The Progress Principle*, 59.

22. Ibid., 71.

23. Ibid.

24. S. E. Asch (1951), "Effects of Group Pressure on the Modification and Distortion of Judgments," in *Groups, Leadership and Men*, ed. H. Guetzkow (Pittsburgh: Carnegie Press), 177–90.

25. L. Festinger (1954), "A Theory of Social Comparison Processes," *Human Relations* 7: 117–40.

26. J. Brockner et al. (1997), "The Effects on Layoff Survivors of Their Fellow Survivors' Reactions," *Journal of Applied Social Psychology* 10: 835–63.

27. H. J. Leavitt (1951), "Some Effects of Certain Communication

Patterns on Group Performance," *Journal of Abnormal and Social Psychology* 46: 38–50.

28. R. M. Kanter (1982), "Dilemmas of Managing Participation," *Organizational Dynamics* 11: 3–21.
29. S. Brill, "Code Red," *Time*, March 10, 2014.
30. A. P. Knight and M. E. Baer (2014), "Get Up, Stand Up: The Effects of a Non-Sedentary Workspace on Information Elaboration and Group Performance," *Social Psychological and Personality Science* 5: 910–17.
31. D. Ames, L. B. Maissen, and J. Brockner (2012), "The Role of Listening in Interpersonal Influence," *Journal of Research in Personality* 46: 345–49.
32. L. C. Miller, J. H. Berg, and R. L. Archer (1983), "Openers: Individuals Who Elicit Intimate Self-Disclosure," *Journal of Personality and Social Psychology* 44: 1234–44.

Chapter 4 → Taking the Process Personally

1. Steele, "The Psychology of Self-Affirmation," 262.
2. Agency and influence reflect two of the main ways in which psychologists have discussed the concept of *control*. For self-determination theorists such as Edward Deci and Richard Ryan, control refers to agency, that is, how much people see themselves as being the initiators of their own behavior. To be agentic means that people see themselves as choosing what to do or not do. To not be agentic means that people see their behavior as due to forces outside of themselves. For other control theorists such as Julian Rotter and Martin Seligman, control refers to being influential, that is, how much people see a connection between what they do and the outcomes of what they do. To be influential means that people see their behavior as having an effect on their outcomes. To not be influential means that people perceive little or no relationship between their behavior and their outcomes; instead, outcomes are controlled by powerful others or by chance events; E. L. Deci and R. M. Ryan (1985), *Intrinsic Motivation and Self-Determination in Human Behaviour* (New York: Plenum Press); J. B. Rotter (1966), "Generalized Expectancies for Internal versus External Control of Reinforcement," *Psychological Monographs* 80: Whole No. 609; M.E.P. Seligman (2006), *Learned Optimism: How to Change Your Mind and Your Life* (New York: Alfred A. Knopf).
3. L. Festinger (1957), *A Theory of Cognitive Dissonance* (Stanford: Stanford University Press).

4. P. G. Zimbardo, M. Weisenberg, I. Firestone, and B. Levy (1965), "Communicator Effectiveness in Producing Public Conformity and Private Attitude Change," *Journal of Personality* 33: 233–55.
5. Steele, "The Psychology of Self-Affirmation."
6. B. M. Wiesenfeld, J. Brockner, and C. Martin (1999), "A Self-Affirmation Analysis of Survivors' Reactions to Unfair Organizational Downsizings," *Journal of Experimental Social Psychology* 35: 441–60.
7. Beer, "Leading Change."
8. Cable, Gino, and Staats, "Breaking Them in or Eliciting Their Best?"
9. J. R. Hackman and G. R. Oldham (1980), *Work Redesign* (Reading, MA: Addison-Wesley).
10. A. Grant, E. M. Campbell, G. Chen, K. Cottone, D. Lapedis, and K. Lee (2007), "Impact and the Art of Motivation Maintenance: The Effects of Contact with Beneficiaries on Persistence Behavior," *Organizational Behavior and Human Decision Processes* 103: 53–67.
11. D. Kraft, "Radiologist Adds a Human Touch: Photos," *New York Times*, April 6, 2009.
12. A. Grant (2007), "Relational Job Design and the Motivation to Make a Prosocial Difference," *Academy of Management Review* 32: 393–417.
13. A. Wrzesniewski, J. M. Berg, A. M. Grant, J. Kurkoski, and B. Welle (2015), "Job Mindsets: Achieving Long-Term Gains in Happiness at Work" (unpublished manuscript).
14. Langer and Rodin, "The Effects of Choice and Enhanced Personal Responsibility for the Aged."
15. A. Wrzesniewski and J. E. Dutton (2001), "Crafting a Job: Revisioning Employees as Active Crafters of Their Work," *Academy of Management Review* 26: 179–201.
16. Wrzesniewski et al., "Job Mindsets."
17. Ibid.
18. Ibid.
19. S. Shim, A. Crum, and A. Galinsky (2015), "The Grace of Control: How Reflecting on What We Can Control Increases Physiological and Psychological Well-Being" (unpublished manuscript).
20. C. M. Steele and J. Aronson (1995), "Stereotype Threat and the Intellectual Test Performance of African-Americans," *Journal of Personality and Social Psychology* 69: 797–811.
21. S. J. Spencer, C. M. Steele, and D. M. Quinn (1999), "Stereotype Threat and Women's Math Performance," *Journal of Experimental Social Psychology* 35: 4–28.
22. G. L. Cohen, J. Garcia, N. Apfel, and A. Master (2006), "Reducing the Racial Achievement Gap: A Social-Psychological Intervention,"

Science 313: 1307–10; G. L. Cohen, J. Garcia, V. Purdie-Vaughns, N. Apfel, and P. Brzustoski (2009), "Recursive Processes in Self-Affirmation: Intervening to Close the Minority Achievement Gap," *Science* 324: 400–403.

23. D. A. Stinson, C. Logel, S. Shepherd, and M. P. Zanna (2011), "Rewriting the Self-Fulfilling Prophecy of Social Rejection: Self-Affirmation Improves Relational Security and Social Behavior Up to 2 Months Later," *Psychological Science* 22: 1145–49.

24. G. B. Walton and G. L. Cohen (2011), "A Brief Social-Belonging Intervention Improves Academic and Health Outcomes of Minority Students," *Science* 331: 1447–51.

25. C. S. Dweck (2006), *Mindset: The New Psychology of Success* (New York: Random House).

26. W. Bridges (1988), *Surviving Corporate Transition: Rational Management in a World of Mergers, Start-Ups, Takeovers, Layoffs, Divestitures, Deregulation and New Technologies* (New York: Doubleday).

27. Wrzesniewski et al., "Job Mindsets."

28. S. Chen and H. Boucher (2008), "Relational Selves as Self-Affirmational Resources," *Journal of Research in Personality* 42: 716–33.

29. S. Lyubomirsky (2008), *The How of Happiness: A Scientific Approach to Getting the Life You Want* (New York: Penguin Press).

30. J. Brockner, G. Spreitzer, A. Mishra, W. Hochwarter, L. Pepper, and J. Weinberg (2004), "Perceived Control as an Antidote to the Negative Effects of Layoffs on Survivors' Organizational Commitment and Job Performance," *Administrative Science Quarterly* 49: 76–100.

31. C. D. Zatzick and R. D. Iverson (2006), "High-Involvement Management and Workforce Reduction: Competitive Advantage or Disadvantage?" *Academy of Management Journal* 49: 999–1015.

32. Brockner, Senior, and Welch, "Corporate Volunteerism."

33. M. DeMichele (1994), "Overcoming Barriers with a Change-Ready Culture" (paper presented to the Academy of Management Conference, Dallas).

34. K. Roloff, J. Brockner, and B. M. Wiesenfeld (2012), "The Role of Process Fairness Authenticity in 21st Century Negotiations," in *The Psychology of Negotiations in the 21st Century Workplace: New Challenges and New Solutions*, ed. B. M. Goldman and D. L. Shapiro (New York: Routledge/Taylor & Francis Group), 45–73.

35. Zatzick and Iverson, "High-Involvement Management and Workforce Reduction."

36. J. Schimel, J. Arndt, K. M. Banko, and A. Cook (2004), "Not All Self-Affirmations Were Created Equal: The Cognitive and Social

Benefits of Affirming the Intrinsic (vs.) Extrinsic Self," *Social Cognition* 22: 75–99.

37. D. K. Sherman, G. L. Cohen, L. D. Nelson, A. D. Nussbaum, D. P. Bunyan, and J. Garcia (2009), "Affirmed Yet Unaware: Exploring the Role of Awareness in the Process of Self-Affirmation," *Journal of Personality and Social Psychology* 97: 745–64.

38. E. G. Clary, M. Snyder, R. D. Ridge, J. Copeland, A. A. Stukas, and J. Haugen et al. (1998), "Understanding and Assessing the Motivations of Volunteers: A Functional Approach," *Journal of Personality and Social Psychology* 74: 1516–30.

39. Brockner, Senior, and Welch, "Corporate Volunteerism."

40. D. K. Sherman, D. P. Bunyan, J. D. Creswell, and L. M. Jaremka (2009), "Psychological Vulnerability and Stress: The Effects of Self-Affirmation on Sympathetic Nervous System Responses to Naturalistic Stressors," *Health Psychology* 28: 554–62.

41. Sherman et al., "Affirmed Yet Unaware."

Chapter 5 → For Ethicality, the Process Also Matters

1. B. L. Toffler with J. Reingold (2003), *Final Accounting: Ambition, Greed, and the Fall of Arthur Andersen* (New York: Broadway Books).

2. L. K. Treviño and M. E. Brown (2004), "Managing to Be Ethical: Debunking Five Business Ethics Myths," *Academy of Management Executive* 18: 69–81, quote on p. 74.

3. Greenberg, "Employee Theft as a Reaction to Underpayment Inequity."

4. L. K. Treviño and G. R. Weaver (2001), "Organizational Justice and Ethics Program Follow Through: Influences on Employees' Helpful and Harmful Behavior," *Business Ethics Quarterly* 11: 651–71, quote on p. 74.

5. Leventhal, Karuza, and Fry, "Beyond Fairness."

6. R. Folger (2001), "Fairness as Deonance," in *Research in Social Issues in Management*, ed. S. W. Gilliland, D. D. Steiner, and D. P. Skarlicki (Greenwich, CT: Information Age), 3–31.

7. Thibaut and Walker, *Procedural Justice*.

8. Lind and Tyler, *The Social Psychology of Procedural Justice*.

9. K. Aquino and A. Reed II (2002), "The Self-Importance of Moral Identity," *Journal of Personality and Social Psychology* 83: 1423–40.

10. D.X.H. Wo and M. L. Ambrose (2014), "A Multiple Mediator Model of Trickle-Down Effects," in *The Social Dynamics of Organizational Justice*, ed. S. W. Gilliland, D. P. Steiner, and D. P. Skarlicki (Charlotte, NC: Information Age Publishing).

11. D. P. Skarlicki, D. D. van Jaarsveld, and D. D. Walker (2008), "Getting Even for Customer Mistreatment: The Role of Moral Identity in the Relationship between Customer Interpersonal Injustice and Employee Sabotage," *Journal of Applied Psychology* 93: 1335–47.
12. M. L. Ambrose, M. Schminke, and D. M. Mayer (2013), "Trickle-Down Effects of Supervisor Perceptions of Interactional Justice: A Moderated Mediation Approach," *Journal of Applied Psychology* 98: 678–89.
13. A. W. Gouldner (1960), "The Norm of Reciprocity: A Preliminary Statement," *American Sociological Review* 25: 161–78; E. Fehr and J. Henrich (2003), "Is Strong Reciprocity a Maladaptation? On the Evolutionary Foundations of Human Altruism," in *Genetic and Cultural Evolution of Cooperation*, ed. P. Hammerstein (Cambridge, MA: MIT Press), 55–82.
14. Wo and Ambrose, "A Multiple Mediator Model of Trickle-Down Effects."
15. Bandura, *Social Learning Theory*.
16. Ambrose, Schminke, and Mayer, "Trickle-Down Effects of Supervisor Perceptions of Interactional Justice"; L. Altizer (2013), "Turn Culture into Competitive Advantage: Lessons from Recent Risk Management Failures," *Life Science Compliance* 2: 6–15.
17. F. Gino, M. I. Norton, and D. Ariely (2010), "The Counterfeit Self: The Deceptive Costs of Faking It," *Psychological Science* 21: 712–20, quote on p. 712.
18. E. Aronson and D. R. Mettee (1968), "Dishonest Behavior as a Function of Differential Levels of Induced Self-Esteem," *Journal of Personality and Social Psychology* 9: 121–27.
19. K. D. Vohs and J. W. Schooler (2008), "The Value of Believing in Free Will: Encouraging a Belief in Determinism Increases Cheating," *Psychological Science* 19: 49–54.
20. E. Boshoff and E. S. van Zyl (2011), "The Relationship between Locus of Control and Ethical Behaviour among Employees in the Financial Sector," *Koers* 76: 283–303.
21. J. B. Pryor, F. X. Gibbons, R. A. Wicklund, R. H. Fazio, and R. Hood (1977), "Self-Focused Attention and Self-Report Validity," *Journal of Personality* 45: 513–27.
22. L. L. Shu, N. Mazar, F. Gino, D. Ariely, and M. H. Bazerman (2012), "Signing at the Beginning Makes Ethics Salient and Decreases Dishonest Self-Reports in Comparison to Signing at the End," *Proceedings of the National Academy of Sciences* 109: 15197–200.
23. W. B. Swann Jr. (2012), "Self-Verification Theory," in *Handbook of Theories of Social Psychology*, ed. P. Van Lang, A. Kruglanski, and E. T. Higgins (London: Sage), 23–42.
24. Aquino and Reed, "The Self-Importance of Moral Identity."

25. W. James (1890), *The Principles of Psychology* (New York: H. Holt and Company).
26. R. F. Baumeister, E. Bratslavsky, M. Muraven, and D. M. Tice (1998), "Ego Depletion: Is the Active Self a Limited Resource?" *Journal of Personality and Social Psychology* 74: 1252–65.
27. M. S. Hagger, C. Wood, C. Stiff, and N.L.D. Chatzisarantis (2010), "Ego Depletion and the Strength Model of Self-Control: A Meta-Analysis," *Psychological Bulletin* 136: 495–525, quote on p. 496.
28. A. Hochschild (1983), *The Managed Heart: The Commercialization of Human Feeling* (Berkeley: University of California Press).
29. K. DeCelles and S. Sonenshein (2015), "Temper or Tempered? How Anger Stifles Motivation among Social Change Agents in Organizations" (unpublished manuscript).
30. Baumeister et al., "Ego Depletion."
31. F. Gino, M. E. Schweitzer, N. L. Mead, and D. Ariely (2011), "Unable to Resist Temptation: How Self-Control Depletion Promotes Unethical Behavior," *Organizational Behavior and Human Decision Processes* 115: 191–203.
32. M. Kouchaki and I. Smith (2014), "The Morning Morality Effect: The Influence of Time of Day on (Un)ethical Behavior," *Psychological Science* 25: 95–102, quote on p. 95.
33. I. L. Janis (1982), *Groupthink: Psychological Studies of Policy Decisions and Fiascoes* (Boston: Houghton Mifflin).
34. S. Danziger, J. Levav, and L. Avnaim-Pesso (2011), "Extraneous Factors in Judicial Decisions," *Proceedings of the National Academy of Sciences* 108: 6889–92.
35. H. Xu, L. Bègue, and B. J. Bushman (2012), "Too Fatigued to Care: Ego Depletion, Guilt, and Prosocial Behavior," *Journal of Experimental Social Psychology* 48: 1183–86.
36. Gino et al., "Unable to Resist Temptation."
37. B. L. Toffler (1986), *Tough Choices: Managers Talk Ethics* (New York: Wiley).
38. A. C. Merritt, D. A. Effron, and B. Monin (2010), "Moral Self-Licensing: When Being Good Frees Us to Be Bad," *Social and Personality Psychology Compass* 4: 344–57, quote on p. 344.
39. J. J. Clarkson, E. R. Hirt, L. Jia, and M. B. Alexander (2010), "When Perception Is More than Reality: The Effects of Perceived versus Actual Resource Depletion on Self-Regulatory Behavior," *Journal of Personality and Social Psychology* 98: 29–46.
40. D. M. Tice, R. F. Baumeister, D. Shmueli, and M. Muraven (2007), "Restoring the Self: Positive Affect Helps Improve Self-Regulation Following Ego Depletion," *Journal of Experimental Social Psychology* 43: 379–84.

41. B. J. Schmeichel and K. Vohs (2009), "Self-Affirmation and Self-Control: Affirming Core Values Counteracts Ego Depletion," *Journal of Personality and Social Psychology* 96: 770–82.

42. M. Muraven and E. Slessareva (2003), "Mechanisms of Self-Control Failure: Motivation and Limited Resources," *Personality and Social Psychology Bulletin* 29: 894–906.

43. Ibid.

44. X. Zhou, K. D. Vohs, and R. F. Baumeister (2009), "The Symbolic Power of Money: Reminders of Money Alter Social Distress and Physical Pain," *Psychological Science* 20: 700–706.

45. H. C. Boucher and M. N. Kofos (2012), "The Idea of Money Counteracts Ego Depletion Effects," *Journal of Experimental Social Psychology* 48: 804–10.

46. M. Kouchaki, K. Smith-Crowe, A. P. Brief, and C. Sousa (2013), "Seeing Green: Mere Exposure to the Concept of Money Triggers Unethical Behavior," *Organizational Behavior and Human Decision Processes* 121: 53–61.

47. Grant et al., "Impact and the Art of Motivation Maintenance."

48. E. L. Deci, R. Koestner, and R. M. Ryan (1999), "A Meta-Analytic Review of Experiments Examining the Effects of Extrinsic Rewards on Intrinsic Motivation," *Psychological Bulletin* 125: 627–68.

49. A. Wrzesniewski, B. Schwartz, X. Cong, M. Kane, A. Omar, and T. Kolditz (2014), "Multiple Types of Motives Don't Multiply the Motivation of West Point Cadets," *Proceedings of the National Academy of Sciences* 111: 10990–95.

50. C. Barnes, J. Schaubroeck, M. Huth, and S. Ghumman (2011), "Lack of Sleep and Unethical Conduct," *Organizational Behavior and Human Decision Processes* 115: 169–80.

51. E. Abrahamson (2004), *Change without Pain: How Managers Can Overcome Initiative Overload, Organizational Chaos, and Employee Burnout* (Boston: Harvard Business School Press).

Chapter 6 → A High-Quality Process: Easier Said Than Done

1. A. Hartocollis and E. G. Fitzsimmons, "Tested Negative for Ebola, Nurse Criticizes Her Quarantine," *New York Times*, October 25, 2014.

2. Langer and Rodin, "The Effects of Choice and Enhanced Personal Responsibility for the Aged."

3. Cable, Gino, and Staats, "Breaking Them in or Eliciting Their Best?"

4. Cohen et al., "Recursive Processes in Self-Affirmation."

5. Kouchaki and Smith, "The Morning Morality Effect."
6. A. L. Molinsky and J. D. Margolis (2005), "Necessary Evils and Interpersonal Sensitivity in Organizations," *Academy of Management Review* 30: 245–68.
7. Brockner and Wiesenfeld, "An Integrative Framework for Explaining Reactions to Decisions."
8. A. L. Molinsky and J. D. Margolis (2006), "The Emotional Tightrope of Downsizing: Hidden Challenges for Leaders and Their Organizations," *Organizational Dynamics* 35: 145–59.
9. Ibid.
10. D. B. Whiteside and L. J. Barclay (2014), "The Effects of Depletion on Fair Behavior: When Wanting to Be Fair Isn't Enough" (paper presented to the Academy of Management Conference, Philadelphia).
11. K. DeCelles, S. Agasi, and A. Rafaeli (2015), "Antecedents of Air Rage: Examining the Contextual Predictors and Psychological Mechanisms of Customer Mistreatment" (unpublished manuscript).
12. N. B. Rothman, S. Wheeler-Smith, B. M. Wiesenfeld, and A. Galinsky (2015), "Gaining Power but Losing Status: Why Unfair Leaders Are Selected over Fair Leaders" (unpublished manuscript).
13. Ibid.
14. Lind and Tyler, *The Social Psychology of Procedural Justice*.
15. Rothman et al., "Gaining Power."
16. A. L. Molinsky, A. M. Grant, and J. D. Margolis (2012), "The Bedside Manner of Homo Economicus: How and Why Priming an Economic Schema Reduces Compassion," *Organizational Behavior and Human Decision Processes* 119: 27–37.
17. Ibid.
18. B. M. Wiesenfeld, J. Brockner, and V. Thibault (2000), "Procedural Fairness, Managers' Self-Esteem, and Managerial Behaviors Following a Layoff," *Organizational Behavior and Human Decision Processes* 83: 1–32.
19. S. G. Barsade (2002), "The Ripple Effect: Emotional Contagion and Its Influence on Group Behavior," *Administrative Science Quarterly* 47: 644–75.
20. Wiesenfeld, Brockner, and Thibault, "Procedural Fairness."
21. Rothman et al., "Gaining Power."
22. M. Van Dijke, N. Van Quaquebeke, and J. Brockner (2015), "In Self-Defense: Reappraisal but Not Suppression Buffers the Negative Impact of Low Procedural Justice on Cooperation" (unpublished manuscript).
23. J. J. Gross and O. P. John (2003), "Individual Differences in Two Emotion Regulation Processes: Implications for Affect, Relationships,

and Well-Being," *Journal of Personality and Social Psychology* 85: 348–62.

24. Molinsky and Margolis, "The Emotional Tightrope of Downsizing."

25. D. P. Skarlicki and G. P. Latham (2005), "Can Leaders Be Trained to Be Fair?" in *Handbook of Organizational Justice*, ed. J. Greenberg and J. Colquitt (Mahwah, NJ: Lawrence Erlbaum Associates), 499–524.

26. Ibid.

27. J. Greenberg (2006), "Losing Sleep over Organizational Injustice: Attenuating Insomniac Reactions to Underpayment Inequity with Supervisory Training in Interactional Justice," *Journal of Applied Psychology* 91: 58–69.

28. J. P. Wanous (1980), *Organizational Entry: Recruitment, Selection, and Socialization of Newcomers* (Reading, MA: Addison-Wesley).

29. Molinsky and Margolis, "The Emotional Tightrope of Downsizing."

30. Ibid.

31. Van Dijke, Van Quaquebeke, and Brockner, "In Self-Defense."

32. D. A. Thomas and S. Creary (2009), "Meeting the Diversity Challenge at PepsiCo: The Steve Reinemund Era," Harvard Business School Case 410-024.

33. Allan Church, personal communication with the author.

34. M. Darling, C. Parry, and J. Moore (2005), "Learning in the Thick of It," *Harvard Business Review* 83: 84–92.

35. Skarlicki and Latham, "Can Leaders Be Trained to Be Fair?"

Index of Names

Index of Subjects